The Social Constructions and Experiences of Madness

At the Interface/Probing the Boundaries

VOLUME 96

The titles published in this series are listed at *brill.com/aipb*

The Social Constructions and Experiences of Madness

Edited by

Monika dos Santos
Jean-François Pelletier

BRILL
RODOPI

LEIDEN | BOSTON

Cover illustration: "The Heart of Psychiatry." Illustration by Martin Fortier. Copyright belongs to Jean-François Pelletier. Description of the painting by the painter: "The artist has just been diagnosed with a schizoaffective disorder. The hand which plays with his heart is that of the psychiatrist, of whom he says to be in love. Her gesture "removes the identity of the person as a person". The patient-artist is nevertheless larger than psychiatry, as personified by the doctor in the background, who happens to be topless. Is the patient-doctor relationship a castrating relationship? The artist felt torn, hence the emotion, hence the tear flowing from his right eye: he mourns his lost youth."

Library of Congress Control Number: 2018931030

Typeface for the Latin, Greek, and Cyrillic scripts: "Brill". See and download: brill.com/brill-typeface.

ISSN 1570-7113
ISBN 978-90-04-35078-6 (paperback)
ISBN 978-90-04-36189-8 (e-book)

This book is printed on acid-free paper and produced in a sustainable manner.

Table of Contents

Introduction: Whose Lived Experience Is It Anyway?

Monika dos Santos and Jean-François Pelletier

What's madness but nobility of soul at odds with circumstances?
- 'In a Dark Time', Theodore Roethke[1]

In this volume we explore the intersection of the social construction of madness with the institution as well as with broader power dynamics, arguing that such constructions elide the workings of power, often by drawing on discourses of ahistoricity. Post-Structuralist accounts of madness illustrate that categories of madness are not fixed or objective, but rather participate in productive and exclusionary practices in the exercise of power by some over others. The charge that madness is historically located and not universal is sublimely illustrated by Foucault (1967) in *Madness and Civilization: A History of Insanity in the Age of Reason*,[2] where he traces a radical disjuncture between conceptualizations of madness in the middle ages (when it was possible for madness to be constructed as the voice of genius or divine inspiration, and when insanity was in a relational dialogue with sanity) and conceptualizations which influence our current understandings.

The historicity argument has been explored in the first chapter by Oisín Wall entitled *Madness: A Revolutionary Rear-Guard*, and is confirmed by the observation that the International Statistical Classification of Diseases and Related Health Problems (ICD) is in its 10th revision and the Diagnostic and Statistical Manual of Mental Disorders (DSM) in its 5th, and that categories have not remained stable over time. What we understand 'madness' to be, continues Oisín Wall, changes from place to place and generation to generation. Its meaning has shifted regularly as political, religious, and cultural expectations changed, madness being in fact co-created both in interpersonal interactions and communities (e.g., the asylum) and through the process of reading and interpreting texts – whether those texts are the human body, verbal communication or the words of a writer.[3]

Although madness as mental illness seems to be the dominant Western view of madness, it is by no means the only view of what it means to be 'mad'. The argument here is that madness cannot be universal because different cultures exhibit different manifestations – madness takes on a distinct symptomatology, which is only found in a particular culture. The symptoms of madness or mental illness occur in all cultures of the world, but have different meanings in different cultural contexts. Evidence suggests that meanings of mental illness have a significant impact on the subjective experience thereof, the idioms used in the expression thereof, the indigenous treatment, and the outcome.[4] Thus the societal understandings and representations of madness are central to the problem of mental illness, as they can be used as a basis for social control.[5] In the second chapter, subtitled *The Consumer Movement and the Social Construction of Mental Illness*, Kara Holmes and Fiona Ann Papps arguably discuss such techniques of control, or what Foucault (1967) names 'procedural techniques' of recording information and prescribing the rules of conduct for professionals and consumers in an institution of mental healthcare.[6] This is just another type of impact that the meanings of mental illness can have over the finalities of the institution.

Another focus interrogates the contested boundaries of madness. Russell (1995) shows that a major epistemological concern is that the objects of study, namely *mental illnesses* or *mental disorders* are by no means conceptually clear.[7] Nor is this epistemological concern diminishing as categories shift and change with each new edition of the major classificatory systems.[8] In examining these issues it becomes useful to identify three contested changing boundaries or oppositions to mental disorder: physical illness, social deviance and mental health. David Lewis Wilson and Monika dos Santos note in *Psychology's Madness: Solipsistic Denial of Relational Dependency* (third chapter), that mental disorder stands in a difficult and precarious position between bodily illness and social deviance, and there is an ongoing struggle between various professionals and social theorists as to where the boundaries should be set.

From a linguistic paradigm and postmodern perspective we see how language *creates* realities as opposed to 'discovering' them.[9] What this means for the mental health profession is that 'mental illness', diagnoses, and associated concepts are social constructions … and the vocabularies of the medical and psychological models, indeed the idea of 'mental illness' itself, are social constructions – *they are made up*. Furthermore, the medical and psychological vocabularies that describe disease and deficit. They view a human being as something that can be 'assessed', 'diagnosed', and 'treated' much like a machine – hence comes the obsession with 'compliance.' These models make distinctions between 'normal' and 'pathological.' They position practitioner as expert and client as more or less passive recipient of 'treatment.' The focus of 'treatment' is on the elimination of 'symptoms.' These vocabularies invisibly and insidiously support the old paternalistic roles. From a postmodern perspective these medical and psychological vocabularies are not representing reality, but, in fact, creating a 'reality' or perspective. The fact is that words simply 'carve up' our undifferentiated sensory experience leading to many possible interpretations of the human condition. The question then becomes 'What is the best "reality" or perspective with which to help people reach their goals?' John Walter and Jane Peller (2000), both prominent leaders in postmodern consultation, describe this shift from *belief* to *utility*.[10]

This stance is supported in the fourth chapter on autism by Simon Cushing, in which he asks *Has Autism Changed?*, arguing that there is indeed no realistic reasons to justify the changes in the diagnostic criteria of autism, and furthermore, that the only way the changes could be justified is if one takes the position that the DSM categories are evolving social constructs.

In an article by Mirowski and Ross (1989), the authors furthermore focus on how the linguistic legacy of the eighteenth century development of biology and epidemiology has influenced the development of psychiatric definitions and explanations of mental illness.[11] According to these authors, superimposing a diagnosis on a person's symptoms and situation does not add information; rather, it removes information. Worse still, it entices us to think, talk, and act as if a hidden entity has been revealed. The mythical entity insinuates itself into the role of a named actor, and the symptoms and situation dissolve into mere signs of its presence. These 'hidden entities' that the authors refer to are the presupposed biological basis for mental illness. Although studies have not conclusively indicated biological causes for mental illness, the model of the language used to conceptualise it presupposes such a basis, and therefore justifies the use of biochemical treatment.[12] These 'hidden entities' are the presupposed biological basis for mental illness. These authors also reflect on the socially constructed need for a diagnostic system. Government agencies and insurance companies want to know exactly where the boundaries for reimbursement are drawn. Psychiatrists and other physicians want to sell their services to some costumers. The pharmaceutical industry wants to sell its drugs. For actuarial purposes, government and the insurance industry want to know and to be able to predict as precisely as possible what it is all going to cost. Insurance companies will only pay for specific cases of mental illness. In this way society has constructed the need for an official and legal classification system.

In terms of diagnosis and the biological approach to mental illness, an observation by Palmer (2000) represents an intriguing paradox in medical psychiatry.[13] He states that symptoms or 'disorderly conduct' are identified on a social rather than a biological basis. The importance of biological knowledge in diagnosis is undermined by the fact that symptoms could be identified long before the biological origins of the condition were known. Palmer asserts that how a symptom is identified and what causes it are separate issues. The judgment of 'pathology' involves ascribing meaning to a person's actions and how they make sense in a particular social setting. So some actions acquire symptomatic significance not because they contravene the laws of biological functioning but because they infringe on the social order. Palmer further states that the social constructionist worldview reconceptualises delusions as the product of a power relationship where the views of the less powerful patient are pathologised, for them to be 'treated'. Notwithstanding, not everyone has this negative view of the use of psychiatric language in order to define madness/mental illness. Gough (1971) states that the goal of diagnosis is not to label or stigmatise those with a mental illness, although it may be an unfortunate byproduct or effect of diagnosis or the abuse thereof.[14] He feels that the goal of diagnosis is rather to identify the problem a patient has presented in such a way that the appropriate treatment for the restoration of the functioning of the patient, in this or that culture and at this or that particular time point, can be carried out. According to Gough, there are three levels of diagnosis. The first level is aimed at identifying and clustering certain symptoms together to be able to identify a disorder. Treatment that results from a diagnosis at level one is aimed at relieving and not curing symptoms. Gough believes that most diagnoses aim toward at least a level two diagnosis, which is concerned with the underlying pathology that causes symptoms. Thus, the treatment at this level is curative and brings about more than only symptomatic relief. However, the ideal is for clinicians to strive towards a level three diagnosis. This is the most basic level of diagnosis, and at this level, aetiological factors are identified. Once the aetiological factors are identified, there is the possibility of designing interventions aimed at prevention. At this level lies the value of careful conceptualisation and understanding of mental disorders.

As per its title, the fifth chapter by Jonathan Appel, Dohee Kim- Appel, Erin Snapp, Claire Whiteman, Mary Cassidy and Rebecca Stanic addresses the relationship between *Creativity and 'Madness'* – the relationship between mental states and creativity, both as the construction and an expression of neurological and psychological diversity, and as a tool for healing a wounded psyche. Even though we are aware that the psychiatric diagnosis are first and foremost social constructs, we also acknowledge that they can often be adopted by people who experience mental distress in order to structure and explain their experiences.[15] Some people find that having a name for their problems provides them with a sense of order and a way to reconstruct their lives. Reconstructing one's life implies the expression of a specific experiential type of knowledge about overcoming adversity and facing invalidating social representations of mental illness and madness. Individuals diagnosed with mental illness are frequently stigmatised and excluded from society and thus unable to claim and exert full citizenship. Finding ways and new meaning in which they can participate in community and re-write their own personal and collective histories, enables a reclamation of voice; a re-naming that encourages re-positioning and the gaining of power and agency. In second last chapter, Jean-François Pelletier suggests that this reviving experience and the experiential knowledge that ensues are intellectual properties of consumers. They can come together in a *Social Enterprise* (subtitle) to position themselves profitably in research and academia as important economic sectors and in the business of conceptual reconstruction.

Mills (2003) reflects that although the understanding of madness as a mental illness has resulted in the alleviation of suffering for many people, it has also resulted in a greater stigmatisation of mental illness, and has placed responsibility for the 'cure' of madness in the hands of professional psychiatrists and psychologists.[16] Research shows that persons with severe mental illness must cope not only with the symptoms of their disease but also with social and self-stigma: the recovery process is only partial if it is only clinical.[17] Societal attitudes toward severe mental illness lead to lost opportunities for education, employment and housing.[18] Self-stigma occurs when individuals assimilate social stereotypes about themselves as persons with severe mental illness. In an article by Corrigan (2007), he discusses the ways in which diagnosis can increase the stigma of mental *illness*.[19] He shows that many people who are in need of mental health services avoid using them so as not to be labelled a 'mental patient' or suffer the prejudice and discrimination the label brings. People with mental illness who live in a society that widely accepts stigmatizing ideas may internalise these ideas and believe that they are less valued than others because of their mental illness. According to Corrigan, the process of diagnosis both accentuates the 'groupness' of those with a mental illness and simultaneously emphasises their 'differentness' from the general public. The hospitalisation of persons with mental illness also has another and important effect. A study by Corrigan, Green, Lundin, Kubiak and Penn (2001) has shown that unfamiliarity with mental illness heightens stigmatising attitudes.[20] The segregation of the mentally ill into mental institutions to which the general public have no access heightens stigma towards those with a mental illness and classifies them as dangerous and incompetent. But the fact is that many did develop some valuable competencies to share with the general public on various ways of overcoming inaccurate social representations and constructions.

In the final chapter, concerning a institutionalised relative of his, Carlo Orefice movingly emphasises that our research efforts should be focused on what we *have in common* as individuals: our capacity to symbolize bodily inclinations; our ability to define ourselves through the experiences of pleasure, pain, and decision-making; and our inescapable need to inhabit a space. Only if we preserve all this from the categorizing and disjunctive language of *disease* (a language that still has a surprising amount of currency today) will we be able to prevent loss from becoming a clinical incident - for mental illness is often the result of an experience of loss, whether real or perceived; only then will loss be understood instead as a *constitutive* experience of human existence.

In the last 20 years media studies have also started to address the problem of stigmatisation of mental illness in the media. One of the most important of such studies is Otto Wahl's 1995 book *Media Madness: Public Images of Mental* Illness.[21] He enlists a vast range of popular texts and genres to support his argument on the treatment of madness in the media. He argues, for example, that newspaper stories that link mental illness and violence contain the same stock characters as those found in popular fiction, namely, insane killers who prey on multiple innocent victims.[22] He argues that the media over-represents a link between mental illness and violence. In reaction to Wahl's book, Harper (2005) examines the mental illness, violence and media discourse.[23] He agrees with Wahl in stating that the media in all their forms often present the mentally ill as violent. In film and television drama, for example, the mentally ill are often presented as unpredictable killers, which create misleading impressions that people with mental illness are to be feared. This is the reason that one of the main contentions of the anti-stigma discourse is that media images of mental illness imply an association or link between mental illness and violence that does not exist – and if such a link does exist it is in the other way around with the mentally ill being more often victims than perpetrators of violence.[24] However, Harper states that a fundamental problem with such critiques is that a correlation between mental illness and violence has been demonstrated in several studies. According to Harper, the concern here is that while anti-stigma critics rightly point out the ways in which the media contribute to public misconceptions about mental illness, their own arguments can have a similarly distorting effect.[25]

In conclusion, it is clear that the meanings attached to mental illness are varied and have changed many times throughout history. They are shaped by the dominant political, scientific and cultural discourses of the day. They also reflect social inequalities and imbalances of power. Throughout history the meanings attached to madness have had far-reaching effects on the experience of mental illness and the reaction of society towards those defined as having a mental illness. In this volume, we postulate that madness and psychiatric diagnoses as well are first and foremost social constructs. The succession of chapters we proposed aimed at deconstructing these constructs for a possibly less invalidating and more inclusive reconstruction process. Indeed, deconstruction[26] is a school of contemporary philosophy and a method of textual analysis applied to various types of writings like philosophy, literature, or newspapers – or even family photos as with the last chapter. Deconstruction reveals the gaps and sense of confusion that these documents convey with a reading grid centered on implied assumptions and with special attention on omissions that are revealed by the discourses themselves. The real meaning of a given message, the meaning that confers effective power to this message, is thus the result of the difference between the words that are used, rather than the reference to the things they are presumably representing directly. This difference is a very active one, and deconstruction is therefore a way of criticizing not only both literary and philosophical texts but also political institutions and power differentials. We thus proposed an attempt to re-conceive the difference that divides self-reflection or self-consciousness. This re-conception of difference works towards preventing the worst hidden violence,[27] such as the unjustifiable social exclusion of the mentally ill. Their experience is their knowledge, an experiential knowledge which can be operationalised and canalised to their advantage in deconstructing-reconstructing the meaning of this authentic and genuine human experience.

Notes

[1] Theodore Roethke, 'In a Dark Time', *Collected Poems of Theodore Roethke* (NY: Knopf Doubleday Publishing Group, 1961).

[2] Michel Foucault, *Madness and Civilization: A History of Insanity in the Age of Reason* (New York: Pantheon books, 1965).
[3] Fiona Ann Papps, 'Introduction: *And Then the Monsters Come Out*', *And Then the Monsters Come Out: Madness, Language and Power*, ed. Fiona Ann Papps (Oxford: Inter-Disciplinary Press), ix.
[4] Richard J. Castillo, ed., *Meanings of Madness* (Thousand Oaks, CA: Brooks/Cole, 1998).
[5] Thomas Szasz, *Law, Liberty, and Psychiatry: An Inquiry into the Social Uses of Mental Health Practices* (Syracuse: Syracuse University Press, 1989), 251.
[6] Michel Foucault, *Madness and Civilization: A History of Insanity in the Age of Reason* (New York: Pantheon Books, 1965).
[7] Denise Russell, *Women, Madness and Medicine* (London: Polity Press, 1995).
[8] Ibid.
[9] Michael Walker, 'The Social Construction of Mental Illness and Its Implications for the Recovery Model,' *International Journal of Psychosocial Rehabilitation* 10.1 (2006): 71-87.
[10] John Walter and Jane Peller, *Recreating Brief Therapy: Preferences and Possibilities* (New York: Norton, 2000).
[11] John Mirowski and Catherine E. Ross, 'Psychiatric Diagnosis as Reified Measure,' *Journal of Health and Social Behavior* 30.1 (1989): 11-25.
[12] Ibid., 12.
[13] Derrol Palmer, 'Identifying Delusional Discourse: Issues of Rationality and Power,' *Sociology of Health & Illness* 22.5 (2000): 661-678.
[14] H. Gough, 'Some Reflections of the Meaning of Psychodiagnosis,' *American Psychologist* 26 (1971): 160-167.
[15] B. Casey and A. Long, 'Meaning of Madness: A Literature Review,' *Journal of Psychiatric and Mental Health Nursing* 10 (2003): 89-99.
[16] Sara Mills, *Michel Foucault* (London: Routledge, 2003).
[17] Jean-François Pelletier, Marc Corbière, Tania Lecomte, Catherine Briand, Patrick Corrigan, Larry Davidson and Michael Rowe, 'Citizenship and Recovery: Two Intertwined Concepts for Civic-Recovery', *BMC Psychiatry* 15 (2015): 1-7.
[18] P. E. Holmes and L. P. River, 'Individual Strategies for Coping with the Stigma of Severe Mental Illness,' *Cognitive and Behavioral Practice* 5.2 (1998): 231-239.
[19] Patrick W. Corrigan, 'How Clinical Diagnosis Might Exacerbate the Stigma of Mental Illness,' *Social Work* 52.1 (2007): 31-39.
[20] Patrick W. Corrigan, A. Green, R. Lundin, M. Kubiak and D. L. Penn, 'Familiarity with and Social Distance from People who have Serious Mental Illness,' *Psychiatric Services* 52.7 (2001): 953-958.
[21] Casey and Long, 'Meaning of Madness,' 89-99.

[22] Otto F. Wall, *Media Madness: Public Images of Mental Illness* (New Brunswick, New Jersey: Rutgers University Press, 1997).
[23] Stephen Harper, 'Media, Madness and Misrepresentation: Critical Reflections on Anti-Stigma Discourse,' *European Journal of Communication* 20.4 (2005): 460-483.
[24] Heather Stuart, 'Violence and Mental Illness: An Overview,' *World Psychiatry* 2.2 (2003): 121-124.
[25] Stephen Harper, 'Media, Madness and Misrepresentation: Critical Reflections on Anti-Stigma Discourse,' *European Journal of Communication* 20.4 (2005): 460-483.
[26] Jacques Derrida, *Force de loi : le 'Fondement mystique de l'autorite'* (Paris: Galilée, 1994). Published in English as 'Force of the Law: The "Mystical Foundation" of Authority', *Acts of Religion*, ed. Gil Anidjar (New York: Routledge, 2002).
[27] Leonard Lawlor, 'Jacques Derrida' The Stanford Encyclopedia of Philosophy (Spring 2014), viewed on 21 October 2015, http://plato.stanford.edu/archives/spr2014/entries/derrida; Leonard Lawlor, 'From the Trace to the Law: Derridean Politics,' *Philosophy & Social Criticism* 15.1 (1989): 1-15.

Bibliography

Casey, B. and A. Long. 'Meaning of Madness: A Literature Review.' *Journal of Psychiatric and Mental Health Nursing* 10 (2003): 89-99.

Castillo, Richard J., ed. *Meanings of Madness*. Thousand Oaks, CA: Brooks/Cole, 1998.

Corrigan, Patrick W. 'How Clinical Diagnosis Might Exacerbate the Stigma of Mental Illness,' *Social Work* 52.1 (2007): 31-39.

Corrigan, Patrick W., A. Green, R. Lundin, M. Kubiak and D. L. Penn, 'Familiarity with and Social Distance from People who have Serious Mental Illness.' *Psychiatric Services* 52.7 (2001): 953-958.

Derrida, Jacques. *Force de loi: le 'Fondement mystique de l'autorite'*. Paris: Galilée, 1994.

———. 'Force of the Law: The "Mystical Foundation" of Authority.' *Acts of Religion*, edited by Gil Anidjar. New York: Routledge, 2002.

Foucault, Michel. *Madness and Civilization: A History of Insanity in the Age of Reason*. New York: Pantheon Books, 1965.

Gough, H. 'Some Reflections of the Meaning of Psychodiagnosis.' *American Psychologist* 26 (1971): 160-167.

Harper, Stephen. 'Media, Madness and Misrepresentation: Critical Reflections on Anti-Stigma Discourse.' *European Journal of Communication* 20.4 (2005): 460-483.

Holmes P. E., and L. P. River. 'Individual Strategies for Coping with the Stigma of Severe Mental Illness.' *Cognitive and Behavioral Practice* 5.2 (1998): 231-239.

Lawlor, Leonard. 'Jacques Derrida.' *The Stanford Encyclopedia of Philosophy*. Spring, 2014. Viewed on 21 October 2015. http://plato.stanford.edu/archives/spr2014/entries/derrida.

———. 'From the Trace to the Law: Derridean Politics.' *Philosophy & Social Criticism* 15.1 (1989): 1-15.

Mills, Sara. *Michel Foucault*. London: Routledge, 2003.

Mirowski, John and Catherine E. Ross. 'Psychiatric Diagnosis as Reified Measure.' *Journal of Health and Social Behavior* 30.1 (1989): 11-25.

Palmer, Derrol. 'Identifying Delusional Discourse: Issues of Rationality and Power.' *Sociology of Health & Illness* 22.5 (2000): 661-678.

Papps, Fiona Ann. 'Introduction: *And Then the Monsters Come Out*'. *And Then the Monsters Come Out: Madness, Language and Power*, edited by Fiona Ann Papps, vii-xii. Oxford: Inter-Disciplinary Press, 2015.

Pelletier, Jean-François, Marc Corbière, Tania Lecomte, Catherine Briand, Patrick Corrigan, Larry Davidson and Michael Rowe. 'Citizenship and Recovery: Two Intertwined Concepts for Civic-Recovery.' *BMC Psychiatry* 15 (2015): 1-7.

Roethke, Theodore. 'In a Dark Time', *Collected Poems of Theodore Roethke*. NY: Knopf Doubleday Publishing Group, 1961.

Russell, Denise. *Women, Madness and Medicine*. London: Polity Press, 1995.

Stuart, Heather. 'Violence and Mental Illness: An Overview.' *World Psychiatry* 2.2 (2003): 121-124.

Szasz, Thomas. *Law, Liberty, and Psychiatry: An Inquiry into the Social Uses of Mental Health Practices*. Syracuse: Syracuse University Press, 1989.

Walker, Michael. 'The Social Construction of Mental Illness and Its Implications for the Recovery Model.' *International Journal of Psychosocial Rehabilitation* 10.1 (2006): 71-87.

Wall, Otto F. *Media Madness: Public Images of Mental Illness*. New Brunswick, New Jersey: Rutgers University Press, 1997.

Walter, John and Jane Peller. *Recreating Brief Therapy: Preferences and Possibilities*. New York: Norton, 2000.

Madness: A Revolutionary Rear-Guard

Oisín Wall

Abstract
Madness is a common theme in avant-garde and counter-cultural writing. Many groups have even attempted to deploy it as a revolutionary tactic. This chapter examines one such attempt made by the British anti-psychiatrists in the 1960s. It explores how the anti-psychiatrists first came to see the revolutionary potential of madness and how they attempted to use it as a tactic to challenge or even overthrow bourgeois society. Building on these explorations this chapter will argue that while the deployment of madness provides an interesting critical approach to society, it inevitably fails as a sustainable revolutionary position. Madness is a historically unstable subject, its meaning changes according to prevailing ideologies, power structures, and discourses. This is its attraction for counter-cultural writers, but it is also its fatal weakness.

Key Words: Madness, counter-culture, anti-psychiatry, 1960s.

*****

1. Introduction

Throughout the twentieth century many European avant-garde and counter-cultural groups were fascinated and troubled by the idea of madness as a liberatory force. This chapter will explore some features of this avant-garde conception of madness as well as its success and failure as a tactical challenge to dominant cultural forces.

Madness entered into the world of the avant-garde in many different ways. For instance, for the futurists it was simply another cultural taboo to be broken; for the surrealists and the situationists it had a personal foundation in friends and comrades who had been committed to asylums; and for the anti-psychiatrists, who had all been psychiatrists or psychiatric patients, it was both a professional interest and a personal one. Moreover, each group's engagement with madness was different. The Futurists saw madness as a spontaneous version to their own project and fantasised about riding into battle against society with madmen by their side;[1] the surrealists argued that madness was a way of understanding and engaging with the world which had been arbitrarily excluded from bourgeois normality;[2] the Situationists denied that madness was a disease-process and demanded the liberation of asylum inmates;[3] and for the British anti-psychiatrists madness was the result of an aborted attempt at social liberation.[4]

While each group approached madness from a different direction and for different reasons there are certain identifiable lines of influence and commonalities between many of these groups and their conceptions of madness. This chapter will examine the British anti-psychiatric group of the 1960s as an example of an avant-garde engagement with the idea of madness. It will examine why madness appears to be an exciting and avant-garde weapon in the right hands because it is an unstable concept – more on their concept of 'instability' later. However, it will also argue that this instability is a weakness as well as a strength, and that inevitably it robs avant-garde groups of their momentum and forces them into rear-guard positions.

In the late 1950s three young, ambitious, but then unknown psychiatrists, became friends, they were R.D. Laing, Aaron Esterson, and David Cooper. As psychiatrists they had all been heavily influenced by the therapeutic community and group analytic movements that had emerged in post-war psychiatry. They also shared a range of other interests including communal living, left-wing politics, and French existentialism. In the early 1960s they collaborated on a handful of research projects, publishing their research on the group- and family-orientated treatment of schizophrenics[5] as well as a book excellently, if somewhat unreadably, summarizing the previous ten years of the writings of Jean Paul Sartre.[6] In the early 1960s their research was seen as a contribution to mainstream psychiatric research on schizophrenia and family dynamics. Slowly the friends began to gather a tight-knit group of followers, some of whom were young psychiatrists while most were current or former psychiatric patients. During the mid-1960s the group became increasingly interested in the counter-culture that was beginning to bloom in London. They began to befriend hip artists, activists and writers like Alexander Trocchi, John Latham, Jeff Nuttall, and Allan Ginsberg. In 1965 they opened Kingsley Hall, a community in East London where people could come to openly act out or work through their thoughts, feelings, and phantasies, without risking psychiatric incarceration or social stigmatisation.[7] From 1965 to 1970 Kingsley Hall was a base of operations for the counter-culture. Huge international events, like the Congress on the Dialectics of Liberation, and cultural revolutionary experiments, like the Anti-University of London, were organised from inside its walls. In this period the anti-psychiatrists became well known public figures. Laing regularly appeared on television; he, Cooper and Esterson gave public lecture tours in the United States of America and around the world, and they spoke at many of the most important societies and conferences of the time. Ultimately, however the group collapsed between 1969 and 1970. As their popularity grew the personal lives of the three main anti-psychiatrists became increasingly strained. Their friendships began to fall apart. Laing withdrew from public life and went to an ashram in Ceylon for a year, Esterson returned to his private practice and withdrew from public life, and Cooper moved to South America, pausing in Canada along the way to declare that his association with Laing was at an end, Laing, he said, 'was on a spiritual trip… [and] He, David, was on a political one.'[8]

In the course of this chapter we will examine how the anti-psychiatrists developed a conception of madness as a construct of dominant cultural forces. We will see that they argued that the purpose of this construction was to exclude deviant world views and activities, or critical perspectives. The chapter will then explore how the anti-psychiatrists attempted to mobilise madness against these same cultural forces by inverting their exclusionary logic and positing madness not only as a valid state of mind, but a state which is, in some sense, more insightful than sanity. As such they mobilised madness as a tactic through which the foundational principles of society could be destabilised. Finally this chapter will argue that while this liberatory conception of madness began as a van-guard action, leading an attempt to liberate peoples' minds and explore the radical possibilities of cultural revolution, it leaves itself open to cultural co-option. In spite of their avant-garde beginnings, these liberatory deployments of madness became rear-guard actions which constantly shifted their position as they retreated from an advancing front of normality and sanity. The chapter will conclude that this approach to madness inevitably leaves itself open to co-option precisely because of the historical instability of the idea of madness, the same instability that these avant-garde groups attempted to exploit in order to advance their cultural revolutionary project.

2. Historically Unstable Madness

If we are to understand the anti-psychiatric attempt to mobilise madness as a liberatory tactic we must first understand their conception of madness as historically unstable. The principle is that what we understand 'madness' to be changes from place to place and generation to generation. Its meaning has shifted regularly as political, religious, and cultural expectations changed.

The British anti-psychiatrists of the 1960s based their entire conceptual framework on the social construction of madness. Heavily influenced as they were by existential Marxism, they argued that all social life was alienated in some sense. Sanity, they argued, was the acquiescence to 'statistically "normal" forms of alienation.'[9] By extension they saw madness as any form of alienation that was 'out of step' with such normality.[10] The identification of the 'normal,' therefore was arbitrary. It relied on the establishment of a socially agreed limit to normality – whether this is identified through the subjective assessment of socially mandated experts, like psychiatrists, or the identification of more objective, but still arbitrary, statistically defined ranges of behaviour.

They also argued that the identification of madness was a socially sanctioned buttress to 'normal' forms of alienation. They argued repeatedly that 'madness' was the result of subtly destructive double-binding social relations. Social groups, they argued, often silently 'elected' one of their number to be the outlet for the group's dysfunction.[11] For instance Cooper described one of his patients who

> proclaimed the delusional idea that he was Jesus Christ. At that time, as on the present occasion he was bearing vicariously the

> full load of his mother's guilt, and in the micro- social family world he was dying in order that the others, principally his mother, might be saved. We all die partial deaths in order that others, for whom we are the sacrificial offerings, may live. The archetypical Christ, in so far as he has any reality at all, is in each of us. In this sense the patient's delusional proclamation was quite true, but it was a truth that no one else could allow himself to see. If one reads the score this way, one appreciates the dictum of the American psychiatrist who defined delusion as a true idea held by a patient which the psychiatrist deludes himself into accepting literally. But the opposite of the literal is not necessarily the metaphorical. The existential reality of a person transcends this opposition.[12]

One of the things that Cooper draws attention to is that his patient's alienation is a manifestation of the alienation of those around him. The identification of this particular person as mad, when he is simply attempting to cope in a coherent way with the dysfunction of his social world, is an entirely arbitrary decision, but a necessary one for the continued functioning of the 'normal' group.

The anti-psychiatrists saw this delimination of mad and sane as fundamental to their contemporary social organisation. In *The Death of the Family* (1970), a text which largely summarizes the ideas that the anti-psychiatrists developed during the 1960s, Cooper wrote:

> If, then, we wish to find the basic level of understanding of repression we have to see it as a collectively reinforced and institutionally formalized panic about going mad, about the invasion of the outer by the inner and of the inner by the outer, about the loss of the illusion of self.
> The Law is Terror put into words.[13]

For Cooper and his comrades the limits of sanity were tightly drawn by a variety of powerful social institutions, not least of which were the law and the psychiatric asylum system. These institutions attempted to stabilise the social system and legitimise their arbitrary categorization of normality by creating systems which invalidate the actions of those considered mad. Like the many avant-garde groups before them from the surrealists to the situationists, the anti-psychiatrists argued that psychiatric hospitals transformed people into caricatures of madmen. Psychiatric hospitals, the anti-psychiatrists claimed, systematically denyed any possibility of validity in the person's world view, by enforcing and rewarding self-identification as a patient and classic patient behaviours, and also by institutionally denying any genuine human interaction between staff and patients.

3. Madness as a Liberatory Tactic

Building on the idea that madness was historically unstable and constructed by powerful social and political forces, many avant-garde groups expressed solidarity with those identified as mad. In 1960, for instance, the German section of the Situationist International released a statement declaring:

> we refuse in all circumstances to let the behavior of men who want to change society be qualified as madness. In particular, we will oppose by all means the qualification of the members of the Situationist International as mad, as well as the consequences that such a qualification can involve. For modern psychiatry, the difference between reason and madness in the final analysis is only social success, and so we also absolutely refuse the qualification of "madness" with respect to every modern artist. The current psychiatric system, in theory, authorizes the internment of all artists. Confronted with this menace, all artists are in solidarity.[14]

This solidarity was an important part of the avant-garde conception of madness. However, there was more than solidarity at play for many avant-garde groups, not least the anti-psychiatrists. They saw madness itself as a liberatory tactic.

From the outset the British anti-psychiatrists argued that madness itself was essentially a social critique. As already mentioned they believed that madness was a manifestation of a dysfunctional social environment. The basic premise of this view was that madness was in some sense intelligible. Indeed this is one of the claims that the anti-psychiatrists are most often remembered for, and the clearest example of this is Laing's reinterpretation of a description of a catatonic patient by Emil Kraeplelin, the psychiatrist viewed by many as the founder of modern psychiatry. In his *Lectures on Psychiatry* (1905) Kraepelin described an incident in which he brought a 'catatonic' patient into a lecture theatre to illustrate to his students some of the characteristics of dementia praecox, a now obsolete diagnosis which was very similar to schizophrenia.[15] Kraepelin proceeded to interview the patient and then discussed his apparently senseless ramblings with his audience of doctors and medical students. In *The Divided Self* (1960) R.D. Laing described this incident again.[16] However, Laing offered a new interpretation of the incident in which the patient's ramblings were actually intelligible. Laing argued that the patient was openly mocking the venerable psychiatrist – refusing, for instance, to perform for Kraepelin in front of the audience by refusing to 'whore' for him. The audience, according to Laing, were either unwilling or unable to acknowledge that what he was saying might be sensible partially because the man's status as mad invalidated anything that he said. Thus they concluded that 'he has not given us a single piece of useful information' other than further signs of his illness.[17] This single piece of interpretation, lasting no longer than two pages has, for many commentators summed up the entire contribution of the British anti-psychiatric movement and almost all of the major commentators on that group refer to the event.[18] Even Sedgwick, whose crushing account of Laing's writing, *Psycho Politics* (1982) finds Laing lacking in almost every possible way, acknowledges the importance of this commentary.[19] It was this insistence on the intelligibility of madness that was the guiding light of the anti-psychiatric group.

This insistence on intelligibility had more than psychiatric implications. It became the basis of the anti-psychiatrists' entire social theory. We saw earlier that they argued that madness was socially mandated and determined, this intelligibility is the other side of that coin. By identifying a person as mad they are, the anti-psychiatrists claim, put in a social position to which there is no 'sane' response. The person's subsequent words and actions, therefore, ought to be thought of as a commentary on their untenable social situation. They argued that madness was not simply a manifestation of social relationships, but an embodied critique of them. Madness was essentially, they argued, an acting out of the contradictions and subtle violences that make up everyday life in modern society. The nuclear family they argued was an 'ideological conditioning device.'[20] At the heart of the anti-psychiatric political critique lay the relationship between the specific conditions of individual small-group relations – families, lovers, etc. – and the complex relationships between the individual and powerful institutions like the state, hospitals and universities.[21] The anti-psychiatrists' argued that throughout society political, economic and cultural institutions present an array of apparent personalities with which the individual may identify. By presenting this array the institution enables the individual worker, customer, client etc. to map their own internalised family relations from the domain of their consciousness onto the domain of the institution in question. This is a development of Stanislav Grof's ideas of mapping of perinatal events to later psychopathology.[22]

This mapping has two functions, according to the anti-psychiatrists. The first is that it 'anonymises' individuals within this structure. Thus, for instance, when a patient in a psychiatric hospital talks to a nurse and a psychiatrist he does not engage with them as individuals on an equal level but does so in their role as nurse and doctor, in that sense dehumanizing them.[23] Moreover, in their roles as nurse and doctor they are, in many ways, caricatures of the patient's mother and father.[24] This anonymisation is reciprocal. The institution, as what Laing refers to as 'conditioning... media,' enables anyone who engages with it to anonymise anyone he encounters through the medium of the institution.[25] In many ways Laing's formulation is a reworking of the Freudian idea of transference in mathematical language; the mathematical process of mapping is focused on relations, in that it maps the relations from a set of points in one domain onto a different set of points in another domain, while transference is focused on the externalisation of specific internal objects. Thus, in a hospital setting for instance, a patient would map their relationship with their father onto their relationship with their doctor, rather than attributing personality traits or characteristics of their father to their doctor. However there is also a linguistic break with the Freudian tradition which enables the anti-psychiatrists to shed some Freudian ideological baggage and re-embed themselves in a different tradition of quantitative social sciences – a tradition that they made repeated attempts, although sometimes half-hearted ones, to enter – for instance with the coding structure in *Interpersonal Interpretation*.[26]

The second function of this mapping is that it enables the institution to exercise the power of the family over those who engage with it. Thus if a psychiatric patient engages with a nurse and doctor as though they were his mother and father then he will react to their exercise of power in the same way as he would to that of his parent. Indeed this analysis, put forward by Michael Conran in his discussion of Villa 21,[27] is particularly apt when one considers that the kind of power exercised by the nurse and doctor in this case was extremely like that exercised by parents – the prescription of bedtimes and mealtimes, the limitation of free movement off the ward, punishment for inappropriate behaviour etc. This exercise of power is elementary to the anti-psychiatrists' political critique because it was, as they saw it, a fundamentally inauthentic exchange – an inauthenticity that they tried to redress in their own communities.[28] The anti- psychiatric idea of inauthenticity was heavily indebted to Sartre and they tended to rely on his idea that to be inauthentic was to lie in some fundamental way.[29] Thus the exploitation of people's internalised family relations by institutions was seen as inauthentic because it lies about what the individual's true relationship to the institution actually is. The anti-psychiatrists fetishised the idea of authenticity and spent most of the 1960s locking for authentic selves, experiences and relationships. This extended into their engagement with social institutions and, as will be discussed, they spent much of the period investigating ways of 'liberating' people from this inauthenticity. At the Congress on the Dialectics of Liberation Cooper summed up their conception of authenticity and their liberatory project:

> Schizophrenia is a half-completed, half-chosen retreat from the precariously and artificially stabilized level of highly differentiated experience that passes as sane in our culture at this time. Schizophrenia is a simple project – usually an abortive one thanks to social interference – to rediscover a pristine wholeness that really lies outside one's history but which is pointed to by one's history. This wholeness undercuts the differentiation of experience. It undercuts all the false divisions within and between arts and sciences, and the whole process of bringing people up – education.[30]

Thus, for Cooper, schizophrenia was, in some ways, an aborted attempt at liberation by breaking through the oppression of inauthentic experience. Nor was he the only anti-psychiatrist to hold this position. In 1967, the same year as the Congress, Laing wrote in *The Politics of Experience*: 'Madness need not be all breakdown. It may also be break-through. It is potentially liberation and renewal.'[31] Later in *The Death of the Family* Cooper expanded on this conception of liberatory madness, suggesting that it could be more than merely gestural or abortive:

> In a sense all we have to do first in our first-world context is to liberate ourselves personally by a Madness Revolution... Madness, which is the individual tentative on the part of the actual identifiable people to make themselves ungoverned and ungovernable – not by undisciplined spontaneity but my systematic reformation of their lives that refuses aprioristic systematization but moves through phases of de-structuring, un-conditioning, de-education and de-familializing ourselves so that we at last get on familiar but unfamilial terms with ourselves and are then ready to re-structure ourselves in a manner that refuses all personal taboos and consequently will revolutionize the whole society.[32]

The anti-psychiatrists' position was a wildly romantic one which seemed to flatly ignore the difficult realities of mental illness.[33] Encountering a position like this so baldly stated in the anti-psychiatric canon is simultaneously unsurprising and shocking. It is unsurprising in that, for many years, their counter-cultural comrades, like Trocchi and Leary, had been talking about similar forms of revolution based on liberation through consciousness transformation. This position coupled with the anti-psychiatrists' fascination with the intelligibility of schizophrenia to produce rallying cries like 'If I could turn you on, if I could drive you out of your wretched mind, if I could tell you I would let you know.'[34] However, this fascination is shocking considering their lived experience of the grim realities of schizophrenia and other disorders – realities that are scarcely recognisable in Cooper's description of schizophrenia as the 'systematic reformation' of a life. Moreover the ham-fisted approach to the subject adopted by Cooper here is jarring, coming from a writer and a group who were adept in the adaptation and application of theoretical subtleties, and who were famous for their empathy and understanding of people in extreme mental states. Indeed their conception of liberation itself is a subtle one which they explored in detail throughout the 1960s.

The idea of liberation, for the anti-psychiatrists, was intimately linked with their multi-layered political critique. They believed that the locus of liberation must be fundamentally interstitial. It must take place, they argued, in the relationships between people and institutions. It is only through changing these relationships that one can be liberated. They argued that on a fundamental level this liberatory change must take place in the relationships between the individual and his immediate surroundings. This is clearly indicated in the contributions of Laing and Cooper to The Congress of the Dialectics of Liberation (1967), and the subsequent collection *The Dialectics of Liberation* (1968),[35] or in *The Politics of Experience* (1967), one of Laing's most popular books, in which he echoed the question posed by Lenin: *What is to be done?*[36]

What is to be done? We who are still half alive, living in the often fibrillating heartland of senescent capitalism – can we do more than reflect the decay around and within us? Can we do more than sing our sad and bitter songs of disillusion and defeat? The requirement of the present, the failure of the past, is the same: to provide a thoroughly self-conscious and self-critical human account of man. No one can begin to think, feel or act now except from the starting point of his or her own alienation.[37]

4. Avant-Garde Becomes *arrière-garde*

The engagement with madness as a liberatory tactic was a double-edged sword. On one hand, such engagements were a source of strength in that they enabled an avant-garde groups to develop a social critique which starkly revealed the instability of fundamental concepts in bourgeois society, like sanity. The corollary of this was that something vital had been marginalised or even expelled from society – whether it was the immediacy longed for by the futurists, the irrational knowledge of the surrealists or the personal and collective freedom that the anti-psychiatrists demanded. On the other hand, for many such groups it also proved to be their Achilles heel. This is particularly clear in the history of the anti-psychiatrists.

As already discussed, the anti-psychiatrists' engagement with madness began with a fundamental revaluation of the idea of madness as a categorization of social deviance. However, this re-evaluation also demands a basic acknowledgment that madness, as a category, is defined by the dominant social structures from which these groups seek liberation. Madness in Western societies, they argued, is a medico-juridical construct defined and limited by a considerable weight of literature. The practical implication of this is that the use of madness as a liberatory tactic is always in danger of being outflanked by a shift in the dominant conception of madness.

During the Second Word War the first 'therapeutic communities' had been formed to treat soldiers. These were residential groups based on the principle that the doctor-patient relationship was not the only possible therapeutic relationship. Psychiatrists encouraged or manipulated the relationships between patients so that the entire community became a therapeutic network. Although the reforms were initially limited, the therapeutic community movement grew during the late-1940s and 1950s. As it grew it became increasingly tied to the liberalisation of psychiatric hospitals, 'open door' policies which unlocked wards, and a degree of levelling of staff-patient distinctions. The therapeutic community movement found support in high places, in 1953, for instance, the World Health Organisation released the third report of the Expert committee on Mental Health which called for all psychiatric hospitals to be reformed along therapeutic community lines. Three years later, in 1956, T.P. Rees, president of the Royal Medico-Psychological Association the forerunner of the Royal College of Psychiatrists, inextricably bound the therapeutic community movement to the movement that would become known as deinstitutionalisation. He speculated:

> The other day an Infectious Disease Hospital closed down and was put up for sale, not for lack of staff, but for lack of patients. Perhaps those who are coming after us will regard this period through which we are now passing in psychiatry as the mental hospital era, and maybe at the Annual Meeting of the Royal Medico-Psychological Association in 2056, a coach trip will be arranged to pay a visit to the last of the big custodial care long-term mental hospitals before it is finally converted into a holiday camp![38]

By 1965 D.H. Clark was able to declare the therapeutic community's 'dominance in institutional psychiatry'[39] and support for deinstitutionalisation had grown with the therapeutic community movement. By the early 1960s the case against the hospital had been taken up by those outside the psychiatric milieu. In the past, liberal psychiatric reforms had often been met with suspicion and even protest by the lay community. At Shenley Hospital, in Hertfordshire where Cooper opened the Villa 21 community in 1962, for instance, the fence that had enclosed the estate was removed as part of an 'open door' policy. However by the early 1960s it had to be rebuilt because of a campaign of complaints by the residents of Shenley village. In 1961 an important step was taken to make the case for the hospital abolition discourse in the public eye.[40] Enoch Powell, the then Conservative Minister of Health, delivered, what would become known as 'The Water Tower Speech' to the annual conference of the National Association of Mental Health.[41]

Powell's speech brought together several strands of the argument for hospital reform. Although he did not directly discuss the therapeutic community movement he clearly engaged with many of the movement's themes. Like Maxwell Jones and D.H. Clarke he pointed to the consistent reduction in in-patient numbers and argued that this must not only be continued but accelerated; that the number of inpatients should be, at the very least, halved by 1975; he proposed the 'elimination of by far the greater part of... [Britain's] mental hospitals as they exist today.'[42] Even the remaining in-patient facilities, he argued, would have to be changed. Like T.P. Rees and Maxwell Jones he called for new hospital buildings which would reflect and facilitate new treatment methods. Like M.J. Heron, he argued that psychiatrists and administrators need to make use of the provisions of the 1959 Act and to move psychiatric facilities into 'wards and wings of general hospitals.' But this was not the only structural reform he proposed. Like Joseph Bierer, T.P. Rees and T.F. Main he called for psychiatrists outside mental hospitals to have a progressive attitude: without the growth of new psychiatric services and practices outside the hospital the reduction of in-patient services, he argued, would make 'no sense.'[43] Here he follows Heron who explicitly argues that the 1959 Act can only be understood if the proposed new psychiatric facilities that would replace the old mental hospitals were intended to be therapeutic communities.

This political shift towards deinstitutionalisation, which was already common currency in the political exchanges of the 1960's and which, in the 1980's, would entirely redefine what it meant to be mad in Britain, had gradually robbed the Anti-Psychiatrists of their institutional critique.[44] During the 1960s the great symbol of the asylum began to lose its power and no longer clearly connected the exercise of political power with the definition of madness. Moreover, by the end of the 1970s, forms of half-way houses and therapeutic communities, which the Anti-Psychiatrists had endorsed, looked as though they would become psychiatric orthodoxy. For a variety of mainly personal reasons, but also because the Right had stolen their thunder, the leaders of the group began to fade away. Laing began advocating non-violent birthing techniques and denying that he had ever been a Socialist;[45] Cooper moved to South America and, after a brief spell as an inmate in an asylum himself, began writing about broader Public Policy issues;[46] Esterson had given up on politics to develop his private practice. Many of the practical features of the Anti-Psychiatric programme had not only become psychiatric mainstream,[47] but, in a manner that hollowed out the political purpose and meaning of the theory, to the extent that they had actually become conservative party policies. Thus we can see how the shifts in legal and psychiatric orthodoxy were able to neutralise the anti-psychiatric idea of madness by superficially adopting many of the anti-psychiatric ideas, while negating the politics that lay behind them.

There is a certain inevitability to all of this because the revaluation of madness which is at the origin of most liberatory deployments of the idea, necessarily cedes the definitive power over the concept itself to psychiatrists, jurists and politicians, even though these are the very social forces from which these groups seek liberation. The structure is simple: The law (in conjunction with medicine etc.) defines X as madness: those in the avant-garde believe that this definition is a social construct of a hegemonic class and embrace X as a weapon for fighting that social class. A change in the definition decommissions the weapon. The hegemony will always be able to adjust its position on madness and co-opt certain features of the radical position – through a change in mental health law, a new Diagnostic and Statistical Manual, new treatment guidelines, or a change in the social welfare system. Once the hegemony adopts a position similar to that of the avant-garde, that position is no longer tenable and the avant-garde must retreat to new ground. In other words, the avant-garde is now the rear-guard. For the Anti-Psychiatrists that meant the partial disbandment and total depoliticisation of the group.

Notes

[1] F. T. Marinetti, 'Let's Murder the Moonlight,' *Futurism: An Anthology*, eds. Lawrence Rainey, Christine Poggi and Laura Wittman (New Haven: Yale University Press, 2009), 54-61.
[2] André Breton, *Nadja* (New York: Grove Press, 1960), 141.
[3] Anon, 'Declaration of the German Section of the Situationist International on Madness,' *Spur* 2 (1960): NP.
[4] David Cooper, ed., *The Dialectics of Liberation* (Harmondsworth: Penguin Books, 1968).
[5] Aaron Esterson, David Cooper and R. D. Laing, 'Results of Family-Orientated Therapy with Hospitalized Schizophrenics,' *British Medical Journal* 21462 (1965); R. D. Laing and Aaron Esterson, *Sanity, Madness and the Family* (Harmondsworth: Penguin, 1972).
[6] R. D. Laing and David Cooper, *Reason and Violence: A Decade of Sartre's Philosophy, 1950-1960* (London: Tavistock Publications, 1971).
[7] Robert Boyers and Robert Orrill, *Laing and Anti-Psychiatry* (Harmondsworth: Penguin Books, 1973), 205.
[8] Stephen Ticktin, 'Brother Beast: A Personal Memoir of David Cooper,' *Asylum Magazine for Democratic Psychiatry* 1-2 (1986).
[9] R. D. Laing, *The Politics of Experience and the Bird of Experience* (London: Penguin Books, 1990), 24.
[10] Laing, *The Politics of Experience*, 24.
[11] David Cooper, *Psychiatry and Anti-Psychiatry* (London: Tavistock Publications, 1967), 2.
[12] Cooper, *Psychiatry and Anti-Psychiatry*, 26.
[13] David Cooper, *The Death of the Family* (Harmondsworth, Penguin Books, 1971), 34.
[14] Anon, 'Declaration of the German Section of the Situationist International on Madness.'
[15] Edward Shorter, *A History of Psychiatry: From the Era of the Asylum to the Age of Prozac* (New York: John Wiley, 1997), 272-73.
[16] R. D. Laing, *The Divided Self: A Study of Sanity and Madness* (Chicago: Quadrangle Books, 1960), 30-31.
[17] Laing, *The Divided Self*, 30.

[18] For instance: Peter Sedgwick, *Psycho Politics* (London: Pluto Books, 1987), 74-75; Elaine Showalter, *The Female Malady: Women, Madness and English Culture, 1830-1980* (London: Virago, 1996), 227; Zbigniew Kotowicz, *R.D. Laing and the Paths of Anti-Psychiatry* (Routledge, 1997), 37; Edgar Z. Friedenberg, *Laing* (London: Fontana/Collins, 1973), 16-17; Daniel Burston, *The Crucible of Experience: R.D. Laing and the Crisis of Psychotherapy* (Harvard: Harvard Univeristy Press, 2000), 67.
[19] Sedgwick, *Psychopolitics*, 74-75.
[20] Cooper, *The Death of the Family*, 5.
[21] Burston, *The Crucible of Experience*, 51-52.
[22] Theodore Itten and Courtney Young eds., *R.D. Laing: 50 Years since the Divided Self* (Ross-on-Wye: PCCS Books, 2012), 154.
[23] Cooper, *Psychiatry and Anti-Psychiatry*, 94-95.
[24] Michael Conran, 'The Family as a Model in an Application of Psychoanalysis to the Care and Treatment of Young Male Schizophrenics' (PhD Diss., University of London, 1971), 29.
[25] David Cooper, ed., *The Dialectics of Liberation* (Harmondsworth: Penguin Books, 1968), 16.
[26] R. D. Laing, H. Phillipson and A.R. Lee, *Interpersonal Perception: A Theory and Method of Research* (London: Tavistock Publications, 1966), 37-130.
[27] Conran, 'The Family as a Model,' 52.
[28] Kotowicz, *R.D. Laing and the Paths of Anti-Psychiatry*, 77.
[29] Itten and Young, *R.D. Laing: 50 Years since the Divided Self*, 48.
[30] Cooper, *The Dialectics of Liberation*, 200-01.
[31] Laing, *The Politics of Experience and the Bird of Experience*, 110.
[32] Cooper, *The Death of the Family*, 106-07.
[33] Incidentally, this is not the only romantic position that Cooper adopted on the topic of schizophrenia. In 1965 Cooper wrote: 'There is, relatively speaking, something remarkably healthy about the chronic schizophrenic preoccupied with his inner world, spending the day hunched over the central heating fitting in a decrepit back ward. If he does not have the solution to the riddle of life at least he has fewer illusions.' David Cooper, 'The Anti-Hospital: An Experiment in Psychiatry,' *New Society*, 3 May 1965, 11-16, 13.
[34] Laing, *The Politics of Experience*, 156.
[35] Cooper, *The Dialectics of Liberation*, 10, 16, 197.
[36] V. I. Lenin, *What Is to Be Done?* (New York: International Publishers, 1929). While Lenin borrowed this formulation from Chenschevsky and conceivably Laing came to the question through Dostoyevsky's *Notes from Underground* it seems more likely that Laing came to the question through Lenin when we consider that he regularly carried a volume by Lenin under his arm around Kingsley Hall (1965-1970).

[37] Laing, *The Politics of Experience*, 11.
[38] T. P. Rees, 'Back to Moral Treatment and Community Care: The Presidential Address Delivered at the One Hundred and Fifteenth Annual Meeting Held at Warlingham Park Hospital,' *British Journal of Psychiatry* 103 (1957): 302-13, 313.
[39] D. H. Clark, 'The Therapeutic Community: Concept, Practice and Future,' *British Journal of Psychiatry* 111 (1965): 947-54, 947.
[40] D. D. Rambarran, 'Relocating the Out-of-Area Treatments: Service Users' Perspective,' *Journal of Psychiatric and Mental Health Nursing* 20 (2013): 696-704, 697.
[41] Enoch Powell, 'Address to the National Association of Mental Health Annual Conference (9 March 1961),' (London: National Health Service, 1961), viewed 11 December 2015, http://www.nhshistory.net/watertower.html.
[42] Powell, 'The Watertower Speech.'
[43] M. J. Heron, 'Functions and Problems of Psychiatric Units in General Hospitals,' *British Medical Journal*, 5318 (1962): 1529-31, 1529.
[44] In 1983 Douglas Bennett and Isobel Morris traced the beginnings of deinstitutionalisation back to the 1950's. in their article 'Deinstitutionalization in the United Kingdom' they showed the development of this idea from an institutional and demographic tendency to a clearly articulated ideology in the late 1960's and early 1970's. Douglas Bennett and Isobel Morris, 'Deinstitutionalisation in the United Kingdom,' *International Journal of Mental Health* 11.4 (1982/1983): 5-23.
[45] Sedgwick, *Psycho Politics*, 103.
[46] For instance, see his later work David Cooper, *Qui Sont Les Dissidents* (Paris: Galilée, 1977).
[47] Kotowicz, *R.D. Laing and the Paths of Anti-Psychiatry*, 111-112.

Bibliography

Anon. 'Declaration of the German Section of the Situationist International on Madness.' *Spur* 2 (1960): NP.

Bennett, Douglas and Isobel Morris. 'Deinstitutionalisation in the United Kingdom.' *International Journal of Mental Health* 11.4 (1982/1983): 5-23.

Boyers, Robert, and Robert Orrill. *Laing and Anti-Psychiatry.* Harmondsworth: Penguin Books, 1973.

Breton, André. *Nadja*. New York: Grove Press, 1960.

Burston, Daniel. *The Crucible of Experience: R.D. Laing and the Crisis of Psychotherapy*. Harvard: Harvard Univeristy Press, 2000.

Clark, D. H. 'The Therapeutic Community: Concept, Practice and Future.' *British Journal of Psychiatry* 111 (1965): 947-54.

Conran, Michael. 'The Family as a Model in an Application of Psychoanalysis to the Care and Treatment of Young Male Schizophrenics.' Unpublished doctoral thesis. London: University of London, 1971.

Cooper, David, ed. *The Dialectics of Liberation*. Harmondsworth: Penguin Books, 1968.

Cooper, David. 'The Anti-Hospital: An Experiment in Psychiatry.' *New Society* 3 (1965): 11-16.

———. *Psychiatry and Anti-Psychiatry*. London: Tavistock Publications, 1967.

———. *Qui Sont Les Dissidents*. Paris: Galilée, 1977.

———. *The Death of the Family*. Harmondsworth: Penguin Books, 1971.

Esterson, Aaron; David Cooper and R.D. Laing. 'Results of Family-Orientated Therapy with Hospitalized Schizophrenics.' *British Medical Journal* 21462 (1965): 1462-65.

Friedenberg, Edgar Z. *Laing*. London: Fontana/Collins, 1973.

Heron, M. J. 'Functions and Problems of Psychiatric Units in General Hospitals.' *British Medical Journal* 5318 (1962): 1529-31.

Itten, Theodore; and Courtney Young, eds. *R.D. Laing: 50 Years since The Divided Self*. Ross-on-Wye: PCCS Books, 2012.

Kotowicz, Zbigniew. *R.D. Laing and the Paths of Anti-Psychiatry*. London: Routledge, 1997.

Laing, R. D. *The Divided Self: A Study of Sanity and Madness*. Chicago: Quadrangle Books, 1960.

———. *The Politics of Experience and the Bird of Experience*. London: Penguin Books, 1990.

Laing, R. D. and Aaron Esterson. *Sanity, Madness and the Family*. Harmondsworth: Penguin, 1972.

Laing, R. D. and David Cooper. *Reason and Violence: A Decade of Sartre's Philosophy, 1950-1960*. London: Tavistock Publications, 1971.

Laing, R. D., H. Phillipson, and A. R. Lee. *Interpersonal Perception: A Theory and Method of Research*. London: Tavistock Publications, 1966.

Lenin, V. I. *What Is to Be Done?* New York: International Publishers, 1929.

Powell, Enoch. 'Address to the National Association of Mental Health Annual Conference (9 March 1961).' London: National Health Service, 1961. Viewed 11 December 2013. http://www.nhshistory.net/watertower.html.

Rainey, Lawrence; Christine Poggi and Laura Wittman, eds. *Futurism: An Anthology*. New Haven; London: Yale University Press, 2009.

Rambarran, D. D. 'Relocating the Out-of-Area Treatments: Service Users' Perspective.' *Journal of Psychiatric and Mental Health Nursing* 20 (2013): 696-704.

Rees, T. P. 'Back to Moral Treatment and Community Care: the Presidential Address Delivered at the One Hundred and Fifteenth Annual Meeting Held at Warlingham Park Hospital.' *British Journal of Psychiatry* 103 (1957): 302-13.

Shorter, Edward. *A History of Psychiatry: From the Era of the Asylum to the Age of Prozac*. New York: John Wiley, 1997.

Showalter, Elaine. *The Female Malady: Women, Madness and English Culture, 1830-1980*. London: Virago, 1996.

Ticktin, Stephen. 'Brother Beast: A Personal Memoir of David Cooper.' *Asylum Magazine for Democratic Psychiatry*, 1986, 1-2.

Oisín Wall is an Associate Curator of Medicine at the Science Museum, London. He was the first UCL CLASH Fellow at the Hackney Museum, London, where he ran an AHRC funded research and public engagement project on the Anti-

University of London (1968). He holds a PhD in History from King's College, London, as well as an MRes and a BA.

'You can't label it and there's no umbrella': The Consumer Movement and the Social Construction of Mental Illness

Kara Holmes and Fiona Ann Papps

Abstract
The mental health Consumer Movement of the 1970s challenged the status quo of the dominant psychiatric discourse of mental illness that is furnished with pathologising and deficit-based language. The present research investigates how the language used in contemporary mental healthcare settings sustains the social construction of mental illness and explores whether the dominant discourse about mental health has shifted in response to critiques framed by the Consumer Movement. Semi-structured interviews were conducted with three consumers, three mental health professionals, and two consumer professionals. Data were analysed using Foucauldian discourse analysis. Two primary sets of findings emerged from the analysis. First, the social construction of mental illness is drawn up by two principle discourses: professionals pathologise mental illness and consumers contextualise mental illness. Second, analysis of the social practices of mental healthcare settings as revealed in language foregrounded central concerns around administration. Mental healthcare as an institution has produced what Foucault names 'procedural techniques' for recording information. These are techniques of control that prescribe the rules of conduct for professionals and consumers in the institution of mental healthcare. These techniques reduce the agency and personal responsibility of professionals and marginalise the self-knowledge of consumers. Overall, the dominant discourse of mental healthcare has retained paramount status by incorporating parts of the Consumer Movement on its own terms. Positioning mental health consumers as individuals with participation rights is a political euphemism that disguises the dominant paradigm that is still built upon deficit-based constructions of mental illness.

Key Words: Mental illness, consumer movement, Foucauldian discourse analysis, qualitative, social construction.

*****

1. Introduction

The sudden and unexpected death in 2014 of popular actor, Robin Williams, and his publicised struggle with what has been termed 'mental illness', has led to the concept of mental illness being given an unprecedented amount of attention by the public, the media and the government in contemporary Western societies. This attention has occurred despite psychosocial suffering being reported in almost all known existing world cultures, and at all points in recorded history; a point noted by many of the contributors to this volume.[1] Our awareness of psychosocial suffering, and the multiplicities of frameworks that have been used in our attempts to make sense of such suffering, has influenced theorists such as Michel Foucault to argue that the conceptualisation of psychosocial suffering as mental illness is a social construction.[2] Over the course of history, discourses have positioned individuals with mental illness as subjects to be segregated, controlled, and of biological inferiority and of needing care. In Australia, the Consumer Movement, a diverse association of individuals, organisations, networks, national and local groups, which campaign for improved services for individuals with mental illness, began to gain momentum in the 1970s.[3] This movement has promoted contestation of the discourse of psychiatry, with its pathologising and deficit-based language. It has furthermore allowed individuals with mental illness to represent and understand themselves as self-governing agents with rights and responsibilities, promoting claims to full citizenship and consequent restoration of dignity.[4] This chapter offers an exploration of the ways in which the Consumer Movement has impacted language and power relations in the domain of mental illness. Through a Foucauldian Discourse Analysis of data obtained from semi-structured interviews with consumers, mental health professionals, and consumer-professionals, we show that despite the advocacy attempts of members of the Consumer Movement, the dominant discourse of mental healthcare has retained paramount status by incorporating parts of the Consumer Movement on its own terms. Indeed, positioning mental health consumers as individuals with participation rights is a political euphemism that disguises the dominant paradigm that is still built upon deficit-based constructions of mental illness.

A. The Mental Health Consumer Movement in Australia

In the 1970s, recipients of mental healthcare in Australia were re-named *consumers*, a term that originated in business and market discourse to recognise that consumers of services have a range of rights and expectations of service providers.[5] This reconstruction of identity challenged the relations of power in the institution of mental healthcare, and became part of a larger movement designed to mobilise and challenge the dominant discourse of psychiatry by advocating for consumers of mental health services to recover their rights, to protest the devaluing language used to describe them and to abnegate their roles as powerless subjects.[6] For Meagher, the catchphrase 'nothing about us without us' expressed the central manifesto of consumers at the time. The Consumer Movement strove to transform the social order via two key mechanisms: participation and the concept of recovery.[7]

Anglicare describes the spectrum of participation as 'the micro level of individual decision-making about treatment to macro level involvement in service planning, evaluation, training and research,' capturing the essence of participation as a mechanism by which an existing system can be reformed.[8] The concept of recovery arose in response to the belief that people with a mental illness would never recover.[9] To redress this belief that had become reified as truth, the Consumer Movement advocated for language to shift from a focus on deficit and illness to a focus on wellness and strengths. Consequently, the movement posited the tenets of recovery as taking responsibility, taking control and exercising choice, challenging both the language and the role typologies of the institutional order.[10] This resistance produced new kinds of knowledge, as contestation of the practices of psychiatry produced oppositional frames of reference such as self-determination/coercion, recovery/chronicity, and human rights/paternalism. As a consequence, new social practices (including consumer participation) have emerged, and, as Pelletier observes in this volume, new roles have been made available for consumers to take up.[11]

B. Contemporary Mental Healthcare in Australia

In Australia, clinical care is provided in acute psychiatric units by mobile mental health teams, residential rehabilitation units and community mental health services. Currently, the promotion and availability of primary care means that General Practitioners are typically the first point of contact for psychosocial problems.[12] General Practitioners codify psychosocial problems as anxiety and depression, thereby translating problems into medically diagnosed conditions. Treatment options include both psychopharmacology and the provision of subsidised access to psychology services through the Better Access program.[13] Therefore, the balance between biological and psychological interventions remains skewed toward the former for most consumers, reflecting the dominance of the bio-medical discourse of mental illness in the 21st century. Furthermore, mental health promotion has emerged as a final layer of mental health policy, grounded in neo-liberalist policy.[14] Public education consequently promotes happiness, the absence of mental illness, the right to freedom and the fulfilment of an individual's emotional, intellectual and spiritual potential, clearly aligning with a neo-liberalist agenda of competition, freedom, self-fulfilment, self-agency and consumerism.[15] The relationship between these particular discourses and the all-time-high prevalence of mental illness in current society can be readily imagined. These units of discourse are socially distributed through the language that is the instrument by which we make sense of the world, and thus an analysis of discourse as coded in language, is the focus of our research.

C. Our Research

It has now been over forty years since the Consumer Movement mobilised. An investigation of the movement's impact on language, power relations and experience is therefore timely. Our research was conducted using the framework provided by social constructionism, which replaces *cogito ergo sum*–I think, therefore I am–with *communicamus ergo sum*–we relate, therefore I am.[16] Social constructionism endorses a post-structuralist view of language whereby meaning is always contestable.[17] Because language is a major site where identities can be challenged or changed, our research focuses on the ways in which the characteristics of mental illness have been identified, defined, classified and contested in and through language.[18] The roles of consumer and mental health professionals are key in this process, as consumers and mental health professionals engage in habitualised actions that are reciprocally typified. Hence, the social practices around mental illness are furnished by role typologies in an institutional order that is sustained through language.[19] We are consequently offering a qualitative investigation constructed around two questions: first, how the language used by consumers and mental health professionals sustains the social construction of mental illness; and second, whether the dominant discourse about mental health has shifted in response to the critique framed by the Consumer Movement.

2. Method

A. Participants

Purposive sampling was oriented to two groups whose perspectives on mental illness seemed to be the most relevant to the research questions: mental health professionals and consumers. Three participants identified as mental health professionals, three participants identified as consumers and two participants identified as both mental health professionals and consumers. Participants ranged in age from 30 to 60 and disclosed their occupations in the interviews. Professionals included Neo, a general practitioner in medicine and psychotherapist; Mao, a former psychiatric nurse and senior manager of an inpatient psychiatric unit in a public hospital; and Una; a social worker in a public mental health service. Consumers included Arc, a high school teacher; Xiu, a retired linguist; and Gyp, an engineer. Consumer professionals included Dex, a consumer consultant at a public hospital-based mental health service; and Hans, a Jungian psychologist in private practice. Participants have been identified using pseudonyms in order to preserve anonymity.

B. Method and Analytic Strategy

The research was approved by the Australian College of Applied Psychology HREC, Approval 008290512. Data were generated using semi-structured interviews, based on ten open-ended, non-directive questions about participants' understandings of mental illness (see Appendix A), the Consumer Movement and their experiences of receiving and providing care, and were analysed using Willig's steps for Foucauldian discourse analysis (see Appendix B).[20] We chose Foucauldian discourse analysis as our analytic strategy because of Foucault's recognition of the way in which discourse, knowledge and power are intimately bound.[21] For Foucault, discourses define the world or a person in such a way that a particular form of knowledge is produced, and particular versions of truth come to be dominant.[22] Power is an effect of discourse, and the power to act, and what in ways, depends upon the prevailing discourses of the time.[23] Furthermore, Foucault argues that power and resistance operate in tandem, as dominant discourses are always subject to contestation.[24] Consequently, Foucauldian discourse analysis enabled us to elucidate the ways in which the dominant discourses of mental illness as framed by psychiatry might sustain the social construction of mental illness but also might be contested in response to the critique framed by the Consumer Movement.

C. Reflexivity

As researchers, we were not independent of the social context of the research.[25] We both work in the discipline of psychology, teaching at a mid-size, private college dedicated to the training of counsellors, psychologists and social workers. We are both white and relatively privileged. In order to maintain an awareness of the ways in which our standpoints might have affected the outcomes of our research, KH maintained a reflexive diary during the process of the research to critically self-reflect on thoughts that arose during the research process, particularly when interpreting and analysing data. Furthermore, since social constructionism is a theory that is itself a social construction and regards objectivity as an impossibility, we make no claims that the present research is objective.[26] Our research is a social construction of our own accounts as researchers and it is not the only possible truth. The data are open to reinterpretation. We would argue that although the results from our research are not generalizable, they are transferable. Drawing on post-structuralist theory and social constructionism, the language used by participants is assumed to have some degree of consistency and compatibility with wider discourses about mental health, mental illness, psychiatry, care, and treatment, and so will serve the same functions in a variety of settings and when used by a range of speakers.[27]

3. Analysis

Analysis of the data was structured around two research questions: First, how the language used by consumers and mental health professionals in contemporary mental healthcare settings sustains the social construction of mental illness; and second, whether the dominant discourse about mental health has shifted in response to the critique framed by the Consumer Movement. Therefore, the first stage of analysis is a language deconstruction that addresses the question of how the social construction of mental illness is sustained in language used by participants. This analysis locates two overarching discourses and examines the relationship between them. The second stage of analysis addresses the question of whether the Consumer Movement has made any alterations to the dominant discourse. This stage of the analysis gives attention to social practices and focalises two further aspects of discourse: institutions and power. Sample extracts are presented at each stage of analysis, and our results are presented next.

A. Stage One of the Analysis

In this stage of the analysis, we identified both discursive constructions of the object of mental illness and the discourses use to talk about this object (Willig's Steps One and Two; see Appendix B). The analysis drew up two overarching principle discourses, which we have termed the Dominant Discourse and the Contextualisation Discourse.

i. The Dominant Discourse

This first discourse draws up mental illness as an object that is real. This real object can be objectively defined, classified, distinguished and categorised in language. This discourse does not go beyond these taken-for-granted assumptions. Mental illness is constructed with deficit-based language: profound loss, sickness, interruptions in a person's life, damaged. Accordingly, mental illness is the legitimate object of intervention. This discourse tends towards drawing up mental health and mental illness as dichotomous states that are located inside a person. The following four extracts are samples of this discourse constructed by mental health professionals.

> Extract Neo:
> It's a bit like medicine where we need to distinguish a broken bone from a respiratory infection, from a heart attack … it is important to categorise … it's important to distinguish, broadly speaking, between what is psychotic illness, that is a major categorisation and a major difference to the rest and the rest are various forms of what used to be called neurotic and they are a different category, a different phenomena [sic].

This analogy draws institutional support from the discourse of medicine and functions to validate the assumption that mental illness can be identified in the way that physical illnesses can. Mental illness is constructed as an object that can be distinguished and categorised.

> Extract Mao:
> Mental illness means to me … profound sickness, profound interruptions of a person's life … I see people with profound, you know, bipolars, schizophrenias, early psychosis and young people too. That's what it means to me.

Mao constructs mental illness using pathologising and deficit-based language: 'sickness' and 'interruptions.' His repetition of 'profound' emphasises the intensity and depth of these deficits. Mao constructs mental illness drawing on psychiatric categories that belong to people: 'people *with* [italics added] … bipolars.'

Embedded in this construction is the taken-for-granted assumption that mental illness can be identified and categorised.

> Extract Mao:
> Mental illness defines us, you know, if you, are, you know, I'm, how do I say, am I kind of, am I normal, sane because I am not mentally ill, you know, like, so, my God, is this the, I'm not sure which is the default position there so, you know, so I know, ok I'm sane, no-one's on me, no-one is trying to schedule me, no-one is trying to treat me, I'm not on the street, so I've got a job blah, blah, blah, so ok, I'm not mentally ill.

Mao constructs mental illness as an object that 'defines us.' Mao asks how to define normality and then answers his question by drawing on the discourse of psychiatry. If the practices of psychiatry are not present, i.e., 'no-one's on me, no-one is trying to schedule me, no-one is trying to treat me' then 'I'm sane.' Hence the position of being 'mentally ill' or 'sane' is to be distinguished by psychiatry's response to it. Implanted in this construction is the assumption that mental illness and sanity are dichotomous positions.

> Extract Una:
> Mental illness is a group of disorders and illnesses, um, that are classified from a medical model. It's usually the domain of psychiatrists, psychologists and people in a clinical setting. Um, they can be psychotic disorders, mood disorders, conduct disorders.

Una constructs the object of mental illness using pathologising and deficit-based terms: 'disorders and illnesses.' Una's construction is also dependent on the taken-for-granted assumption that the object can be classified. Una places the task of classification in the domain of a 'clinical setting' populated by professionals: 'psychiatrists, psychologists.' This construction produces institutionalised roles for the application of expert knowledge.

This discourse produces psychiatric knowledge that is operationalised by the 'mental healthcare system.' We refer to this discourse as the *dominant discourse* in recognition of its hegemonic status, and its implication of historicity and control. The dominant discourse draws institutional support from the discourse of medicine and is indistinct from the discourse of psychiatry. The inherent assumptions of the dominant discourse make it difficult to escape the conceptualisation that mental illness is a real object that can be defined, measured, classified and treated (see Figure 1).

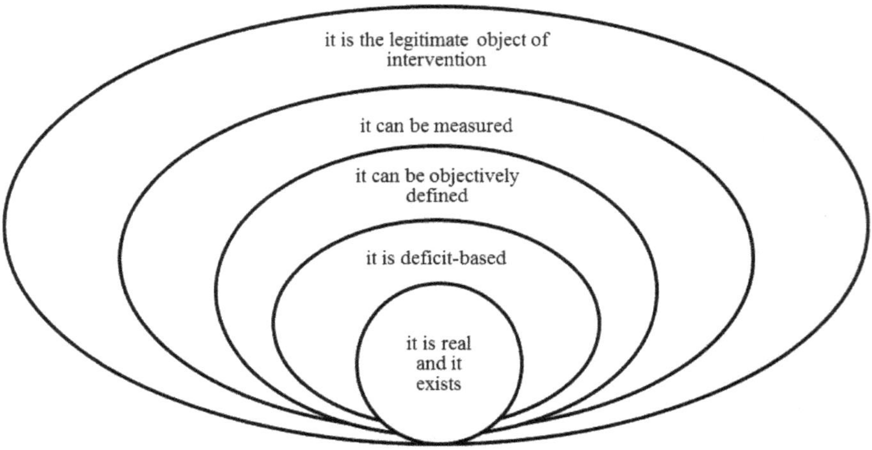

Figure 1: The social construction of mental illness drawn up by the dominant discourse © Kara Holmes. Used with permission.

ii. The Contextualisation Discourse

The *contextualisation discourse* draws up mental illness as an object that might not exist. It is an object that is difficult to identify, is socially defined, is non-dichotomous, is not a pathology and is not always located in the individual. The following extracts are samples of this discourse and are constructions that were drawn up by consumers and a consumer professional.

> Extract Xiu:
> I think mental illness maybe doesn't exist, or doesn't exist in the way that we think it does, and that maybe it's just, everyone is on a spectrum of sanity or insanity or whatever you call it but there's no extremes, you are not at one end and you are sane and at the other end you're insane, everyone is on the spectrum somewhere, even if there is such a thing as insanity, and I really don't think there is.

Xiu constructs mental illness an object that 'maybe doesn't exist.' The phrase 'doesn't exist in the way that we think it does' presupposes that there is an established and mutually available way of thinking about the object, which is an oblique reference to the culturally available dominant discourse. Xiu constructs an alternative using the metaphor 'spectrum': language that invokes a range that prohibits making a distinction between 'sanity' and 'insanity.' This metaphor functions to construct mental illness as non-dichotomous. By saying that 'everyone is on the spectrum somewhere,' Xiu draws up a space that is inclusive of everyone.

> Extract Gyp:
> [Mental illness] is however you define it, where you draw the line … I would say it is entirely socially defined … and groups of people quickly put up boundaries of what's normal and what isn't and what's acceptable behavior and what isn't and that's what mental illness is.

Gyp uses a 'line' metaphor to invoke a boundary of what the object is and what it is not, with the boundary determined by whomever is drawing the line. The object of mental illness is consequently produced as an indeterminate concept that is subject to society's conception of what is 'normal,' thereby undermining the construction that mental illness is a fixed object that can be objectively identified and defined.

> Extract Xiu:
> This thing called bipolar disorder again is not really a pathology as such, it's just people at different points again on that mood continuum … I have been diagnosed as such, I don't actually buy it myself.

Xiu constructs bipolar disorder as a 'thing' and rejects that it is 'a pathology.' He constructs an alternative when he describes a 'continuum.' This produces a sense that no point is perceptibly different from the rest. This everyday language normalises different experiences of mood by placing people on this 'continuum.'

> Extract Arc:
> You can't put it in a box and tie it with a ribbon … it's extreme and it can go from one extreme to the next … you can't label it and there's no umbrella.

Arc constructs the object of mental illness using a metaphor that conveys that it cannot be neatly packaged and sealed. For Arc, the object shifts on a continuum of ordinal classification: 'it can go from one extreme to the next.' Arc denies that the object is fixed and identifiable: 'you can't label it' and 'there's no umbrella.'

This discourse produces different knowledge from the dominant discourse. Consumers drew on this discourse to reject the existence of psychiatric classifications: bipolar affective disorder, attention deficit disorder, Asperger disorder, and depression. Alternative explanations and qualities of the object thrive in this discourse. The following extracts illustrate some of the explanations constructed by consumers and a consumer professional.

> Extract Gyp:
> G: We are just animals, the whole idea that we have a right to be happy and sane and content and everything is just bullshit …
> K: That idea about happiness, where do you think it comes from?
> G: Culture, it has always been an ideal, we have always been told stories about people who are happy or attain happiness.

Gyp constructs humans as 'animals' and in doing so powerfully debases the assumption that 'we have a right to be happy and sane and content.' This assumption resonates with neoliberal discourse that promotes individualism and self-fulfillment. Gyp takes up discourses of cultural stories, anthropology and neo-liberalism to explain the social construction of mental illness.

> Extract Xiu:
> Unfortunately the world has become such a different place that it is hard to look at the world without going mad.

Xiu constructs a world that produces experiences of 'going mad,' which functions to de-pathologise the object of mental illness and locate its cause in the world rather than inside the individual.

> Extract Hans:
> I think it [mental illness] is a result of being shut down emotionally and I think it is a cultural problem, from the point of view that we are all rationalised, it's economic rationalism.

Hans draws on discourses about culture and economic rationalism to construct mental illness.

> Extract Xiu:
> I think that messages about mental health, in some instances far from being reassuring, can actually produce more stress and anxiety because you end up feeling well, the government is telling me that I should be happy and I am not happy so maybe there is something wrong with me and I think anyone who is not insane in this world today, you know, is probably insane.

Xiu constructs mental illness as a product of government directive: 'the government is telling me.' This indirect reference to economic rationalism resonates with Hans's construction in the previous extract.

This second discourse constructs mental illness as a sane response to a mad world, as the product of economics, neoliberalism, fashion, media, psychiatry, and mental health promotion: a construction noted by many of the authors in the chapters in this volume.[28] Drawing on this discourse was typically attended by an awareness of subjectivity that was signalled by participants' use of qualifiers: 'it's just my observation,' 'I wouldn't claim to know,' 'maybe,' 'I would say,' 'I am not an expert' and 'in my understanding.' Thus, this discourse does not make claims to absolute truth in regards to the object of mental illness. This discourse undermines binary classifications of the object by invoking non-dichotomous metaphors: continuums, spectrums, rev counters and scales. We therefore refer to this discourse as the contextualisation discourse (see Figure 2) in recognition of its inclusion of wider discourses to explain the social construction of mental illness.

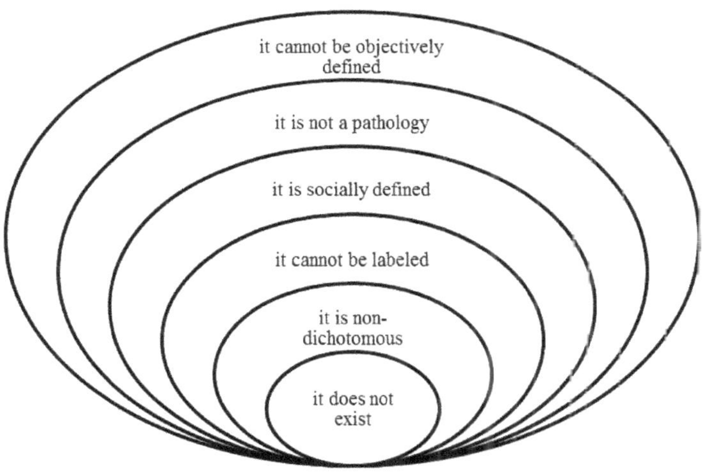

Figure 2: The social construction of mental illness drawn up by the contextualisation discourse © Kara Holmes. Used with permission.

We acknowledge that the contextualisation discourse may be drawn up into secondary discourses (see Figure 3). In this analysis, however, it is sufficient to conceptualise this discourse as a body of knowledge that entails and embeds wider discourses to explain the object of mental illness. The contextualisation discourse locates the object of mental illness in a discursive world that is inclusive of many contributing factors to the social construction of mental illness.

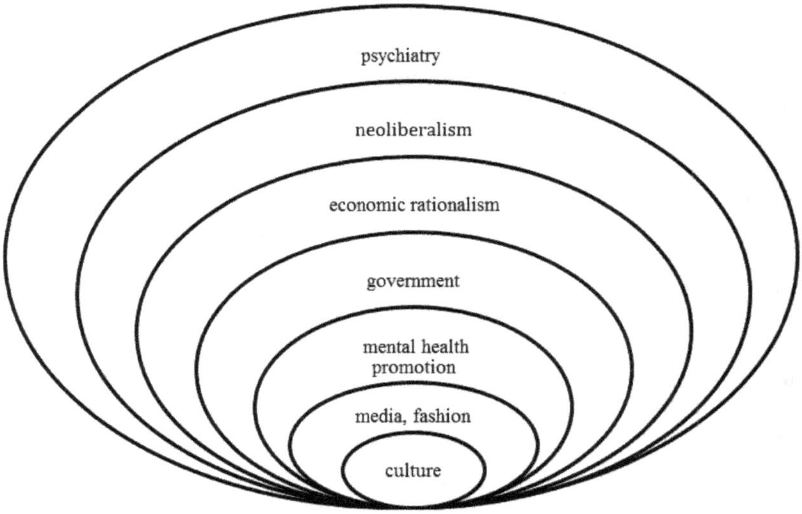

Figure 3: Factors drawn up by the contextualisation discourse to explain the social construction of mental illness © Kara Holmes. Used with permission.

The two discourses produce different types of knowledge and divergent versions of the truth. The hegemonic status of the dominant discourse means that the relationship between the two discourses is one of contestation. The contextualisation discourse contests that mental illness is a real, objective and measurable thing. An inquiry into what is gained from constructing the object of mental illness with either of these discourses reveals relations of power. We discuss these next.

The dominant discourse pathologises mental illness and locates the object of mental illness inside the individual. The discourse brings deviation from 'normality' into the realm of mental health with its proliferation of disorders and categories. The regimes of truth in this discourse are historically located in Australia's social practices of responding to mental illness. Drawing on this discourse obscures the contribution of non-psychiatric factors to explain the social construction of mental illness. Professionals drew almost exclusively on the dominant discourse to construct mental illness. This functions to validate professionals' roles, their practices of treating the consumer and the institution within which these practices take place, maintaining them in a position of significant social power.

In contrast, drawing on the contextualisation discourse gives attention to the factors that are ignored by the dominant discourse (see Figure 3). The contextualisation discourse maps a picture of a world that features an intricate social context. In so doing, it calls for an acknowledgement of the problems with this world. The discourse functions to normalise experiences of mental illness and to ground our experiences in the world in which we live. Tenets of this discourse were shut down in the early 19th century. This is when madness became a disease category and a person's failure to achieve in a society of opportunity was attributed to an underlying pathology.[29] Drawing on the contextualisation discourse subverts the institution of mental healthcare that locates the object of mental illness inside a person. Consumers mostly drew on this discourse and called for an acknowledgment of wider discourses to explain the social construction of mental illness. The contextualisation discourse resists existing power relations. Furthermore, consumers connect the dominant discourse of mental healthcare with other institutions that sanction oppression: neoliberalism, economic rationalism, government, and the media. The contextualisation discourse disputes the legitimacy of the social practices of the dominant discourse. These social practices will be examined in the next stage of analysis.

B. Stage Two of the Analysis

The second stage of analysis follows Willig's procedural guidelines of action orientation for Foucauldian discourse analysis (Willig's Steps Three to Six; see Appendix B).[30] This stage of the analysis will give attention to the social practices of responding to mental illness for it is in these practices that we can address if dominant discourse about mental health has shifted in response to the critique framed by the Consumer Movement. As the Consumer Movement mobilised to challenge the unequal power relations that were inherent in the institutional social practices of mental healthcare, Parker's instructions for focalising institutions and power guide this stage of analysis.[31] This analysis delimits social practices into five areas that emerged from the data: role fulfilment, standardisation, risk management, sharing knowledge, and evaluating care (see Figure 4). As illustrated in Figure 4, the practice of gathering and recording information pervades these social practices. Each practice will be addressed in turn and is accompanied by extracts.

i. Role Fulfilment

Professionals justify the systemic response to consumers by constructing demand and positioning themselves as fulfilling their role in this system. Embedded in these constructions is the taken-for-granted assumption that mental illness can be identified and categorised. The following extracts are a sample of the discursive strategies employed by professionals.

> Extract Una:
> You are meant to be assessing someone's needs and what services they might qualify for or what services would be useful

> but all they end up getting invariably is a risk assessment which you know is what they are not there for and you do the best you can but it is such a workload intensive environment and you're, you know, as a worker you are absolutely slammed.

By using the term 'meant,' Una defers to the systemic demands placed on her when assessing consumers' needs. 'All they end up getting' produces a sense that consumers ought to be responded to with more than 'risk assessment.' She justifies the systemic response by constructing demand and positioning herself as 'absolutely slammed' in a 'work load intensive environment.' Una acknowledges consumer disappointment: 'you know that's not what they are there for' before validating herself as fulfilling her role: 'you do the best you can.'

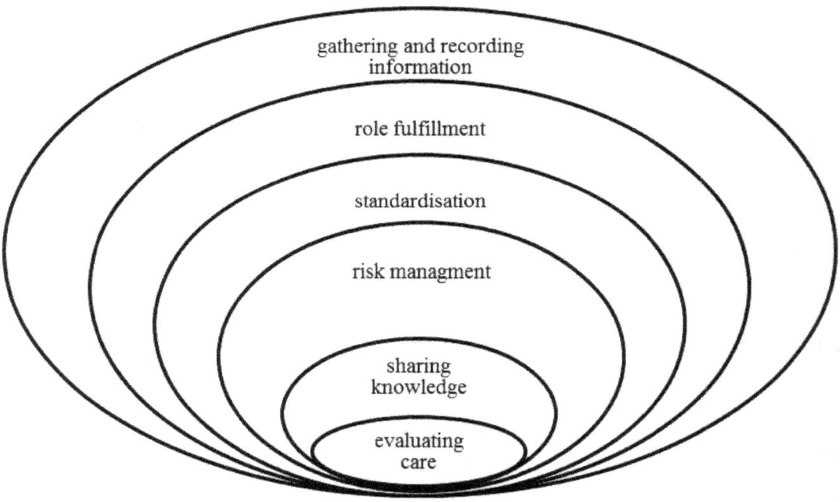

Figure 4: Social practices of the dominant discourse in response to the object of mental illness © Kara Holmes. Used with permission.

> Extract Una:
> I work in, invariably, with triage day once a week, you know, and the purpose of that is to provide a really brief assessment of someone, you know, they're walking in, calling in, or a fax has come across, um from another service, requesting follow-up and your job is to funnel essentially in the right direction. And I guess the reason that comes to mind is that people come in, it can take a lot for people to come in off the street or pick up the phone

> and say that they need help … the pressures on workers in that setting is enormous.

Una scripts the demands placed on her in triage. The verb 'to funnel' depersonalises consumers. Personal responsibility for this impersonal process is alleviated by Una's deference to her 'job.' She then counters the impression that consumers are objectified in this practice by validating their requests for help from the system. Una then repositions herself as a worker under 'enormous pressure.'

> Extract Una:
> I have had, I guess, evidence to support that people feel invalidated and, um, you know, unheard and like numbers at a deli and it's awful but the reality as a worker is that you get it done as quickly as possible.

Una's use of 'I guess' suggests that Una is not committed to what she is about to say. Using the simile 'like numbers at a deli,' she objectifies consumers while also conveying demand. She interactively positions consumers as feeling 'invalidated' and 'unheard.' Una assesses that 'it's awful' which works subtly to manage blame and accountability.[32] Una justifies her position by appealing to the 'reality' of her role as a worker where 'you just get it done as quickly as possible.' This construction distances Una from the consumer as their experiences are mediated by the system.

> Extract Una:
> They won't leave that hospital well, they will leave when they're not sick enough to be there anymore, and that's what you are trying to, trying to argue and it's a tough sell and it's not one that I am saying that they should, or could be able to do any differently, because the bed pressure is huge, absolutely huge, but, you know, you've just got to advocate and try the best you can but you know your patients will leave hospital generally before you think they are ready.

Una's construction first produces a sense of systemic neglect for patients who are discharged before they are 'well' and implies that they are 'sick.' She constructs her advocacy for better care in economic terms: 'it's a tough sell.' Una counters any impression that the system is neglectful by constructing the rationale of 'bed pressure.' She then disclaims the existence of an alternative by saying: 'it's not one that I am saying they should, or could be able to do any differently.' While Una critiques the system's practices, her compliance to the institution is maintained.

These constructions of role fulfilment validate the system's institutionalised response to consumers. This validation is achieved by drawing attention to the demands on the system and by positioning professionals as fulfilling their roles in an institutional order. Moreover, a social structure emerges. The institution responds to demand by placing demands on professionals who then place demands on consumers in order to fulfil the duties of their roles. Power circulates in this structure (see Figure 5). Relations of power feature in the following analyses.

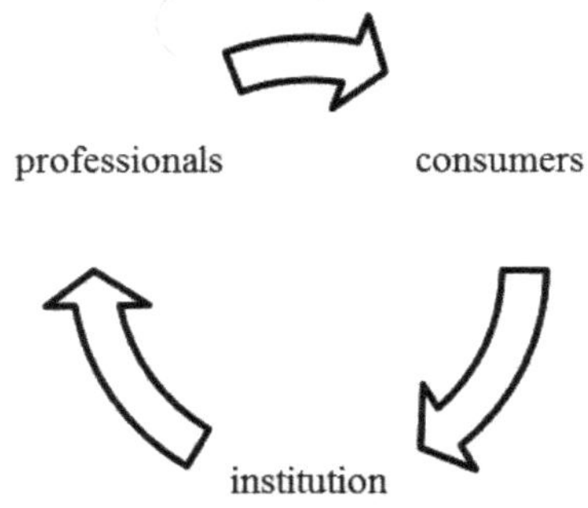

Figure 5: Relations of power in the domain of mental healthcare © Kara Holmes. Used with permission.

ii. Standardisation

The dominant discourse has produced the knowledge that mental illness can be measured, assessed and recorded. Standardised formats are a technique produced by the institution to measure, assess, and record. Relations of power are manifest in constructions of standardisation. The following three extracts are samples of professionals' constructions.

> Extract Una:
> Using standardised formats… you try and have a conversation with people, but even in that the requirement to record it in something so structured can be difficult in itself and you often don't have the space to talk about something clearly that might, that you'd like to really layout and map out.

Una constructs her compliance with the institution's requirements that professionals use standardised formats. Una draws attention to the absence of her personal agency: 'you often don't have the space to talk.' Hence, the institution prescribes the types of conversations that can occur between professionals and consumers.

> Extract Una:
> Sometimes you have to, you really have to, kind of foot note what you say, you have to say in advance, I am going to ask you some things that might seem odd or unusual, they are questions that we ask everyone.

Una uses a footing shift, 'you,' to direct accountability away from her.[33] In so doing, she communicates that standardisation is mandatory and indiscriminate. This positions her as not having agency in this process. Una relays that she 'footnotes' what she says to consumers as a strategy for making standardisation acceptable. Una constructs this explanation as sufficient to garner consumers' co-operation, consequently she positions consumers as complicit in assisting her to meet the demands of her role and hence, the system.

> Extract Una:
> Our clients are incredibly generous with their time, they are incredibly generous and I really think that they are invariably more than accepting of, you know, the person in front of them and that there is some things that they need to do in terms of who their employer is.

This extract follows on immediately from the previous extract. Una now constructs consumers' response to standardisation: 'they are incredibly generous with their time.' She interactively positions consumers as being accepting of the institution's demands on her: 'some things they [professionals] need to do in terms of who their employer is.' This construction de-centres consumers in the system. The institution is integrated into consumers when they participate in standardised dialogues with 'odd or unusual questions' that are inappropriate to their presentation. These constructions reinforce the reality of the institutional response to consumers.

The following extracts are samples of consumers' constructions of receiving care with standardisation processes.

> Extract Arc:
> Do you feel like you are worthless, ah yes, and then tick and that's it … you are ticked off for the plan … It was question and answer and I was like it was fine, because I don't care about you and I know that you don't care about me.

Arc uses active voicing to convey the question that the professional addressed to her: 'do you feel like you are worthless.' Arc relays her answer 'ah yes' and the professional's response was 'tick.' This construction draws attention to the collecting and recording of information in the pursuit of an administrative goal:

completing the plan. Arc constructs this interaction as 'question and answer' and makes an assessment of it: 'I was like it was fine, because I don't care about and I know that you don't care about me.' This assessment produces an impression that the dialogue is attended by a mutual disregard between the professional and the consumer.

> Extract Xiu:
> I have never had a clear diagnosis from anyone, I had a number of symptoms that I wanted to talk about and I mentioned a couple of them, you know, writing down and asking questions and when I wanted to ask questions about what I thought was related, it didn't fit into the checklist so they weren't interested in moving the conversation in the other direction.

Xiu draws on the dominant discourse's incapacity to produce 'a clear diagnosis' by interpreting his 'symptoms.' Xiu reflects that he 'wanted to ask questions' but as they 'didn't fit into the checklist,' they were dismissed.

The analysis of standardisation reveals how power is coordinated. The institution prescribes the format in which professionals are to collect consumers' information. Hence, standardisation practices reduce the personal agency of professionals. However, the professional is positioned as having control over the dialogue. The professional then provides the framework from within which the consumer is to come to understand themselves. Furthermore, dialogues driven by standardisation and information recording processes do not comply with the essence of conversation whereby partners create meanings together.[34] Instead, the consumer's contribution to the dialogue is reified into a 'diagnosis' or a 'mental health plan.'[35] Standardisation practices reproduce the institutionalised role typologies. The professional abandons pragmatics and controls the interaction in order to comply with the institutional practice of information gathering. The consumer is de-centred and dismissed in this process.

iii. Risk Management

Risk management is a social practice of the institution of mental healthcare that was constructed by professionals. The following extracts are samples that contributed to the analysis.

> Extract Mao:
> It's like the biggest thing risk, media coverage, complaints, problems.

Mao constructs risk as an object and uses the adjective 'biggest' to give the object a size. The biggest size conveys that risk is an object that is dominant over other objects in the system. Hence, risk is prioritised. Mao constructs the negative consequences of not attending to risk: exposure, 'media coverage, complaints and problems.' This construction functions to legitimise the institution's practices for managing risk.

> Extract Mao:
> Minimising risk, and it is a risk environment, everyone is thinking risk. Yeah, so that means that there is going to be very little creativity, as it trickles down to the staff, but it is, it's minimising risk.

Mao constructs the system's objective as 'minimising risk.' This objective is internalised by professionals and prevents innovation: 'everyone is thinking risk.' This functions to manage Mao's accountability as he projects outside himself in order to deflect personal responsibility. The metaphor 'it trickles down to the staff' produces a hierarchical structure in which the concept of risk flows through all levels of the system.

> Extract Mao:
> We are in a risk, this sort of high anxiety, that means that creativeness is going to be, creativity is going to be squashed .. the system is shaping me.

Mao locates professionals in a 'high anxiety' place together using the first person plural pronoun 'we.' Mao gives the object of risk a weight that can suppress innovation: 'squashed.' Thus, deviations from the institutionalised practices become highly improbable. Mao's construction that 'the system is shaping me' produces an institutionalised person who has compromised agency. This functions to produce the dominance and power of the system and alleviates Mao from having personal responsibility.

> Extract Mao:
> Risk environment … there's just so much concern … about their careers, concern about being in the media, concerned about … being in somebody's spotlight and keeping out of that as much as possible … so what that means is enormous amounts of briefs, reports … everyone needs to know what everyone, what is going on.

Mao builds a picture of a surveillanced environment by using the metaphor 'spotlight.' He invokes an atmosphere in which professionals are concerned and are held accountable in ways that may be considered excessive 'everyone needs to know what everyone, what is going on.' This produces the hierarchical and political structure of the institution.

> Extract Mao:
> It's a micro-managed situation. So the experience at the moment in terms of mental illness is that it is just tedious and it is highly prescriptive.

Mao constructs the system as a 'micro-managed situation' that is 'tedious and highly prescriptive.' This produces an institutionalised response to mental illness whereby deviations from the institutional order require non-compliance to the prescribed rules of conduct.

Analysis of the social practice of risk management reveals a hierarchical observational structure featuring surveillance and fear of exposure. This structure reduces the agency of the professional as evidenced by professionals' use of discursive strategies to avoid personal responsibility. Deviations from the institutional order are very unlikely as the compliance to the prescribed practices prohibit innovation and creativity. These constructions reinforce the reality of the institutionalised response to mental illness.

iv. Sharing Expert Knowledge

The social practice of sharing knowledge emerged in constructions of providing care. The following extracts are samples of professionals' constructions that contributed to the analysis.

> Extract Neo:
> Labeling something is really for the use of the diagnostician, it is not much use for the recipient of the label, in fact, sometimes the recipient of the label is, in fact, handicapped by that label. And begins to identify with the label so that they are actually boxed in, the label is of no value to the consumer, it is value for discussion amongst colleagues, maybe, I'm not even completely sure about that, but it certainly allows for different categorisations and severity to be discussed in a shorthand way amongst colleagues so that we may distinguish, it's a bit like in medicine where we need to distinguish a broken bone from a respiratory infection, from a heart attack, you know, an abdominal ulcer or category, in these situations it is important to categorise so we may approach it differently.

Neo's construction legitimises the labelling of mental illness by drawing a parallel to the discourse of medicine. This discursive construction positions professionals as the rightful and exclusive appliers of the expert knowledge. In contrast, Neo positions the consumer adversely and renders them incapable of using expert knowledge appropriately as they 'begin to identify with it.' This construction functions to privilege professionals and to undermine consumer capacity.

> Extract Una:
> I really enjoy[ed] today I spent … an hour and a half sitting with a man who has a diagnosis of PTSD but didn't even know what the PT and SD stood for so working through that and having a really slow, deliberate, balanced approach.

Una constructs PTSD is as an object that the consumer 'has.' He 'didn't *even* [italics added] know what the PT and SD stood for' produces a sense that the consumer should know as the diagnosis belongs to him. Una positions herself as the expert who used a 'deliberate approach' which produces control over the interaction. This construction reinforces the institution's role typologies where the professional is the expert.

> Extract Una:
> This particular client … I would much rather spend the hour going through that PTSD psycho-education and him being able to label his distress, be able to articulate his distress.

Una produces an account of why she shared the expert knowledge with the consumer. By calling this 'psycho-education,' Una draws attention to the fact that this practice has been formalised and named by the dominant discourse. The process requires two institutionalised roles: the consumer and the professional. The consumer is positioned as the student and the professional is positioned as the expert. Una formulates that the goal of 'psycho-education' is for the consumer to be 'able to label his distress, be able to articulate his distress.' In effect, Una is colonising his experience with the dominant discourse, illustrating the privileging of professional discourse over the consumer's own language and therefore the consumer's own reality.

> Extract Una:
> I talk much more in terms of recovery and future than I do in terms of treatment, even when I am having discussions around treatment and risk.

Una's construction conveys that the act of talking more about 'recovery' than 'treatment' involves the act of talking about treatment. Central to Una's conceptualisation of recovery is treatment and risk. Thus, the institution has incorporated the Consumer Movement's concept of recovery in name only as the concept is weighed down with the deficit-based language of the dominant discourse: treatment and risk.

> Extract Una:
> A couple of weeks ago a man came in, he says to me … that he believed he had schizophrenia but he was never diagnosed but he in fact had been diagnosed with borderline personality disorder which he very much disagreed with. He had attended a local NGO where he was given a pamphlet of local services one of which included our mental health service, he came along because he hadn't been linked in with a mental health service … yet, and he saw that our co-located service not only involved mental health but homeless health, he came into triage, saying I have seen your board out front, I want to be referred to homeless health and I said well I can't do that, because that's not a pathway that I was able to do. What in fact he needed was … go back to that NGO and attend that homeless health clinic … I guess, you know, the diagnosis of the, of the personality disorder kind of speaks to the, the, he quickly jumped to a maladaptive way of trying to get, you know what he wanted from me which was to yell.

Una formulates a script about a consumer with whom she interacted. Una establishes the consumer's contention with his 'diagnosis.' Una's use of 'in fact' conveys that she privileges the diagnosis that was given to him over the diagnosis that he 'believed he had.' 'In fact' also implies that the diagnosis that was given to him was the reality or the truth. Una interprets his behaviour using the framework of diagnosis given by the system. This version of events reinforces the dominant discourse's pathologisation and management of the object of mental illness. The consumer's self-knowledge is entirely dismissed.

> Extract Neo:
> One client last year who came with a view that her anxiety and panic are to do with her nutritional state and her chemistry, like she had to get the right magnesium, or zinc or copper levels to get the food right and so on, so I was working with her … but she was really not fully committed to working with her emotional state and wanted to continue pursuing medication or metabolic approaches, and I didn't, she stopped seeing me … I kind of have to allow that some people are in a particular state of life when they are ready to look at something and sometimes

> they are not, they are actually psychologically too young for this type of work or because this work is advanced and because some people don't have a clue what the hell I'm talking about.

In this script Neo constructs a hermeneutic circle.[36] The consumer who rejects 'treatment' is constructed as 'not fully committed,' 'not ready,' 'psychologically too young' and not sufficiently 'advanced' for this work. This functions to place blame on the consumer and not on the professional and the professional's type of treatment.

The analysis of professionals' constructions of sharing knowledge reveals the institution privileges expert/professional knowledge, marginalises consumers' knowledge, undermines consumers' capacity, colonises consumers' experiences with discourse, and employs hermeneutic circles to blame the consumer for unsuccessful treatment.

v. Evaluating Care

The social practice of evaluating care emerged in participants' constructions of providing and receiving care. The following three extracts are professionals' constructions that contributed to the analysis.

> Extract Mao:
> The consumer and the family like they are just there, just part, they are not the centre, the centre for the manager is how am I going to, I have got to do this brief, I have to find all the information, I can't stuff up.

Mao de-centres consumers in this construction of the institution: 'they are not the centre.' Mao then positions himself as compliant with the institution: 'I can't stuff up.' This construction reinforces the reality of the hierarchical structure of the institution with central concerns around administration.

> Extract Mao:
> As a manager … my principle concerns are, are the patients moving from ED [Emergency Department], have we got enough beds, what is their length of stay, or this sort of stuff that comes down, so nowhere does anyone say what sort of care are they getting? Everyone says are they out of ED within four hours, have they spent more than 35 days in the ward, have they had this many reviews, this many risk assessments? I'm not saying that gathering assessments is a bad thing.

By constructing an environment that includes 'everyone,' Mao is alleviated from taking personal responsibility for evaluating care. Mao attends to the high demands of administration and scripts this in a way that closes down the possibility that he could also evaluate care: 'nowhere does anyone say what sort of care are they getting.' He then counters any impression that he is suggesting that things could be done differently: 'I am not saying that gathering assessments is a bad thing.' Mao's compliance to the institution is maintained in the presence of an admission that the quality of care is not regarded.

> Extract: Una
> I don't have time in the grand week of getting through my work to [get feedback], we don't, I, don't know, I just try to do the best I can.

Una's use of the adjective 'grand' implies superiority. From this superior position, Una closes down the possibility that she can seek consumer feedback. By using the first person plural pronoun 'we,' she distributes accountability to other professionals. Una's shift to 'I' then counters personal responsibility: 'I just try to do the best I can.' Hence, professionals are positioned to meet the high demands placed on them by the institution. This construction functions to validate professionals' failure to evaluate care.

The following extract is a consumer's construction of care evaluation.

> Extract Arc:
> I felt like I knew I needed to do it and maybe if I went back now it would be different because I wouldn't feel that anxiety and I could probably say, now that I am not so anxious about everything, I could say, hang on, I've done this, this is not what I need, but I wasn't there then.

Arc constructs her experience of not giving feedback to a psychologist. This construction reveals unequal power relations as Arc reflects that she did not feel able to communicate her needs: 'but I wasn't there then.' This draws attention to the potential value of evaluating care in processes that minimise the effects of power relations.

This analysis exposes the institution's failure to make evaluation processes available. One of the key principles of the Consumer Movement is the right for consumers to participate in decision-making at micro and macro levels. The National Standards for Mental Health Services specified how services are to consult consumers in the planning and evaluation of services.[37] This analysis reveals an absence of evaluation practices in this sample of experiences.

vi. Summary of Findings

The second stage of analysis examined five areas of social practices that emerged in the data: role fulfilment, standardisation, risk management, sharing knowledge, and evaluating care. Analysis of each practice reveals that the principles of the Consumer Movement have not made any alterations to the dominant discourse. Indications of the movement's impact may have included non-pathologising language with a focus on wellness and strengths rather than deficit, practices which value the consumer's self-knowledge, practices to evaluate care, and opportunities for consumer participation. The analysis, however, reveals unequal power relations in all areas of practice.

Furthermore, the analysis demonstrates the centrality of administration in the institution. Foucault noted that in the modern era, power is coordinated by the invention of procedural techniques.[38] The techniques of collecting, recording, and standardising information are a form of social control and have dominion over both professionals and consumers. The agency of professionals is negated and personal responsibility is avoided. Consumers are complicit in meeting the needs of the institution when they participate in standardised dialogues. A depersonalised system of bureaucracy has emerged. The institution's procedural techniques alienate the consumer and the professional from one another as their identities and experiences are mediated by the system. Foucault stated that techniques and procedures are accorded value in the acquisition of truth.[39] The procedural techniques of the institution of mental healthcare are limited to acquiring only the truths that are consistent with the dominant discourse's inherent assumptions.

Institutionalised role typologies persist. The professional is positioned as the expert. Expert knowledge is privileged and consumers' knowledge is marginalised. The dominant discourse retains contemporary status by naming this institutionalised process 'psycho-education' and 'psycho-social education.' Furthermore, the dominant discourse has incorporated the concept of recovery on its own terms. Professionals contaminate the concept with pathologising and deficit-based language: 'treatment' and 'risk.' The experiences of consumers are colonised with the language and reality of the dominant discourse.

The social phenomena of mental illness is sustained through the five areas of social practice identified in the interviews. It is evident that an extreme transition would be required in order to abandon the knowledge of the dominant discourse as it has come to be established as reality, and hence deviation from the institutional order appears to be a departure from reality.[40] Despite the rhetoric of consumer participation at national policy levels in Australia, it appears that a genuine power shift has not occurred. The dominant discourse is reinforced in all areas of practice and the social construction of mental illness is sustained in language.

4. Conclusions

In conclusion, professionals pathologised mental illness and consumers contextualised mental illness; a theme also noted by the consumer members of the co-researcher team in Pelletier's research.[41] Professionals in our research looked to the institution of mental healthcare to construct mental illness. In contrast, consumers looked away from the institution of mental healthcare to both construct mental illness and to make sense of their experiences. The contexualisation discourse drawn up by consumers' calls for an acknowledgement of the problems of the world and functions to ground and normalise experiences of mental illness. Consumers connected the dominant discourse of mental health with economic institutions that sanction oppression: economic rationalism and neoliberalism. This tells us something about the way these discourses articulate with each other. Although mental health is receiving an unprecedented amount of attention in contemporary Western societies, what we learn from the contexualisation discourse is that an individual's problems with many institutions have been brought into the realm of mental health.[42]

The analyses of the social practices of the institution of mental healthcare revealed that the institution has central concerns around administration. The institution has produced what Foucault names 'procedural techniques' for recording information.[43] These are techniques of control that prescribe the rules of conduct for professionals and consumers in the institution of mental healthcare. These techniques reduce the agency and personal responsibility of professionals and marginalise the self-knowledge of consumers.

As the discourse of psychiatry has risen to hegemony in Western industrialised societies, alternative knowledges of psychosocial suffering have been occluded. Therefore, the dominant discourse of mental healthcare has retained paramount status; it continues to do so by incorporating parts of the mental health Consumer Movement on its own terms. Positioning mental health consumers as individuals with participation rights is a political euphemism that disguises the dominant paradigm that is still built upon deficit-based constructions of mental illness.

In this research, we have attempted to undermine the familiarity of the present. The dominant discourse of mental health is a version of the truth that is kept in place by language and power. Our research functions to draw attention to the language that maintains unequal power relations in the domain of contemporary mental healthcare. As social constructionism replaces 'I think, therefore I am' with 'we relate, therefore I am,' it is in language that a genuine power shift may occur. The results of our research calls for a reflection on what we do when we speak. We must examine our language to get beyond our entrenched perspective.

Appendices

A. Appendix A: Interview schedule

Can you please tell me what mental illness means to you?

Can you please describe the part that mental illness plays in your life?

Can you please tell me about your experience of mental illness?

Can you please talk me through one of your first experiences of receiving of providing mental health care? What was this like for you?

Can you please talk me through other experiences of receiving or providing mental health care that come to mind? What was this like for you? Why has this particular experience come to mind?

Can you please talk me through one of your more recent experiences of receiving or providing mental health care? What was this like for you?

Can you please tell me about a time when your expectations of mental health care were met?

Can you please tell me about a time when your expectations of mental health care were not met?

Can you please tell me about your understanding of the mental health consumer movement?

Can you please tell me about how the mental health consumer movement may have impacted on your experiences of receiving or providing mental health care?

B. Appendix B: Willig's Guidelines for Foucauldian Discourse Analysis

Discourse in Foucauldian Discourse Analysis (FDA) refers to any particular shared knowledges and corresponding practices, and an *object* refers to an event or any topic of the discourse.[44] Distinct discourses may present the same object in various ways through discursive constructions, and may generate various subject positions.[45] The ways in which specific discourses are confirmed through functional events within society are referred to as material practices.[46] The object investigated in the present research is mental illness.

Although there is no prescriptive format for performing a FDA, the following steps were proposed by Willig[47] as general guidelines, and were drawn upon in this research. These steps are summarised as follows:

Step one: Identifying discursive constructions. Involves locating all variations in how the object is mentioned.

Step two: Locating discourses. Establishing which discourses are being drawn upon through the various discursive constructions.

Step three: Action orientation. Exploring how these discursive constructions produce specific achievements or effects at various points throughout the text.

Step four: Positionings. Acknowledging the resulting subject positions made available through these discursive constructions and discourses.

Step five: Practice. Identifying possibilities for opening up or closing down actions that result from asserting these subject positions.

Step six: Subjectivity. Exploring possibilities for thoughts, emotions and experiences that these subject positions could assume.

Notes

[1] Jean-François Pelletier, 'The Lived Experience of Mental Health Issues as a Constructive Asset for Redefining Citizenship and Social Inclusion,' *And Then the Monsters Come Out': Language, Power and Madness*, ed. Fiona Ann Papps, (Oxford: Inter-Disciplinary Press, 2014), 23; Hans Pols and Stephanie Oak, 'Mental Health in Australia: Current State and New Directions,' *International Journal of Mental Health* 40.2 (2011): 3.

[2] Michel Foucault, *The History of Sexuality Volume 1: An Introduction* (New York: Pantheon, 1978), 25.

[3] Anglicare Tasmania, *Experts by Experience: Strengthening the Mental Health Consumer Voice in Tasmania* (Australia: Anglicare Tasmania, 2009), viewed 29 March 2011, www.slhd.nsw.gov.au/.

[4] Pelletier, 'The Lived Experience of Mental Health Issues as a Constructive Asset for Redefining Citizenship and Social Inclusion,' 22.

[5] Janet Meagher, *Partnership or Pretence? A Handbook of Empowerment and Self-Advocacy for Consumers of Psychiatric Services and Those Who Provide or Plan Those Services* (NSW: Psychiatric Rehabilitation Association, 2002), 3.
[6] Stephen M. Buechler, 'New Social Movement Theories,' *Sociological Quarterly* 36.3 (1995): 443; Frederick J. Frese and Wendy Walker-Davis, 'The Consumer-Survivor Movement, Recovery, and Consumer Professionals,' *Professional Psychology: Research and Practice* 28.3 (1997): 244; Pelletier, 'The Lived Experience of Mental Health Issues as a Constructive Asset for Redefining Citizenship and Social Inclusion,' 22.
[7] Meagher, *Partnership or Pretence?*, 5.
[8] Anglicare Tasmania, *Experts by Experience.*
[9] Frese and Walker-Davis, 'The Consumer-Survivor Movement, Recovery, and Consumer Professionals,' 244; Arnold Kruger, 'Schizophrenia: Recovery and Hope,' *Psychiatric Rehabilitation Journal* 24.1 (2000): 30; Pelletier, 'The Lived Experience of Mental Health Issues as a Constructive Asset for Redefining Citizenship and Social Inclusion,' 22.
[10] Desley Casey, 'Divided Loyalties,' *Australian Journal for the Advancement of Mental Health* 5.3 (2006): 175.
[11] Pelletier, 'The Lived Experience of Mental Health Issues as a Constructive Asset for Redefining Citizenship and Social Inclusion,' 22.
[12] Sebastian Rosenberg, 'True North?' *International Journal of Mental Health* 40.2 (2011): 16.
[13] Ibid., 20.
[14] David Pilgrim, *Key Concepts in Mental Health* (London: Sage, 2005), 19; Joseph E. Stiglitz, *Civilization and Its Discontents* (New York: W.W. Norton, 2002), 5.
[15] Pilgrim, *Key Concepts in Mental Health*, 21; Stiglitz, *Civilization and Its Discontents*, 12.
[16] Kenneth Gergen, *An Invitation to Social Construction* (London: Sage, 1999), 3.
[17] Vivien Burr, *Social Constructionism* (2nd Ed) (New York: Routledge, 2003), 50.
[18] Peter L. Berger and Thomas Luckmann, *The Social Construction of Reality* (New York: Doubleday, 1966), 6; Burr. *Social Constructionism*, 50.
[19] Klaus G. Deissler, 'Psychiatric Language Games: From Objects in Treatment to Partners in Dialogue,' *Systemische Praxis in der Psychiatrie*, ed. Thomas Keller and Nils Greve (Bon: Psychiatrie-Verlag, 1996), viewed 29 March 2011, http://www.deissler.org/pdf/psychiatric_language_games.pdf; Michel Foucault, *Madness and Civilization: A History of Insanity in the Age of Reason* (New York: Pantheon, 1965), 59; Foucault, *The History of Sexuality Volume 1*, 26; Kenneth Gergen, 'The Social Constructionist Movement in Modern Psychology,' *American Psychologist* 40 (1985): 227; Gergen, *An Invitation to Social Construction*, 3; Kenneth Gergen and Fred Newman, 'Diagnosis: The Human Cost of the Rage to

Order,' *Performing Psychology: A Postmodern Culture of the Mind*, ed. Lois Holzman (New York: Routledge, 1995), 45.

[20] Carla Willig, *Introducing Qualitative Research in Psychology*, 2nd Ed. (Berkshire: Open University Press McGraw-Hill, 2008), 109.

[21] Foucault, *The History of Sexuality Volume 1*, 56.

[22] Burr, *Social Constructionism*, 47; Foucault, *Madness and Civilization*, 59; Foucault, *The History of Sexuality Volume 1*, 24.

[23] Burr, *Social Constructionism*, 51; Foucault, *The History of Sexuality Volume 1*, 24.

[24] Michel Foucault, *The History of Sexuality Volume 1*, 27:

[25] Ian Parker, 'Reflexive Research and the Grounding of Analysis: Social Psychology and the Psy-Complex,' *Journal of Community and Applied Social Psychology* 4 (1994): 240.

[26] Burr, *Social Constructionism*, 51.

[27] Virginia Braun and Victoria Clarke, *Successful Qualitative Research: A Practice Guide for Beginners* (London: Sage, 2013), 108.

[28] Jonathan Appel and Dohee Kim-Appel, 'Non-Rational States of Consciousness: Understanding and Counseling "Madness,"' paper presented at Mad-6 Conference (Mansfield College, Oxford, UK: 2013), viewed 30 May 2015, http://www.inter-disciplinary.net/probing-the-boundaries/wp-content/uploads/2013/07/appel-kim-appel-mad6-wpaper.pdf; Monika Dos Santos and David Lewis Wilson, 'Reflections on the Masks and Mirrors of Madness,' paper presented at Mad-6 Conference (Mansfield College, Oxford, UK: 2013), viewed 30 May 2015, http://www.inter-disciplinary.net/probing-the-boundaries/wp-content/uploads/2013/07/dosSantos-Wilson_mad6-wpaper.pdf; Pelletier, 'The Lived Experience of Mental Health Issues as a Constructive Asset for Redefining Citizenship and Social Inclusion,' 27.

[29] Milton James Lewis, *Managing Madness: Psychiatry and Society and Australia 1788-1980* (Canberra: Australian Government Publishing Service, 1988), 100.

[30] Willig, *Introducing Qualitative Research in Psychology*, 110.

[31] Ian Parker, *Discourse Dynamics: Critical Analysis for Social and Individual Psychology* (London: Routledge, 1992), 25.

[32] Sally Wiggins and Sara Riley, 'Doing Discourse Analysis,' *Doing Qualitative Research in Psychology: A Practical Guide*, ed. Michael Forrester (London: Sage, 2010), 140.

[33] Ibid., 145.

[34] Ludwig Wittgenstein, *Philosophical Investigation* (Oxford: Blackwell, 1953), 103.

[35] Deissler, 'From Objects in Treatment to Partners in Dialogue.'

[36] Martin Heidegger, *Being and Time* (New York: Harper Collins, 1927), 128.

[37] Australian Health Ministers, *National Mental Health Plan* (Canberra: Australian Government Publishing Service, 2010).
[38] Foucault, *Madness and Civilization*, 3.
[39] Foucault, *The History of Sexuality Volume 1*, 56.
[40] Berger and Luckmann, *The Social Construction of Reality*, 6.
[41] Pelletier, 'The Lived Experience of Mental Health Issues as a Constructive Asset for Redefining Citizenship and Social Inclusion,' 28.
[42] Ibid., 28.
[43] Foucault, *The History of Sexuality Volume 1*, 58.
[44] Burr, *Social Constructionism*, 53.
[45] Ibid., 53.
[46] Ibid., 53.
[47] Willig, *Introducing Qualitative Research in Psychology*, 109.

Bibliography

Anglicare Tasmania. *Experts by Experience: Strengthening the Mental Health Consumer Voice in Tasmania*. Australia, Anglicare Tasmania, 2009. Viewed 29 March 2011. www.slhd.nsw.gov.au/.

Australian Health Ministers. *National Mental Health Plan*. Canberra, Australia: Australian Government Publishing Service, 2010.

Berger, Peter L. and Thomas Luckmann. *The Social Construction of Reality*. New York, USA: Doubleday, 1966.

Braun, Virginia and Clarke, Victoria. *Successful Qualitative Research: A Practice Guide for Beginners*. London, UK: Sage, 2013.

Buechler, Stephen M. 'New Social Movement Theories.' *Sociological Quarterly* 36.3 (1995): 441-464.

Burr, Vivien. *Social Constructionism*, 2nd Ed. New York, USA: Routledge, 2003.

Casey, Desley. 'Divided Loyalties.' *Australian Journal for the Advancement of Mental Health* 5.3 (2006): 171-176.

Deissler, Klaus. 'Psychiatric Language Games: From Objects in Treatment to Partners in Dialogue.' *Systemische Praxis in der Psychiatrie*, edited by Thomas Keller and Nils Greve, 1 - 20. Bonn, Germany: Psychiatrie-Verlag, 1996. Viewed 29 March, 2011, http://www.deissler.org/pdf/psychiatric_language_games.pdf.

Foucault, Michel. *Madness and Civilization: A History of Insanity in the Age of Reason.* New York: Pantheon, 1965.

———. *The History of Sexuality Volume 1: An Introduction.* New York: Pantheon, 1978.

Frese, Frederick and Wendy Walker-Davis. 'The Consumer-Survivor Movement, Recovery, and Consumer Professionals.' *Professional Psychology: Research and Practice* 28.3 (1997): 243-245.

Gergen, Kenneth. 'The Social Constructionist Movement in Modern Psychology.' *American Psychologist* 40 (1985): 226-275.

———. *An Invitation to Social Construction.* London: Sage, 1999.

Gergen, Kenneth and Fred Newman. 'Diagnosis: The Human Cost of the Rage to Order.' *Performing Psychology: A Postmodern Culture of the Mind*, edited by Lois Holzman, 73-86. New York: Routledge, 1995.

Kruger, Arnold. 'Schizophrenia: Recovery and Hope.' *Psychiatric Rehabilitation Journal* 24.1 (2000), 29-37.

Lewis, Milton James. *Managing Madness: Psychiatry and Society and Australia 1788-1980.* Canberra: Australian Government Publishing Service, 1988.

Meagher, Janet. *Partnership or Pretence? A Handbook of Empowerment and Self-Advocacy for Consumers of Psychiatric Services and Those Who Provide or Plan Those Services.* NSW: Psychiatric Rehabilitation Association, 2002.

Parker, Ian. *Discourse Dynamics: Critical Analysis for Social and Individual Psychology.* London: Routledge, 1992.

———. 'Reflexive Research and the Grounding of Analysis: Social Psychology and the Psy-Complex.' *Journal of Community and Applied Social Psychology* 4 (1994): 239-252.

Pelletier, Jean-François. 'The Lived Experience of Mental Health Issues as a Constructive Asset for Redefining Citizenship and Social Inclusion.' *And Then the Monsters Come Out': Language, Power and Madness*, edited by Fiona Ann Papps, 21-33. Oxford: Inter-Disciplinary Press, 2014.

Pilgrim, David. *Key Concepts in Mental Health.* London: Sage Publications, 2005.

Pols, Hans and Stephanie Oak. 'Mental Health in Australia: Current State and New Directions.' *International Journal of Mental Health* 40.2 (2011): 3-7.

Rosenberg, Sebastian. 'True North?' *International Journal of Mental Health* 40.2 (2011): 8-24.

Stiglitz, Joseph. E. *Globalization and Its Discontents.* New York: W.W. Norton, 2002.

Wiggins, Sally and Riley, Sara. 'Doing Discourse Analysis.' *Doing Qualitative Research in Psychology: A Practical Guide*, edited by Michael Forrester, 135-153. London: Sage, 2010.

Willig, Carla. *Introducing Qualitative Research in Psychology*, 2nd Ed. Berkshire: Open University Press McGraw-Hill, 2008.

Wittgenstein, Ludwig. *Philosophical Investigations.* Oxford: Blackwell, 1953.

Kara Holmes is a registered psychologist with a private practice that specializes in providing services to people experiencing homelessness in Sydney, Australia. Kara completed her Masters in Clinical Psychology in 2014. She also tutors psychology at the Australian College of Applied Psychology. Her research projects are attentive to subjugated ways of being and to the relations of power that hold society in place; to the benefit of some and to the disadvantage of others.

Fiona Ann Papps is a senior lecturer in Psychological Sciences at the Australian College of Applied Psychology. Her research interests include representations of madness, the body and sexuality in the popular media and qualitative and quantitative research methods. She also writes poetry and creative non-fiction.

Psychology's Madness: Solipsistic Denial of Relational Dependency

David Lewis Wilson and Monika dos Santos

Abstract
As psychologists, we have a duty to inform as to what it means to be human. If nothing else, we can speak and write about the dehumanisation that we encounter within the mental health field. As exponents of the talking cure, we should consider seriously the power of speech to transform - although it may be seductive for us to comfortably peddle our wares from behind closed doors. Surely every therapist is in a position to ask radical questions about the relationships between the deformation of the human psyche, and the profit-motivated, hedonistic, narcissistic and even 'psychopathic' values which dominate political and economic practices. Issues of psychiatric medication occur within invidious debates and conceptual acrobatics involved in the processes of diagnosis. The questions of psychiatric medication often evoke extreme and vitriolic positions regarding what psychiatric practices are allowed under the guise of rationality and medical help. These accounts sometimes amount to claims of flagrant abuse of human rights, dehumanising forms of social control, and the forced administration of psychiatric drugs which some critics describe as chemical lobotomies. Do these living dead, or 'mad,' represent our supposedly advanced and humane psychiatric medical care? Unlike prison, committal to a psychiatric facility can be a Kafkaesque experience at the State President's pleasure; there is no way of knowing when incarceration will end. The writers realise that many of the questions do not have a clear, unequivocal answer, and rather than present this chapter as a claim to having resolved the complexities of the debate, we hope to render the questions more accessible, by presenting clinical experiences that have raised relevant concerns. The writers propose exploring aspects of the debates by referring to specific psychological conditions commonly encountered, often controversially raised as 'madness' in both the popular press and professional literature.

Key Words: Psychopathology, psychiatry, dehumanisation, institutionalisation, madness, psychology, medicalisation.

*****

1. Introduction

Our initial idea was to present a seemingly simple set of arguments and basic ideas for a chapter to illustrate the challenges of integrating psychological practices with advancing medical and biological technologies. Between this idea and the process of writing this chapter, we soon realised, with some trepidation, that many complexities and paradoxes need to be tolerated in order to avoid reducing the questions to simplistic polemical platitudes.

To do full justice to a debate that has its roots in ancient philosophy, requires raising questions involving concepts from fields as diverse as genetics, biology, neurology, chemistry, physics, numerous schools within psychology, philosophy, sociology, politics, economics etc. We realise that many of the questions do not have a clear unequivocal answer, and rather than present this chapter as a claim to having resolved the complexities of the debate, we hope to render the questions more accessible, without providing a final mythical answer.

2. Medical and Scientific Hegemony

Science affords us an opportunity to admire our technological progress and perceived mastery of nature, and despite the explicit aim of prediction and control, we have never been more out of control socially, as is evident in crime, violence, addiction, and the plundering and destruction of nature. Despite a common sense logic that the ruthless laws of profit and over-production and consumption are not sustainable, nobody is willing to let go of the power of wealth. Medicine largely panders to our inability to accept mortality and ageing in a social- spiritual vacuum. The aged themselves cling to envy of youth. Psychiatric medication masks symptoms and is to the benefit of employers, as employees spend less time in absenteeism and less time away from the workplace by going to therapy. These legal psychiatric drugs are nowadays being directly marketed to the public and often fit well with patient's preference for a medicalised 'chemical imbalance' explanation of their problems. Thus these patients are saved from ever confronting difficult psychologically and morally challenging questions that might slow the restless, constantly disturbed minds rhythm of consumption, production and the quest for excitement misused to hide the void. However, the benefits of psychotherapy in the long-term, if it addresses the major causes and consequences of psychosomatic problems have in the past revealed longer term benefits to health due to less smoking, over-eating, obesity, sleep disturbances and intoxication and other abuse of the self. In combination with sedentary work in which fight- flight stress responses have no release in activity, hormonal and autoimmune diseases seem to proliferate. Medicine, as organised largely in the West, still appeals to a so-called elite motivated by prestige and money and, for patients, the myth of longevity. Of course enough great and inspiring exceptions exist to keep the dream alive.

Despite so-called technological progress, working conditions for the majority of people have been rendered more destructive in terms of time and quality that affects the individual's stress levels and intrude through the interconnectivity of technology into people's 'private' home lives. Bigda-Peyton speaks of the splitting of 'being' versus 'nature,' which is viewed as something to be conquered, and 'that humans have inherent tendencies to destroy and use up'.[1]

While Schor reports that watching television is directly related to increased spending,[2] Bigda-Peyton proposes that few people accept that they themselves are part of the over consumption competition using the defences of projection and denial onto others.[3] A person in an objectless world has a need to get rid of any feeling that causes frustration, becoming entrapped in a world of taking without giving. Galbraith talks of a world that we have created of over-consumption, in which wants are created in the illusion of abundance and over-consumption.[4] Bigda-Peyton notes further that for some, it is easier to destroy life rather than to surrender to losing it.[5] Children watch and internalise their parent's pre-occupation with work and acquisition. The social ethos forces parents into premature return to work before adequate attachment bonds can be stabilised.

Giddens summarises the vast changes in human conditions and fundamental relations in modern times.[6] The vicissitudes of global capitalism reflect a dynamism that undercuts traditional habits and cultures. Space and time have become fragmented. There is relentless intensified commodification of labour and a loss of security in an increasingly fragile economic system. A sense of meaninglessness and doubt permeates all philosophical systems and all knowledge has taken the form of hypotheses, always subject to revision. The fragility of marriages and the increase of reconstituted families, the supremacy of the abstract systems such as money is no longer even tied to anything 'real' like gold, as we negotiate a so-called 'notional' economy of binary digital wealth. Relationships are what he oddly terms 'pure relationships'- based on mutual discretion (expedience seems an apt synonym), not duty, obligation or kinship.

Shame, a response to loss of attunement to primary attachment figures, usually results in anger, which if not recognised and channelled usually takes pathological self-destructive forms. It can, however, give rise, in the correct conditions to a revolutionary refusal to accept even deeper enslavement to wage slavery. Increased stress and parents trapped in work, as technology intrudes on homes and children are targeted as consumers of endless commodities that increasingly replace human relationships.

3. Medicalisation of Mental Illness

Issues of psychiatric medication occur within polemical debates, and conceptual acrobatics are involved in the processes of diagnosis itself. The question of psychiatric medication also evokes seemingly extreme positions taken regarding what psychiatric practises are allowed under the guise of rationality and medical help. These accounts amount to flagrant abuse of human rights, dehumanising forms of social control, and the forced administration of psychiatric drugs which Weitz describes as chemical lobotomies.[7] In South African psychiatric hospitals, we are accustomed to seeing patients in the so called biological or organic wards shuffling along with varying degrees of Tardive Dyskinesia for example – symptoms with can appear after long-term or high-dose use of antipsychotic drugs. These living dead represent our supposedly advanced and humane psychiatric medical care.[8]

It is widely accepted that the medical model is hegemonic and this view tends to look no further than biology for explanations of psychopathology.[9] A more complex argument is put forward by Szasz, namely that psychological processes have been reduced to disease and mental illness or the medicalisation of morality.[10] At the other extreme of the biologically reductive brain-disease diagnoses, one finds views that dismiss all diagnoses as fictional, a view associated with cultic religious beliefs such as scientology and forms of fundamentalist Christianity.

Regrettably, and possibly inevitably, where human power is unchecked - hiding beneath a mask of rationality - under many psychiatrists (and we would emphasise, the host of us allied professionals), we deferred in the selfishly motivated wish to avoid conflict and suffer the consequences of confronting the psychiatric power stranglehold and their cognitive behavioural therapy entourage. The titled 'real doctors' whose access to medications and the nightmare of the apparatus of electroconvulsive therapy (ECT) seemed the Oedipal father-figures who used their potency whilst we, the allied professionals watched in silent submission while patients, often elderly, often aging, often of little family or social means, were wheeled off for their weekly or bi-weekly experience of the 'treat' button on the ECT machine - one can only wonder darkly what the' trick' could be? There is a body of almost febrile attacks on psychiatry as being nothing but a form of social control, which resorts to inhumane methods to achieve these ends, using methods from the now outdated insulin shock, lobotomies, to ECT and the mental straitjackets of antipsychotics and antidepressants which Weitz describes as chemical lobotomies.[11] It cannot be denied that all medication carries risk. Equivocal though we are about a method such as ECT, discovered in slaughterhouses, we must confess to having seen two dramatic resolutions of psychotic suicidal depressions. On the other hand, the geriatric patients were literally doing somersaults!

A perhaps more reasonable perspective is proffered by Moreira who insists that we acknowledge the realities of biological correlates of emotional distress or individual pathology, as long as we are sure to find ways to keep the social, political and economic context of psychopathology in mind and, we contend, in some form that gives such factors due acknowledgement as causal and/or maintaining the psychological and psychiatric symptoms which patients experience.[12] She also does not simplistically suggest a reductionist link to capitalism, although, certainly the capitalist value system which conditions the Ideological State Apparatuses. Education, the media, the legal system etcetera, cannot be denied the force they bring to bear upon people in immersing us in the immense stress associated with an ahistorical social reality in which profit, competition and individual success are the over idealised supposedly natural forces governing our society. The media feeds a hankering for consumerism in a psychopathic search for new markets, regardless of the real costs to real humans and our world.

Intoxicated by the usually impressively productive and destructive forces unleashed by modern technology, not denying the high tech discoveries in medical equipment and drugs, however, we seem seduced by an illusion of our creative and destructive power and control over nature. In our secular society, it seems to make sense that medicine has been absurdly idealised in contrast to our muteness around the inevitable reality of our deaths. Our rapid exit from this planet; the inevitability of sickness, old age and death, do not sit well with secular consumers and producers to realise they may have bought far more than needed for our short sojourn on this planet. There is a reality in our modern time that the only certainty is change, and that all change, positive or negative, is inherently stressful. The stress of modern living is not ameliorated by any unifying meaningful philosophy or socially acceptable plans for change. In fact the antidote profit seems to be increased consumption, debt, and stress.

Referring back to Moreira's call to bear the social context in mind does find one small concession in the tome of empirical idiocy, the Diagnostic and Statistical Manual (DSM) finally granted an axis devoted to stress in the multi axial diagnosis of psychopathology.[13] Although the Fourth Axis in DSM III- R was promising in this direction, it tended however in practice to be dealt with rather trivially in explaining psychopathology in relationship to the stressors which certainly in Africa and, in different forms in Western countries, must surely rank close to severe forms of dehumanisation, whether there is a glut of money masking this inherent 'chronic trauma.' We do not mean though to suggest that the starvation and structural unemployment that many face in Africa - the AIDS, violence etcetera, can be simply equated or trivialised by comparison to 'First World' countries.

The psychoanalyst Nguyhen, who specialises in severe Post Traumatic Stress Disorder (PTSD), makes the point that there are many aspects taken for granted daily regarding the reality that we live that may well be abnormally normal, and therefore many symptoms of PTSD such as absence of desire, hope, maybe more ubiquitous than we would like to admit.[14] It has always been one of the important aspects of psychoanalysis that is nicely stated in the simple title of Freud's *'The Psychopathology of Everyday Life.'*[15] This is the contention that the distinction between abnormal and normal is largely a statistical normality- more than a qualitative one- and that there is no obvious radical dichotomy between madness and sanity.

4. Educational Influences

As Illich proposed, the educational system is more about 'taming' people to accept as normal an unquestioned acceptance of external control of the time and space in which we live, rather than the instillation of a true curiosity and love of knowledge.[16] In reality, much so-called education consists in reproducing social inequality, to link learning to individual competiveness and accept ongoing public shaming or praise, by marking school-work publically in an emotionally questionable way. Intellectual knowledge is a form of intellectual capital, to be used to get scarce jobs. The knowledge acquired does little, if anything, to raise awareness of consciousness itself and to manage people's beliefs, prejudices or emotions. For these, there is no cheap and quick fix, an academic course in Life Orientation cannot alter foundational irrationally-based beliefs acquired in earliest life. The school system serves to integrate the human into a society identified as itself pathogenic and addictive in its very essence. The payment of teachers, despite a few startling exceptions, speaks of the undervaluation of teaching, and cannot contribute to a teacher's motivation in the face of repetition of dead facts to children barely socialised or coming from homes in which learning is valued. At a tertiary level, academics have largely been reduced to machines to publish and attract funds. Costs are prohibitive. Professors no longer profess truth but a social academic arrogance. Research is often deadened by bureaucratic rules and dissertations gather dust as sad relics of social irrelevance in the game of academic competition.

5. The Patient's Experience of Psychology and Psychiatric Medication

Most research nowadays recommends combined psychiatric treatment and psychotherapy as 'best practice.' An immediate concern, however, is that contemporary recommendations seem to have Cognitive Behavioural Therapy (CBT) in mind, which does not imply the degree of controlled regression etcetera which are often part of psychoanalytic approaches, for example. Secondly, in almost all cases psychotherapy and pharmacotherapy are administered by different people. This may in itself reinforce and add to confusion in both the patient and therapists mind as to who is ultimately responsible for treatment, and unwittingly feed into a Cartesian-Newtonian body-mind split. We note the debate claiming that psychiatry itself is an over-priced speciality in the view of some neuroscientists, given the relative safety of modern antidepressants, which can be easily managed by general practitioners.[17]

Despite our sense of high technology, the FDA requirements for treatment effect size are rather dismally low, and the performance of many well-known psychotropic medications is much less impressive than the widespread advertising would suggest.[18] Shedler claims that the only other treatment strategy in the psychiatrists' arsenal, is the mastery of the simplistic platitudes of CBT, which again, the authors contend requires no specific qualification or advanced understanding, or experience.[19] Psychoanalytic therapy is dismissed as only reliably expensive. Clearly a nasty little article, yet it does capture something about the ignorance of many neuroscientists, particularly regarding the endless repetition that there is a total lack of evidence for psychodynamic approaches, which is certainly being addressed and now boasts some reliable research, meeting the most exacting criteria of empirical research, even showing effect sizes which surpass those of medication, where positive gains increase with time after treatment, rather than decay.[20]

Many patients come to us referred by a medical practitioner and are already diagnosed and on medication. Others are self-referred and are all too eager to find a 'quick fix' which will cure their symptoms and relieve them of their pain. We have looked with horror at photographs of patients who have been subjected to a few years of polypharmacy, reduced to retarded overweight dull- eyed lumps of chemical inertia, yet who claim to have maintained 'functionality.' A fair number of therapists raise their concerns as to whether their medication is simply blocking symptoms of problems of a broader psycho-social dimension. The authors struggle with the frequent and glib advice from some medical doctors' that they will need medication for the rest of their lives. Unfortunately, this is seldom suggested as opinion, but as having the full weight of scientific evidence and authority behind it.

Whenever medication is part of the picture, we are faced with the dilemma of whether the medication, while suppressing pain, is also suppressing other complex aspects of the symptom which may be necessary to fully engage with the real person, or be an integral part of their complex pathway to healing, for example, the cases of the psychoses such as schizophrenia - we nowadays rarely encounter a patient in whom any natural course can be discerned. Instead we witness patients shuffling along in total chemical suppression, not only from the antipsychotics, but often added drugs to increase compliant sedation and those for side-effects. Those already diagnosed and who are on medication regimens and which they find acceptable, even though they may have been told by their physicians that this optimal position will require medication for the rest of their lives pose complex questions for the psychologist. Our intuitive psychological bias usually leads the authors to question more precisely what the patient's acceptance of lifelong medication will mean for them. In many cases, we have noted with concern that the medication is suppressing a painful symptom, which we consider a meaningful communication or response to a life which it is doubtful that the patient should tolerate. This entails the question as to whether successful interventions involve the patient's adaption to life circumstances, for example, abusive relationships at work or home. Surely, this is the equivalent of chemically removing a life preserving reflexive removal of one's hand from being incinerated by leaving it on a hot stove plate. To rephrase the critical point, is it not the task of successful therapy to assist the patient bear their pain in such a way as to make adaptions to their lives - rather than to adapt passively to pain and to remove the source of pain? Or where it is part of inevitable existential nature, such as the inevitability of death and loss, to develop an attitude of mastery (not pseudo control or denial) toward the pain, using it to enrich rather than denude life of its meaning and sink into futility and despair and depression? This is the central thrust of Bion's (1962) exposition of our capacity to think about loss, rather than simply evacuate or project and split it off.[21]

Some patients present with such pain or risk of self-harm, or with anxiety that is so overwhelmingly debilitating, that there is a serious ethical question raised as to whether discouraging access to medication that we know will provide fairly rapid relief of pain, is not a violation of the principle of basic mercy. At least temporarily, medication can be used to create a therapeutic window, allowing access to a patient who literally cannot hold even a most basic conversation. Even basic structured CBT techniques may not be learnable when anxiety is at a 'thalamic' level, preventing even most basic cognitive functions such as reading a text on relaxation techniques problematic.

For the psychoanalytic purist, in an ideal world, it might be a small victory to show right from the start that it is human connection which is the ultimate healing factor. Unfortunately, for most of us and our patients, we strive for a compromise, recommending the temporary use of pills in place of the person.

Twelve-step models have become almost standard unquestioned parts of almost all drug rehabilitation strategies, and the pontification and medicalisation of addiction as a lifelong disease which has been incorporated into 12-step programmes. There does seem to be an obvious danger in reciting daily weekly monthly yearly repeating 'I'm X and I'm an addict' day after day after week after month after year! Does this not foreclose any development or fly in the face of what we know about natural 'maturing out' process of addictions? This evokes the simply potent observation by Thomas, that if people define a situation as real, it is real in its consequences.[22] In terms of diagnosis, problems associated with self-fulfilling prophecy cannot be underestimated.

O'Brien asserts that at a clinical level addiction may be considered similar to an infectious disease such as tuberculosis, depending on an interaction of host, agent and environment.[23] Drugs dampen limbic system activation, he concludes, somewhat abruptly and confidently, that these findings support a biological basis for addiction. He further describes the vast array of aids to make it possible even for the heroin addict to detoxify without experiencing the disabling effects of withdrawal, allowing for outpatient psychotherapy. Despite the impressive armamentarium of drugs to cushion the horrors of detoxification, and his confident assertion of the involvement of brain biology in the problem (which is not being contested!), O' Brien continues and ends his paper with the sad lament that despite the advances in detoxification, the relapse rate remains extremely high.[24] The point of singling out this article is precisely to bring attention to the usually confident assertions which with researchers make sweeping claims as to the brain biological bases of a vast number of problems, only to peter out when it comes to finer analyses, or to look for evidence of cure, or even longer term maintenance. In fact, it should be almost common knowledge that sudden creations and changes are easy- it is the long-term maintenance of change that is the acid test. O'Brien laments that the relapse rate over time is depressing.[25] We have witnessed the effects of such detoxification aids. As we have noted, maybe we need to query whether a more benign experience of withdrawal does the disservice to the patient by so masking the pain but possibly depriving the patient of feeling the sense of mastery and power of having tolerated the pain i.e. the consequences of the addiction and value the accomplishment more because the price was so high.

Closely linked to addictions in terms of levels of controversy, as well as possible comorbidity, is the diagnosis of Attention Deficit Disorder (ADD). One of the more controversial diagnoses, it provides a useful example of the extreme polarised approaches taken by patients and families and various treatments. The prevailing psychiatric view seems to be that it is a lifelong problem, requiring treatment usually using Ritalin, or, interestingly, even responding to some of the SSRI's which in itself should give some hint that our understanding of what pharmacological systems are involved and how remains unknown.

At one extreme we find arguments such as those proposed by Keirsey that no such disorder exists, that the child usually shows perfect attention when it is in an activity they enjoy, and that subjecting children to mind disabling narcotics verges on the criminal.[26] Clearly ADD has a lot to do with a capacity for delay of gratification, perseverance and procrastination. All of these are behaviours that can be modified with clear consequences and the acceptance of the aspect of life called maintenance or regulated activity according to a routine that is inherent to any aspect of life. It suggests an over-reliance on external pleasant stimuli, rather than a capacity to find happiness in inner mastery. Keirsey takes a radical 'abuse it or lose it' stance. He also implicates a poor educational system.[27] Indeed, Illich's point that the hidden curriculum of school is not about information acquired, but preparation for reluctant enslavement to work for the rest of one's life.[28] However, we believe the problem goes much further than academic or work achievement but the capacity for delay of gratification and use of symbolisation, specifically language, to talk through one's emotions without destructive acting out. In essence to a degree what Foucault referred to as taming our animal instinctive behaviours.[29] The point, however, is to show the child that rather than simple conformity to often arbitrary rules, this capacity can be liberating from enslavement to instincts. The problem does seem to be multifactorial, parental consistency, self-esteem and fear of failure, acceptance of limits and habits such as regulated sleep in accord with natural diurnal rhythms. An unsubstantiated thought is the degree to which there is over diagnosis in pre-adolescent boys may reflect different hormonal surges. One imagines boys a few hundred years ago did not learn via passive auditory means, but by doing.

We have no doubt all encountered children literally bouncing off the walls, who cannot listen for long enough to hear one meaningful statement from the therapist. In such cases short term carefully monitored drug therapy may be useful to give the child's preview of ability if only they were capable of listening. Listening is not a modality much emphasised in today's action, visually- dominated society. It takes patience, inner serenity, humility, a curiosity - which in itself requires a tolerance for not knowing which the envious may find it hard to acknowledge. And given the abuses of authority, the age of hypocrisy where we are told to do what the teachers themselves do not is not without profound consequences. Similar dynamics exist in therapy-patients can go no further than we ourselves can. However, time limited use of medication, provided that skills and feelings are dealt with using the window created through minimal effective medication seems justifiable provided the host of techniques all readily available to the concerned educator and parent in addition to the therapy.

The efficacy of Ritalin could be explained in many ways besides a neurological one, the first being that as a stimulant, we should recall that its initial intent was as an antidepressant. Unlike most stimulants like cocaine, it has a long (half ?) life so does not involve the dramatic crash associated with drugs of abuse. It may well be the case that the stimulant effect is sufficient to enable a child to pay attention to poorly motivated teachers teaching mind numbing facts, remembering Illich's important work on the hidden curriculum of school being to condition or tame humans to future reality of having time and place controlled by demands of work.[30] Possibly the greater flexibility in terms of options for home schooling also reflect technology's development such that confinement to particular work places are no longer necessary in many cases. An extensive internet search reflected just how dominated by the medical Ritalin/ positing an understanding of ADD as related to depression and manic defences mobilised by the child against the depression.[31] In our experience, and despite our admission of the limited usefulness of a stimulant in gaining initial access to the child, we regret to say that our overall sense is that ADD represents one of the clear examples of blatant 'disease mongering.'[32] The concept of ADD as a manic defence needs to be considered in the light of Bion's seminal work on thinking as a means to tolerate frustration and symbolise lack, such that the actual situation or reality can be modified.[33] Overall the writers suggests that a review of even the most basic references will provide compelling arguments for understanding the process in a complex set of behavioural, emotional and cognitive systems indicating disturbance in the synthetic, organising, and integrating effects of the ego. The body-mind split here may help ameliorate parental guilt regarding aetiological factors.

Furthermore, many patients are diagnosed and on what they consider to be a comfortable confection of medications, which frequently they are told they may be expected to accept for the rest of their lives, especially with the ever so popular and to the writers' dismay, proliferation of varieties of bipolar disorder diagnoses now being so frequently applied. In this regard, consider bipolar type III- a patient who responds to antidepressants with symptoms of mania is lumbered with a bipolar diagnosis.

Lastly, Kandel won the Nobel Prize years ago for his discovery with sea slugs which led to evidence for the enormously important findings linked to neuroplasticity.[34] At one level there is incontrovertible proof that environment may affect how genes are expressed, or switched on or off. Secondly, evidence exists that changing the environment, either through CBT, other therapies and pharmacotherapy, meditation etcetera, results in definite changes in the neurological system such as strengthening of synaptic connections and the interconnections between brain nerve cells. Kandel states that learning produces changes so that 'nurture becomes represented in nature.'[35] He posits that genes have two functions, one being the template, which contains all the DNA information which may be altered by mutation, but certainly not experience. Their transcriptional function is, however, responsive to environmental factors and experiences. Overall, he argues for abandonment of Cartesian dualism as inimical to the development of psychiatry - and that psychoanalysis and biology can enter into a fertile interchange.

We need to recognise that for many, it is also just how appealing it is to receive a 'medical' diagnosis, with all the blame and responsibility shifted to genetics and 'my nerves or chemical imbalance.' On whose authority do we, especially if committed to truth versus ignorance, share our beliefs that these medical imbalances are not of the same order of physical medicine, where a blood test can unambiguously assert the presence of the illness? That although the drugs work on serotonin and noradrenalin, the exact ways through which they work may involve other, perhaps still unknown neurochemical pathways.

6. Psychiatric Diagnosis

Our pragmatic complicity in using the DSM system and attempts to even pursue research using these diagnoses as key variables raises some questions.[36] In fact the whole question of which power relationships and ideologies dominate research is a problem unto itself. Without getting involved in the over simplistic anti-capitalistic debates that often seem to undermine interesting and valid criticisms of the psychiatric and pharmaceutical industry's dangerously close relationship, a fairly recent experience of a point seminar for psychiatrists made some aspects of the power of that relationship patently obvious. No charge to the attending psychiatrists, state of the art presentation materials, free pens, papers, meal and even a little gift bag of take way medication with the serene company logo made it somewhat enviably clear as to what a powerful ally being the target of pharmaceutical sales can be. While more obvious abuse is legally eliminated, we understand that 'legitimate' assistance in terms of attending conferences, for example, is considered fair. Surely the ease with which the dissemination of medically based information makes a vast difference? Ultimately, so many neurotransmitters are being modified, who knows what's doing what to what? Moreover, the manner in which diagnoses are made, remains notoriously unreliable from practitioner to practitioner and most diagnoses still require clinical diagnosis, not laboratory tests or PET scans or blood tests. The application of a diagnosis is the danger of disempowering the patient. It reifies in the sense that the diagnosis implies a state rather than ongoing part of a dynamic developmental process.

A case study from David Wilson's files

A case study comes to mind, of a young man deeply medicated, having gained weight, mentally and physically almost literally lobotomised, with a caveat of 'don't see him more than once a week.' An enlightened psychiatrist still somehow labouring under a misconception that I would be regressing and dragging out unconscious fantasies of Oedipal murder, or who knows what, with an already overwhelmed patient. The patient was diagnosed as schizoaffective. A heavy duty diagnosis indeed! After a few weeks of twice weekly therapy, an initially sinister delusion that his 'face was melting' turned out to be, in context, a construction by a very overprotected young man, developed on a first overseas holiday away from his mother, believing he'd been fed cannabis. His panic and reactions in a foreign country did indeed cause people to stare. Not having mommy close by to reassure, he was quickly on high medication and bundled back to SA. My experience was rather like 'talking through' a person who's having a bad and prolonged overdose of hallucinogens. He persisted in isolation because of a lingering belief that people were staring at him. I decided to take a walk down a street with him to observe his fantasy in action. Stepping out into the street, immediately I was struck - as was he - by two men staring at us very intently. All I could do was affirm they were indeed staring unusually. I was able to point out to him though that in more general way, staring at people, making intense eye contact with passesbys, would evoke a more intense reaction from them, which he failed to realise as precipitating their staring!

The only other evidence he had was of being in a public toilet and being stared at. Whether he was being cruised or perceived to be cruising seemed likely; incredibly naive, he had no conception of these basic assumptions regarding levels of eye contact appropriate for strangers. I refer to this case showing actually how very little I did. He was certainly not cognitively and emotionally ready for deep meaningful therapy. What it did was remind me how an elaborate diagnosis can obscure such simple realities. I believe simply affirming his perception but opening his mind to the myriad possible interpretations including his obliviousness to the amount of information we transmit non- verbally, was a key in anchoring him. From an admittedly over- simplistic perspective I would suggest an acute separation anxiety reaction. Whether he actually was given cannabis remains unknown. However, given what we know from the studies of Bowlby about how frightening stimuli are to an infant when separated from the primary attachment figure, compared to the capacity to tolerate without fear the very same stimuli when the primary attachment figure is in close proximity, is in my experience a critically important observation, especially that in our modern society where the emphasis is on independence, where even the nuclear family is a rare ideal, and parents are forced into premature return to work, and even with the best intentions, are too depleted emotionally after work to be, in my opinion, emotionally optimally available.[37]

Normally with much experience, supervision and healthy self-certainty, we can increasingly make accurate assessments in consultation with the patient to correctly agree as to when to begin gradual tapering off of medication, and to differentiate between the patients re-experiencing tolerable levels of pain versus possible relapse or extreme and severe variations of the serotonin withdrawal syndrome. Adequate knowledge and an acceptance of our limits can also be liberating provided we communicate effectively with and avoid splitting and egotism when working with a potentially thorny issue of meddling in another healthcare practitioner's treatment strategy. Ultimately it is the patient's interest, which is primary, not our haste to prove the efficacy of psychotherapy versus medicine. Ideally we evolve a practise in which we have a trusted network of other professionals who work in close mutually respectful professional relationships.

More subtle masking of the patient's real issues may significantly get in the way of the therapists access to the true needs and emotional defensive structures. A therapy conducted almost entirely with the aid of medication raises serious questions of relapse should therapy and/or medication be stopped. Panic attacks, so responsive to SSRI's, are a good example. Although we may arm the patient with the best range of CBT strategies, it is this practitioner's belief that a key triad, a) anger, b) fear of loss of control and c) fears of separation, need to be resolved to prevent relapse once medication is terminated.

7. The Psychologist

Given the complexity of the work, and given the immensity of our task, we do ourselves a disservice and even potential harm by omnipotently dealing with so many intense feelings. Imagine how much more contained the work of a classical analyst, paid in advance for a year, the patients understanding that there is a specified break when both take holiday simultaneously, not subject to 24 hour cancellations, holidays etcetera which we may strive to accommodate at both financial and emotional stress. The costs entailed in training, even as a clinical psychologists, is hardly the stuff of professional compensation compared to the uncertainties of following undergraduate degrees which at honours and masters level may result in our either giving up, or undergoing further investment in personal therapy to reach the often very dubious selection criteria. To do this almost sacred work is a vocation. Of course many of our own painful issues must be a powerful factor in undertaking work of such complexity but also offering rare opportunities for touching the transcendent. The costs of on-going supervision, personal therapy and even the time required just to digest material is not trivial. To afford training as a psychoanalyst is even more daunting, and not only again because of years of uncertainty and personal analysis. In Europe at least, medical aids seem to reimburse only psychiatrists for providing psychoanalysis. We have no solid information, but it is brought to our attention how few men persist as individual therapists. A few more enterprising therapists have made much money selling continued professional development (CPD) points, groups and or invested in other areas or taken up comfortable position in large corporate where the work bears little resemblance to daily clinical work. We are amazed at our work and sense of discovery and mystery. Yet the reality is also one of absorbing (containing and metabolising) an inevitable amount of emotional toxicity no matter how detached or clinical the approach, such as objective behaviour therapies, or psycho neurological assessments.

The most mediocre general practitioner in few minutes of perfunctory questions and a hasty prescription have waiting rooms in which one waits, usually testimony not to emergency calls but pure profit. Medical aids, notwithstanding our questions about the entire association with medical professions, reimburse at rates hardly consistent with the complex expertise we use. While dissociating from medical practise, the facts of research indicating that almost half of general practitioner consults are attributable to psychological factors. So many patients nowadays manifest with the complex diseases or condition such as fibromyalgia, ulcerative colitis, irritable bowel syndrome and eczemas, and even where the as yet mysterious connections between psyche, neuro and immune systems, but the psychological sequelae of contracting any significant or recurrent illness, excluding the effects of alcohol and other addictions, through accident or disinhibitions. Some studies have attempted to make crude estimates of relative cost efficacy of standard medical treatment versus therapy. Even as therapists we ourselves may have been in position to avoid crises requiring hospitalisations due to therapy being offered at bare minimum.

The low esteem in which we are held in terms of our role in the mental health industry, including hospitalising, prescribing is reflected in our generally low reimbursement. Effects of the capitalistic structure and the profit motive extend also to the manner in which we are all- psychiatrists included- being reduced to interchangeable service providers. The interference in clinical practice of judgements based on cost rather than efficacy and the criteria remain.

8. Conclusion

Our concern with the medical model is that it is often clearly wrong, yet we are so bedazzled by PET scans and so forth that we forget two simple points: the first is that these spectacular machines are in most cases nothing but means of extending our senses. The same imperfect senses which we use in other situations of empirical observation. Even were it not for the limits of the senses, or the stimuli, our minds have been trained to perceive in a given way. So this concern goes beyond medicine to problems inherent to positivistic science itself. The second is that we remain convinced that the studies do not reveal a causal relationship between the variables.

Notions of absolute space and time, and elementary solid particles, the fundamental material substance, the strictly causal nature of physical phenomena and the objective description of nature, has all been brought into serious question.[38] Officially we live in a post structuralist, post Foucault, post- Derrida world in which the myth of objectivity has been thoroughly discredited, supplanted by sophisticated developments in understandings of language itself. We have Lacan's work suggesting that the unconscious is not individual energy, but is dispersed throughout the field of interactions created through language.[39]

Yet despite this, at the middle level of the visible world of bodies and cars and hamburgers, our capacity to quantify and calculate still is highly effective to a society in which actions and measurable results are valued most highly. There is no way we can assume that the reality of global capitalism does not impinge on all aspects of our lives. Reading the young Marx is often pure poetry and his central concerns are still relevant in contemporary society, such as those of alienation, the overriding of all imperatives by the quest for profit, or the concept of 'commodity fetishism.'[40] Without necessitating our repeating old mistakes in search of social renewal, because it does seem clear that our advances in material sciences are almost inversely related to social and political regression in politics, lies, hypocrisy - every social ill seems to be growing. Is there a connection? Certainly concepts such as alienation, the species being of the human, commodity fetishism the arid tedium of attempts to provide a so-called materialistic science of the historical scientific necessity of socialism. Like all simplistic materialists, he ignored the possibilities of consciousness which became, in the hands of his disciples, a site where the delusion of freedom was situated, where through mystification the ideological state apparatuses acted to create an illusion of volitional subjectivity, rather than the realisation that the subject was merely the carrier and reproducer of either capital or labour. Yet who can read his discourse on money and not be moved by the power of his arguments and the relevance it has since by its abstract nature it has become the ultimate power.

As psychologists, we feel that every time we capitulate to the requirement to inserting an ICD X diagnosis, whatever we may have said to a patient, a sense of hypocrisy exists. We warn our patients that people may access this information that is not subject to the ethical standards of the profession. As we recall, a formal complaint was laid with the Health Professionals Council of South Africa (HPCSA) several years ago. Of course, we never heard of any response. On the other hand we do not think that such acts are failures. At least we speak out rather than give an assumption of tacit acceptance.

Again, using the nomenclature may harm the clinician's use of more subtle ways of understanding. Just as we have been surprised that intelligent patients with whom the arbitrary nature of the diagnosis has we thought been clearly understood, yet several return with questions showing that there may be a need to be labelled or curiosity and sufficient symptoms that she or he can identify with to raise concerns as to the power that this name will assume. The realities of psychological and psychiatric practise, when viewed from a personalist perspective, make it much clearer why success and failure of treatment remain so confusing. To find any person both capable and willing to go through the process involved for a profound connection aiming for truth, is not unexpectedly rare event. To be treasured as is any authentic connection nowadays.

It may be irrational to the atheist, yet we are missing the reality that many people are not looking for reason, but need opportunities in which letting go can be expressed in socially sanctioned ways. The pervasion of positivism and rationality may not be what we need - the interlinked goals of prediction and control may thwart just as powerful a need for the numinous. Our educational system devotes years of learning to the memory of facts and skills deemed important to be domesticated animals who succeed in the workplace.[41] Yet consciousness itself is barely acknowledged.

The authors, recognising the essential nature of our underlying beliefs as determining our perceptions and philosophical rationale, are inclined to assert a dualism, which requires acknowledging a spiritual dimension. From this perspective dichotomies are inherent in material reality. Even if one does not subscribe to a spiritual belief, hopefully, we can continue to explore the contradictions that arise from this debate. Some may be artefacts of our culture and language itself. Already in linguistics, the diacritical theory of meaning has shown convincingly that the connection between signifier and signified is arbitrary, and that the meaning of any word depends on all the words which it is not. But this is another debate.

Notes

[1] Tom Bigda-Peyton, 'When Drives Are Dangerous: Drive Theory and Resource Over-Consumption,' *Modern Psychoanalysis* 29 (2004): 251-270.
[2] Julient Schor, 'In Defense of the Consumer Critique: Revisiting the Consumption Debates of the Twentieth Century,' *The Annals of the American Academy of Political and Social Science* 611.16 (2007): 16-30.
[3] Bigda-Peyton, 'When Drives Are Dangerous,' 259.
[4] John Gabraith, *The Affluent Society* (Boston: Houghton Mifflin Company, 1958).
[5] Bigda-Peyton, 'When Drives Are Dangerous,' 268.
[6] Anthony Giddens, *Modernity and Self-Identity* (Standord: Stanford University Press, 1991).

---

[7] Don Weitz, 'Struggling against Psychiatry's Human Rights Violations [An Antipsychiatry Perspective],' *Radical Psychology* 7 (2008), viewed on 26 June 2015, http://www.radicalpsychology.org/vol7-1/weitz2008.html
[8] Weitz, 'Struggling against Psychiatry's Human Rights Violations.'
[9] Virginia Moreira, 'Critical Psychopathology,' *Radical Psychology* (2005), viewed on 22 May 2015, http://www.radicalpsychology.org/vol4-1/moreira.html
[10] Thomas Szasz, *The Myth of Mental Illness* (London: Granada Publishing, 1972).
[11] Weitz, 'Struggling against Psychiatry's Human Rights Violations.'
[12] Virginia Moreira, 'Critical Psychopathology.'
[13] Ibid.
[14] Leanh Nguyen, 'The Question of Survival: The Death of Desire and the Weight of Life,' *The American Journal of Psychoanalysis* 67.6 (2007): 53-67.
[15] Sigmund Freud, *The Psychopathology of Everyday Life.* (London: Fisher Unwin, 1901).
[16] Ivan Illich, *De-Schooling Society* (London: Calder and Boyars, 1971).
[17] Robert Krause, 'Depression, Antidepressants and an Examination of Epidemiological Changes,' *Radical Psychology* 4.1 (2005), viewed on 27 May, 2015, http://www.radicalpsychology.org/vol4-1/krause.html
[18] Jonathan Shedler, 'The Efficacy of Psychodynamic Psychotherapy,' *American Psychologist,* 65.2 (2010): 98-109, American Psychological Association.
[19] Shedler, 'The Efficacy of Psychodynamic Psychotherapy.'
[20] Ibid.
[21] Wilfred Bion, *Learning from Experience* (London: Tavistock, 1962).
[22] William Thomas, *The Unadjusted Girl. With Cases and Standpoint for Behavioral Analysis* (London: Harper & Row, 1967).
[23] Charles O'Brian, 'Treatment of Addiction in the Era of Genomic Medicine,' *Addiction* 102.11 (2007): 1697- 1699.
[24] Charles O'Brian, 'Treatment of Addiction': 1697-1699.
[25] Ibid.
[26] David Keirsey, 'The Great ADD Hoax,' Viewed 10 April 2015, http://www.keirsey.com/add_hoax.aspx.
[27] Keirsey, 'The Great ADD Hoax.'
[28] Ivan Illich, *De-Schooling Society.*
[29] Michel Foucault, *L'Ordine del Discorso* (Torino: Einaudi, 2004).
[30] Illich, *De-Schooling Society.*
[31] Burton Seitler, 'Successful Child Psychotherapy of Attention Deficit/Hyperactivity Disorder: An Agitated Depression Explanation,' *The American Journal of Psychoanalysis* 68.3 (2008): 284-294.
[32] Ravi Shankar and Palaian Subish, 'Disease Mongering,' *Singapore Medical Journal* 4 (2007): 275.
[33] Wilfred Bion, *Learning from Experience.*

[34] Eric Kandel, 'A New Intellectual Framework for Psychiatry,' *The American Journal of Psychiatry* (1998): 155.4: 457-469.
[35] Kandel, 'A New Intellectual Framework for Psychiatry,' 156.
[36] American Psychiatric Association, *Diagnostic and Statistical Manual of Mental Disorders, Fifth Edition (DSM-5 (TM))* (Washington, DC: American Psychiatric Association, 2013).
[37] John Bowlby, 'The Nature of the Child's Tie to His Mother,' *International Journal of Psycho- Analysis* XXXIX (1958): 1-23.
[38] Fritjof Capra, *The Turning Point, Science, Society and the Rising Culture,* (London: Fontana, 1983).
[39] Jacques Lacan, 'Some Reflections on the Ego,' *International Journal of Psychoanalysis* 24 (1953): 11-17.
[40] Karl Marx, *Economic and Philosophical Manuscripts of 1844* (Moscow: Progress Publishers, 1959), 93-109.
[41] Illich, *De-Schooling Society.*

Bibliography

American Psychiatric Association. *Diagnostic and Statistical Manual of Mental Disorders, Fifth Edition (DSM-5 (TM)).* Washington, DC: American Psychiatric Association, 2013.

Bowlby, John. 'The Nature of the Child's Tie to His Mother.' *International Journal of Psycho- Analysis* XXXIX (1958): 1-23.

Bigda-Peyton, Tom. 'When Drives Are Dangerous: Drive Theory and Resource Over-Consumption.' *Stanford: Modern Psychoanalysis* 29 (2004): 251-270.

Bion, Wilfred. *Learning from Experience.* London: Tavistock, 1962.

Capra, Fritjof. *The Turning Point, Science, Society and the Rising Culture.* London: Fontana, 1983.

Foucault, Michel. *L'Ordine del Discorso*. Torino: Einaudi, 2004.

Freud, Sigmund. *The Psychopathology of Everyday Life.* London: Fisher Unwin, 1901.

Gabraith, John. *The Affluent Society.* Boston: Houghton Mifflin Company, 1958.

Giddens, Anthony. *Modernity and Self-Identity.* Stanford: Stanford University Press, 1991.

Illich, Ivan. *De-Schooling Society.* London: Calder and Boyars, 1971.

Keirsey, David. *The Great ADD Hoax.* Viewed 10 April 2015. http://www.keirsey.com/add_hoax.aspx.

Kandel, Eric. 'A New Intellectual Framework for Psychiatry.' *The American Journal of Psychiatry* (1998) 155. 4: 457- 469.

Krause, Robert. 'Depression, Antidepressants and an Examination of Epidemiological Changes.' *Radical Psychology* 4.1 2005, viewed on 27 May 2015, http://www.radicalpsychology.org/vol4-1/krause.html

Lacan, Jacques. 'Some Reflections on the Ego.' *International Journal of Psychoanalysis* 24 (1953): 11-17.

Marx, Karl. *Economic and Philosophical Manuscripts.* Moscow: Progress Publishers, 1959.

Moreira, Virginia. 'Critical Psychopathology.' *Radical Psychology,* 2005, viewed on 22 May 2015, http://www.radicalpsychology.org/vol4-1/moreira.html

Nguyen, Leanh. 'The Question of Survival: The Death of Desire and the Weight of Life.' *The American Journal of Psychoanalysis* 67.6 (2007): 53-67.

O'Brian, Charles. 'Treatment of Addiction in the Era of Genomic Medicine.' *Addiction* 102.11 (2007): 1697-1699.

Schor, Juliet. 'In Defense of the Consumer Critique: Revisiting the Consumption Debates of the Twentieth Century.' *The Annals of the American Academy of Political and Social Science* 611.16 (2007): 16-30.

Seitler, Burton. 'Successful Child Psychotherapy of Attention Deficit/Hyperactivity Disorder: An Agitated Depression Explanation.' *The American Journal of Psychoanalysis* 68.3 (2008): 284-294.

Shankar, Ravi and Palaian Subish. 'Disease Mongering.' *Singapore Medical Journal* 4.275 (2007): 275-280.

Shedler, Jonathan. 'The Efficacy of Psychodynamic Psychotherapy.' *American Psychologist* 65.2 (2010): 98-109. American Psychological Association.

Szasz, Thomas. *The Myth of Mental Illness.* London: Granada Publishing. 1972.

Thomas, William. *The Unadjusted Girl. With Cases and Standpoint for Behavioral Analysis.* London: Harper & Row, 1967.

Weitz, Don. 'Struggling against Psychiatry's Human Rights Violations [An Antipsychiatry Perspective].' *Radical Psychology* 7, 2008, viewed on 26 June 2015, http://www.radicalpsychology.org/vol7-1/weitz2008.html

David Lewis Wilson is a psychoanalytical clinical psychologist. He is currently a doctoral candidate in the Department of Psychology at the University of South Africa, with a focus area on the social construction of narcissism and its manifestations in various psychopathologies. He has spent 25 years exploring the limits of consciousness, and aims to awaken our limits beyond bland platitudes of what passes for human life today- the quest for Commodities. He further aspires to navigate the gulf between East and West, body and mind, spirit and matter.

Monika dos Santos is an associate professor in the Department of Psychology at the University of South Africa. She holds doctoral degrees in Psychology and Clinical Psychology, and is currently completing an MSc in Sustainable Urban Development at the University of Oxford. She is curious about aspects related to human-environment functioning and psychopathology.

Has Autism Changed?

Simon Cushing

Abstract
The fifth edition of the Diagnostic and Statistical Manual of Mental Disorders (DSM) has just been published and it contains the following changes from the previous edition: gone are the subcategories 'Autistic Disorder,' 'Asperger Syndrome' and 'PDD-NOS,' replaced by the single diagnosis 'Autism Spectrum Disorder,' and there is a new category 'Social Communication Disorder.' In this paper I consider what kind of reasons would justify these changes if one were (a) a realist about autism, or (b) one were a constructivist. I explore various analyses of autism in the research literature that portray it as essentially either a psychological, neurological or genetic phenomenon, and discuss these by reference to the diagnostic criteria and by analogy with the way we understand race and sex categories. I conclude that no realist reasons are available to justify the changes in the diagnostic criteria, and further, that the only way the changes could be justified is if one takes the position that the DSM categories are social constructs. I conclude by exploring what implications follow from this.

Key Words: Autism, Autistic Disorder, Asperger Syndrome, PDD-NOS, DSM-5, realism, constructivism, mindblindness, weak central coherence, executive dysfunction, Simon Baron-Cohen, Uta Frith.

*****

1. Introduction

The most notorious change associated with autism in recent decades has been the sharp increase in the number of diagnoses. However, it is a second, more recent change, one that is often claimed to be motivated by the former, which shall concern me here: the alteration in diagnostic criteria in the Diagnostic and Statistical Manual of Mental Disorders (DSM), the standardized reference guide published by the American Psychiatric Association and used by clinicians in the US as a basis for their diagnoses.

On 18 May 2013 the fifth edition of the DSM was published. It had been at least 13 years since the last update (the DSM-IV-TR) and this time there was considerable controversy surrounding the new definitions contained therein. There were two major changes that directly concerned autism:

1. Three separate diagnoses, "Autistic Disorder" (AKA "classic autism"), Asperger syndrome and PDD-NOS (Pervasive Developmental Disorder Not Otherwise Specified) were

unified into the single diagnosis, "Autism Spectrum Disorder [ASD]."

2. A new diagnostic category, "social communication disorder" (SCD) was created that will cover some people who would formerly have been diagnosed as one of the three sub-categories above (probably PDD-NOS).[1]

It is worth noting that this is not the first time the criteria for identifying autism have been tinkered with. To see that, we need to look at the ur-text of our contemporary notion of autism (at least in the English-speaking world): Leo Kanner's paper, 'Autistic Disturbances of Affective Contact.' In that report, Kanner describes 'a unique 'syndrome,' not heretofore reported' marked by a set of common characteristics.[2] Those characteristics include: late speaking; a use of language that is rote and focused mainly on the use of nouns to identify objects, colours or numbers; excellent rote memory; 'delayed echolalia'; personal pronouns 'repeated just as heard, with no change to suit the altered situation'; common failure to attend to people calling on the subject; fussiness about food; adverse reaction to loud noises and moving objects; lack of spontaneity; treatment of people like objects; possession of 'good cognitive potentialities' and 'strikingly intelligent physiognomies'; and clumsiness in gait allied with skill in finer muscle coordination.[3] All or most of these features will seem familiar to anybody with a friend or family member who has been diagnosed as on the autism spectrum and indeed later commentators remarked that Kanner's list stood up remarkably well.[4] However, there have been significant changes both between Kanner's original list and diagnostic criteria in the DSM-IV, and between those criteria and those of the DSM-5.

Since word of these changes leaked before the publication of DSM-5 there has been a flood of articles discussing them, prognosticating about their impending effects both on new diagnoses and on the status of those diagnosed under the former criteria, and wondering about the motivation and/or justification for the changes. For example:

> When the APA publishes the *DSM-5*, people who have already met the criteria for autism in the current *DSM-IV* will not suddenly lose their current diagnosis as some parents have feared, nor will they lose state services. But several studies recently published in child psychiatry journals suggest that it will be more difficult for new generations of high-functioning autistic people to receive a diagnosis because the *DSM-5* criteria are too strict. Together, the studies conclude that the major changes to the definition of autism in the *DSM-5* are well grounded in research and that the new criteria are more accurate than the

> current *DSM-IV* criteria. But in its efforts to make diagnosis more accurate, the APA may have raised the bar for autism a little too high, neglecting autistic people whose symptoms are not as severe as others. The studies also point out, however, that minor tweaks to the *DSM-5* criteria would make a big difference, bringing autistic people with milder symptoms or sets of symptoms that differ from classic autism back into the spectrum.[5]

There is a lot going on in this passage that is of interest. First, why the difference in status between those old enough to be diagnosed under earlier editions of the DSM and those now under the aegis of the DSM-5? Surely either the new standards are right and the old wrong (which is implied by the fact that only the new criteria will be applied to new diagnoses) or both are equally valid, which would seem to obviate the need for the new criteria. There is a similar tension between 'making diagnosis more accurate' and 'raising the bar too high.' If the changes are 'well grounded in research,' in what sense could they 'raise the bar too high?' Are we operating on two sets of standards here, only one of which is supposed to be objective and value-free? Which of the sets of standards would motivate the 'minor tweaks?'

The central question of this paper then, is what are the reasons for the various changes to the diagnostic criteria that I have delineated above?

2. Realism vs. Constructivism

Before we get to the main discussion, I would like to consider and reject one possible way of denying the premise of my question. This is to assert that there *haven't* been any changes of criteria. Notice that each of the three sets of diagnostic criteria, Kanner's and the DSMs IV and 5, are associated with conditions of different names. It may be true that there is significant overlap in the conditions, but they are none-the-less distinct, and it is not the case that any has *superseded* any other, they just all exist in parallel: Kanner's syndrome, PDD-NOS and ASD all exist alongside one another as conditions it is possible to have right now. The advantage of this view is that it allows us to say that Kanner was *right*: he accurately identified a genuine condition and modern advances have not contradicted him.

While this view is certainly coherent, it is not worth much discussion. Why, one would ask, if Kanner's syndrome is a live possibility, is it nowhere to be found in either edition of the DSM discussed here, and why has Asperger syndrome vanished from DSM-5? I shall proceed on the assumption that contemporary researchers and clinicians believe that they are refining what Kanner started: that he noticed *something* and it is that same something that contemporary diagnostic criteria are meant to capture, and capture more accurately. His list itself is not sacrosanct, it was just a set of characteristics (most of which) were the effects of a condition that is distinct from any subset or individual instantiation of those characteristics.

So, given that we are assuming that there has been real change in the diagnostic criteria, and that Kanner and the DSMs *disagree*, what grounds can the compilers of the criteria of the DSM-5 give to defend *their* criteria as an improvement over what came before?

The answer to that question can both depend on and influence our metaphysical stance on what autism is (where I am using 'autism' here to stand in for any and all of the related syndromes described in various diagnostic manuals). Let's crudely divide our metaphysical possibilities into *realism* and *constructivism*. Realism, we shall say, assumes that our conceptual categories 'carve nature at the joints,' or map on to real differences in the mind-independent world, whose existence, while influenced by the way people act towards it, is distinct from the way we think about it. Constructivism, by contrast, assumes that the nature of autism is somehow determined by human intellectual activity, in that the *concept* of, in this case, autism is intimately tied to autism itself.

The controversies and competing positions regarding *race* and racial categories offer instructive parallels. For one thing, the racial categories used on US census forms change with every new census, and millions of US census respondents change their self-identification from one census to the next.[6]

What response should the fact of these changes provoke in us? Clearly it could make us suspicious of *any* racial categories. One would think that race categories should not be like rankings of popular baby names, which can be expected to change from year to year with no public outcry. Nor should one's racial identity vary like the width of one's lapels from season to season. If we find race categories behaving in this way we might suspect that there is no more to them than public perception. Of course, for constructivists, this is neither surprising nor to be regretted. Race categories are *social constructs*, projections of the collective *zeitgeist* on to the world.

On the other hand, it is hard to reconcile such changeability with a robust *realism* about racial categories. Realism about racial categories demands a justification for any alteration in our list of recognized races, ideally one based on improved knowledge of the world, so that our new categories are in some way a *more accurate* reflection of the reality they purport to map. But what kind of reality is it that our concepts are supposed to represent? What is it that divides into groups that our conceptual categories track with increasing accuracy?

For race, the reality would be biological, as racial traits are themselves biological. Indeed, this is why the very concept of 'race' has come to be challenged, because it does not seem that there *is* any biological essence that any of our racial categories map on to. Of course, this does not mean that there is no such thing as *racism*, sadly, as humans persist in acting as if race were a real thing. And this very fact, say the social constructivists, is what *makes* race real, a reality of human making, by which humans who move around in it cannot help to be affected. This means that social constructivists, too, will demand justification for change in categories, particularly given the impact of such categories on people's lives and status. Depending on one's overarching ideology, one might look for the influence of powerful interested manipulators or one might point to certain impersonal engines of cultural change, but certainly the question of whose interests are served by the changes in categories will be raised.

I draw two morals from the foregoing. First, whether or not one is a realist or social constructivist about racial categories can and should be influenced by what one observes about shifts in the categories themselves. Second, whether or not one is a realist or social constructivist will affect what kinds of justifications one will demand for such shifts. I will apply these morals to the changes in the diagnostic criteria for autism and closely associated conditions.

3. Justifying the Changes

Suppose we are realists about autism, and we believe that there really is something out there in the world that we have discovered and can perhaps learn more about, what kinds of reasons would motivate the kinds of changes in diagnostic criteria we have seen?

The most obvious reason would be that we now *know more* about autism, we have discovered *more facts* that necessitate *more accurate* diagnostic criteria. But what is the 'more' that we could know? A radical kind of advance would be if we now know that autism is a different *kind* of phenomenon from what we previously thought, like the shift from thinking about light as a wave to thinking of it as a particle. So, for autism, it might be that we previously thought of it simply as a cluster of behaviours but now we identify autism with, say, a psychological 'module,' or a biological feature of the brain, or a genetic condition.

Alternatively, it might be that we have not changed what *type* of phenomenon we think it is, we just know *more* about the phenomenon, presumably because of improved scientific studies or technological advances.

Finally, it might be that the change is in that the original diagnosticians, beginning with Kanner, were agnostic – neither realists nor constructivists – and the change is that since that time we have *become* realists. That is, Kanner just noticed that he had several patients who could be grouped together, but reserved judgment on what kind of thing explained the similarity.

The kind of reasons that a realist would *not* endorse as reasons to change diagnostic criteria would be reasons that were unrelated to changes in knowledge of the nature of the phenomenon itself. So, for example, a change in attitudes (moral or otherwise) towards autism, like the changes in attitude towards homosexuality or transgenderism that we have seen in the US over the past few decades, would not affect the criteria of diagnosis. Whether or not society regards it as a disorder or a feature should have no bearing on whether or not you *are* autistic, according to the realist. Neither should pragmatic monetary concerns have any bearing. It is certainly true that, should the numbers of people diagnosed as autistic continue to rise exponentially, and insurance companies be required to pay for treatments, then there might be pressure on diagnosticians to narrow the diagnostic criteria or to come up with a greater spectrum of diagnoses and only label some of them as requiring treatment. But this would not be driven simply by knowledge of the phenomenon, as realism requires.

But perhaps it's not that simple. Consider how the criterion of death has changed. Here is the opening paragraph of the Report of the Ad Hoc Committee of the Harvard Medical School to Examine the Definition of Death, which met in 1968:

> Our primary purpose is to define irreversible coma as a new criterion for death. There are two reasons why there is a need for a definition: (1) Improvements in resuscitative and supportive measures have led to increased efforts to save those who are desperately injured. Sometimes those efforts have only a partial success so that the result is an individual whose heart continues to beat but whose brain is irreversibly damaged. The burden is great on patients who suffer permanent loss of intellect, on their families, on the hospitals, and on those in need of hospital beds already occupied by these comatose patients. (2) Obsolete criteria for the definition of death can lead to controversy in obtaining organs for transplantation.[7]

That is, with the old criterion of death, people who were 'brain dead' still counted as alive. This hadn't been a problem before the development of artificial respiration, as the majority would have died anyway, but since that advance, wards were 'filling up' with brain dead patients who could live for months or years longer. At the same time, the technique of heart transplantation had been pioneered by Christiaan Barnard, which was (and remains) only possible with a heart that was beating very recently before the surgery. Before the advent of respirators, such hearts were very hard to come by. The Harvard Committee are openly admitting here that their goal is both to allow hospitals to remove 'patients who suffer permanent loss of intellect' from life support and to provide a source of organs for donation. And so the criterion of death was changed.[8] Notice two things: both the prior and current criteria of death are very much realist: they point to actual phenomena in the world as the signs of death. But at the same time, the change was motivated by pragmatic concerns. And there are signs that the same thing might be happening for autism, as these quotes from reports about the changes between the DSM editions show:

> "We have to make sure not everybody who is a little odd gets a diagnosis of autism or Asperger disorder," said Dr. David J. Kupfer, a professor of psychiatry at the University of Pittsburgh and chairman of the task force making the revisions, which are still subject to change. "It involves a use of treatment resources. It becomes a cost issue."[9]

The changes would narrow the diagnosis so much that it could effectively end the autism surge, said Dr. Fred R. Volkmar, director of the Child Study Center at the Yale School of Medicine and the author of the new analysis of the proposal. 'We would nip it in the bud.'[10]

The effects, in particular, of moving some patients who would have fallen under the DSM-IV definition of 'Autistic Disorder' to the new 'Social Communication Disorder' may indeed have cost-saving effects (although not for the patients or their caregivers, of course):

> For students re-classified into the new proposed diagnosis of Social Communication Disorder or who are otherwise ineligible for an ASD diagnosis under the DSM-5, the IDEA (Individuals with Disabilities Education Act) eligibility process may prove more challenging.[11]

Interestingly, a recent study casts doubt on whether or not the changes between the DSMs have had any effect on rates of diagnosis.[12] What lessons should we draw from the example of the criterion of death and the quotes of Drs. Kupfer and Volkmar above? Can we be realists but have changes in diagnostic criteria still be driven by pragmatic or value-driven concerns? I don't think so. First of all, remember that the criterion of death is not the same as a *definition* of death. Presumably, if we are realists, the definition of death doesn't change, it's just that we don't necessarily know what it is. Assuming that water really is H_2O, it always *was* H_2O, even when we didn't have a conception of atomic structure and even if our criterion for recognizing it was 'potable clear-ish liquid.' Secondly, the fact that our criteria of death both before and after the Committee's recommendations include real-world phenomena doesn't mean that the metaphysical view of *death itself* is realist. It could still be 'whatever we decide death is.' Compare beauty: we can say with perfect consistency that beauty is a socially-constructed phenomenon and changes from culture to culture and epoch to epoch, without denying that the features that make it up (body mass, facial structure, skin texture, et. al.) are *not* socially constructed.

So, I argue that if the reasons motivating the changes in diagnostic criteria *were* really driven by financial worries, then that strongly indicates that the diagnostic categories of the DSM-5 should not be given a realist interpretation. However, consider this claim, published in an article in 'the official newsmagazine of the American Academy of Pediatrics':

> The diagnostic criteria for autism spectrum disorder has been modified based on the research literature and clinical experience in the 19 years since the DSM-IV was published in 1994.[13]

That is, the diagnostic criteria *have* been modified, and in response to knowledge acquired in the interim. This would ring true if there was some emerging consensus about autism, like the consensus that AIDS was caused by the HIV virus, where previously it was just known by its symptomatic effects. But no such consensus can be found when it comes to autism, and certainly not a consensus that would justify the specific rejection of Asperger Syndrome and the introduction of SCD. In fact, according to Harker and Stone, the collapsing of Autistic Disorder, Asperger's Disorder and PDD-NOS into the single category of ASD was 'reflecting research indicating a lack of reliability across clinicians in assigning subcategories,'[14] which suggests that if there was some consensus before DSM-IV that motivated the three separate subcategories, it has vanished. What seems to have been learned by the clinical experience of those trying to apply the DSM-IV criteria is that they were hopelessly vague and open to diverse subjective applications.

But again, if the DSM-IV's criteria were merely intended to give the visible signs of a reality only visible at the brain or genetic level, then the only lesson we could learn from looking at lack of clinical consensus is that the diagnostic criteria needed to be tied closer to the invisible reality. It shouldn't be that *the subcategories themselves* do not apply.

Let me give another analogy to illustrate. It used to be the case that there were clinical 'experts' on the 'disorder' of homosexuality. They believed, not just that homosexuality was a sign of ill mental health, but that it could be recognized from the results of (then) respectable psychological tests – the Rorschach, Thematic Apperception and Make-A-Picture-Story tests, none of which was directly correlated to sexual preference. In other words, it was believed that there was an *essence* to homosexuality which had pervasive effects across all areas of personality, not just on one's preferred love interest or sex object. Indeed, this was part of what made homosexuality a disorder: it disrupted all areas of one's life. Of course this belief was famously debunked by Evelyn Hooker, as she demonstrated that the so-called experts fared no better than blind chance at distinguishing homosexuals from heterosexuals from the results of the tests.[15] Notice, though, that this did not cause us to abandon the notion of homosexuality itself, just the idea that it was a mental disorder. If we think of the results of the three tests above as analogous to the diagnostic criteria for autism, then the lesson of the clinicians' inability to reach consensus on who fits in what subcategory should only be a sign that the criteria themselves are not good indicators (as the results of the Rorschach *et. al.* were not good indicators of homosexuality), but not that the categories themselves are wrong… unless we never had good reason for the categories in the first place. But then, why should we think that current confusion *lends support* for the new categories of the DSM-5. Furthermore, consider the following advice from the same article in AAP News referenced above:

> Because almost all children with DSM-IV confirmed autistic disorder or Asperger syndrome also meet diagnostic criteria under DSM-5, re-diagnosis is not necessary. Referral for reassessment should be based on clinical concern. Children given a PDD-NOS diagnosis who had few DSM-IV symptoms of autism or who were given the diagnosis as a "placeholder" might be considered for more specific diagnostic evaluation.
>
> Patients may wish to continue to self identify having Asperger syndrome, although the DSM-5 diagnostic category will be ASD.[16]

On the one hand this advice is consistent with a realist interpretation of the changes (PDD-NOS as a 'placeholder' for the newer, better diagnoses), but it also allows that one can keep a 'self-identity' of Asperger condition. Why, if it is inaccurate? The answer indicates the minefield the writers of DSM-5 had to traverse: they were not just altering medical diagnoses, but labels that individuals looked to as a source of identity. It is certainly telling to see identity politics seeping into a supposedly value-free clinical enterprise.

4. Psychology, Neurology and Genetics

So much for clinical experience justifying the changes in diagnostic criteria: what about the 'research literature?' Here, if anything, there is even less consensus. There is not even consensus over what level of phenomenon autism might be. The options are as follows.[17] First, autism could be located at the level of behavioural characteristics. That is, on this view, if one exhibits the characteristics described in the DSM, then one is autistic. If not, one is not. On this view, autism would be both treatable and, in theory, curable, if one ceased to exhibit the symptoms. Some do indeed claim that it is possible to 'recover' from autism.[18]

Second, autism could be a psychological phenomenon. This differs from the first option in that one could have the condition but not exhibit it. Compare with homosexuality: if it were at the first level, then anyone having same sex sex, would at least meet a most basic condition for being gay. The idea of a lifelong gay virgin would lack content. However, if homosexuality were a psychological phenomenon –say, 'same-sex sexual attraction'—then one could be gay even while living the same life as someone heterosexual. It allows for one to be closeted to everyone, even possibly oneself.

Third, autism could be a feature of the brain, such that all and only those with the requisite kinds of neural arrangements would be *really* autistic, allowing for the possibility of exhibiting either psychological or behavioural features associated with autism while not being autistic, or conversely, lacking either but being autistic.

Finally, autism could be located at the level of the genes, so that one would need a genetic screening to tell if one were *really* autistic. Some people believe that biological sex is like this, so that one can *appear* female (say) but if one has XY chromosomes, then one is *really* male. It was this view of what sex amounts to that led to the dismissal of a malpractice suit brought by Christie Lee Littleton against the doctors responsible for her husband's death: the Fourth Court of Appeals of Texas ruled that the man who died could not have been her husband because she was actually biologically male because she was XY (Littleton was transsexual, a transwoman) and Texas did not (and does not) recognize same-sex marriage.[19] It also led to the end of Spanish hurdler Maria Patino's athletic career because she failed a 'sex test' at the 1985 World University Games in Kobe, Japan. Unbeknownst to her, Patino had Androgen Insensitivity Syndrome (AIS), so named because typically an XY fetus develops male genitalia as a result of exposure to androgen *in utero*, but AIS individuals do not respond to that androgen. As a result, they are usually designated female at birth, and grow up thinking of themselves in that way.[20]

It is a fairly striking disagreement that researchers have not even settled where autism is to be located. I think the assumption most people have is that these levels will line up, so we don't necessarily have to settle this issue. But the example of sex shows the problems with this: Christie Lee Littleton's and Maria Patino's self-identities as female matched their outward appearances and secondary sexual characteristics, but did not match up with the 'right' kind of chromosomes. What are we to say in these kinds of instances?[21] This is not something that science can help us with. Science can tell us, for example, what genes correlate with what brain types or patterns of behaviour, but it is up to us to decide which represents the 'true essence' of something. With 'water' we appear to have decided that the essence lies at the molecular level. If something is *not* H_2O, then it does not matter how clear or potable it is, or even if it boils at 100°C, it is not water.[22] I think it is assumed, therefore, that science *showed* that 'water' was H_2O. This is not the case: 'water' used to refer to a much wider range of things than simply H_2O (basically anything wet) and still does refer to things that contain a lot more than just H_2O. We have *decided* to alter our usage because H_2O covers a significant chunk of what we were calling water. But we could have gone another way. And it looks like we might with sex: while many are still under the impression that XY=male and XX=female, the emerging acceptance of transgender individuals and the changing societal view that we should honour their self-identifications will mean that decisions like that in *Littleton v. Prange* will soon be as scorned as the one in *Dred Scott v. Sandford.* One's sex will be up to oneself in a way that one's chromosomes are not.

There is a further lack of consensus even between researchers that agree on what level is most basic. For example, assuming autism is a psychological feature most essentially, *what* psychological feature? Simon Baron-Cohen is often cited as a leading expert, but his own theory continues to mutate, from 'mindblindness,' through 'empathizing-systematizing' and the 'extreme male brain.' His various theories all have similar problems, though, in that they only even attempt to explain a subset of the features that the DSM asserts are definitive of autism disorders.[23] Uta Frith has offered 'Weak Central Coherence' as an alternative, but that too has the problem that it would at best explain a subset of the diagnostic criteria (noticeably having nothing to say about motor issues), and furthermore that those features are shared by individuals who are *not* labelled autistic.[24] A third major contender is that autism is 'executive dysfunction.' The features of autism that executive dysfunction is said to explain are the repetitive behaviours, reliance on routine, 'obsessive' interests and (purported) lack of creativity,[25] as well as the inability to plan a schedule for oneself. However, once again, it does not seem equipped to explain any sensory issues or the things the other theories purport to explain, such as social difficulties or enhanced perception of detail, so it is at best incomplete. Also, repetitive behaviours, reliance on routine, *et al.* are features of other distinct psychological conditions, like Obsessive Compulsive Disorder or Tourette's syndrome, so even if executive dysfunction explained these things it would not be a unique indicator of autism.

What we see, then, is that the contenders that offer a psychological account of the 'essence' of autism would, if correct, require a major re-working of the diagnostic criteria, or, failing that, are incomplete. Does it seem likely that any of these theories is behind the changes between DSMs IV and 5? Well, no: if anything they seem tied to the distinction between Asperger's and autism, and they do not seem amenable to underpinning the new category of SCD. Furthermore, the fact that sensory issues are stressed in DSM-5 also counts as a blow against these theories.[26] The prevailing view seems to be that the diagnostic criteria provide the more accurate guide to who fits the syndrome and the theories need to be adapted until they agree with the criteria – in other words, the influence is in the opposite direction from what it would be if the theories explained the changes in diagnostic criteria.

So, if psychological theories cannot explain the changes, what about studies of brains?

Perhaps it will not surprise you to hear that there is as much disunity amongst brain researchers as we have seen amongst psychologists. Jill Boucher provides a reason why this might be:

> The implications of findings on brain function are easily identified because the research is always hypothesis-driven. That is to say, each study is designed to test a specific hypothesis concerning the neural activity that occurs when the person being tested is carrying out a specific task.[27]

In other words, the brain research does not drive the psychological theorizing but rather the reverse. That is, researchers identify a feature that they associate with autism and then do studies to find out if that feature correlates with an identifiable part of the brain. Reading these studies is rather depressing, as the underlying presuppositions of the studies are often rather crude and it is clear that it is less the case that brain studies are advancing our view of autism than that our current view of autism is holding back brain studies.[28]

As a materialist I have to believe that *some* of the phenomena that Kanner noted are associated with particular brain structures, but perhaps it would be fair to say that autism is not located at the neural level. If we speak of an 'autistic brain' then, maybe we can say it is the *result* of a particular genetic structure. Maybe autism, like Down syndrome, has a specific genetic origin. Certainly that would make sense of the fact that 'there is now considerable evidence from family and twin studies that, for a subgroup of autistic individuals, the etiology is mainly genetic.'[29] What recent studies seem to show is that autism is *genetic* (like Down syndrome) because of the high rate of concordance in monozygotic twins, *familial* (unlike Down syndrome), but that *environmental factors* also must play a part (because in 10% of cases one monozygotic twin has autism but the other doesn't at all, and in cases where both have it, the severity can vary widely).[30] But a complicating factor to the notion that autism is 'in the genes' is the now well-accepted notion of 'broader autism phenotype' (BAP). This is

> a behavioral phenotype that is qualitatively similar to but more broadly defined than that which defines autism occurs more commonly in relatives of autistic individuals than in the general population.[31]

Or, as Baron-Cohen puts it, 'mild echoes' of autism:

> This might take the form of being socially withdrawn or confused by social interaction, or mildly obsessive (in the sense of having strong narrow interests or a need for sameness) or having excellent attention to detail and remarkable memory. Although [the close relatives of autistic individuals] don't have autism or Asperger syndrome itself, they have a milder manifestation of the same characteristics.[32]

The existence of 'BAPs' in families of autistic individuals would appear to explain the apparent high incidence of autism in the children of academics in such disciplines as Philosophy and in such places as Silicon Valley: the kind of focus and interest that leads one to succeed in certain intellectual pursuits is itself evidence of BAP. However, I would argue that actually BAP threatens the coherence of the concept of autism because it allows that one can have *some* of the criteria but not all. While this is acknowledged by the DSM (each edition makes clear that there are several conditions, each of which is necessary, none of which is individually sufficient), it also makes each diagnostic category look very arbitrary. Why *that* number of symptoms? What if you have one very severely, but others below the level necessary for a diagnosis? Then you would not meet a diagnosis, but clearly you have some challenges such that you would benefit from assistance of some kind.

What if a genetic test did emerge? It seems very possible that, on the one hand, many people who currently have no diagnosis for ASD would test positive, and at the same time many who do have a diagnosis would lack the gene. By analogy with a genetic definition of biological sex: AIS people like Maria Patino would previously have had the category of 'woman' but lose it on genetic testing, while, conversely, they would *gain* a 'diagnosis' of 'male.' But just as in the case of AIS individuals, science does not make the final decision as to what we regard as definitive of a person's sex. And when we are considering autism, where social services and insurance issues depend on a diagnosis, it would seem perverse to provide services for somebody who does need or want them because of a genetic marker while denying them from somebody who would clearly benefit from them on the basis of its absence.

But we are a long way from that, anyway: a study of over 200 papers published between 1961 and 2003 on the genetics of autism reached the following conclusion:

> Although many genes and proteins have been implicated as causes of autism, too little is known about their functions or their role in brain development to generate a parsimonious hypothesis about the brain dysfunctions that underlie autism. Evidence from multiplex families with the broader autism phenotypes, together with twin studies, indicates that single-gene defects are rare even within families… Despite the profusion of investigations into the genetics of autism, few significant genetic linkages to autism have been identified.[33]

Clearly, then, any changes between DSM-IV and DSM-5 cannot be justified by 'knowledge' of a genetic basis to autism.

5. Conclusion

Realism about the various conditions that could be grouped under the heading of autism would demand that any changes to our diagnostic criteria be motivated by an advance in our knowledge of the real, mind-independent phenomenon that we refer to with that term. I argue that there is no consensus among clinicians or researchers that could possibly justify us claiming better knowledge of such a phenomenon. We don't even know what we're looking for. That would appear to imply that I am denying that people are autistic, just as people who question the biological basis for race deny that individuals really have a race. I am hesitant to go that far. What I will say is that there are no doubt conditions that the diagnostic criteria in the DSMs identify that have a biological realization, just as one's hair texture, skin pigmentation and facial structure have a biological realization, even if race does not. This leaves the door open to the idea that 'autistic,' like, say, 'black,' is amenable to a constructivist analysis. What that would mean, however, is that the kind of questions we would ask about the changes between the editions of the DSM would be about whose interests those changes serve and not assume that scientific impartiality is what is driving them. Indeed, a constructivist would be very suspicious of the medicalization of autism as a category. Those who press for the rejection of any notion that autism is a disorder, and argue that it is simply a different way of being, and that we should talk of 'neurodiversity' instead of 'the normal' and 'the disordered' are motivated by just such a suspicion. Again, I am not going to put myself firmly in that camp, as I believe that there are plenty of people whose 'autistic' symptoms are severe and whose lives are hampered and made miserable by them, such that they would benefit from services that can only be paid for if they meet a medical diagnosis. I just do not think that clustering conditions together under particular headings, and re-ordering them between editions of the DSM is a practice that can be said to be justified by advances in science. Be wary of clinicians who treat the DSM as anything more than a rough guide for locating helpful services.

Notes

[1] For a much more thorough listing of all the differences between the DSM-5 and its immediate predecessor, see Colleen Harker and Wendy Stone, 'Comparison of the Diagnostic Criteria for Autism Spectrum Disorder Across DSM-5, DSM-IV-TR, and the Individuals with Disabilities Act (IDEA) Definition of Autism,' The Iris Center 2014, viewed on 4 November 2014, http://iris.peabody.vanderbilt.edu/wp-content/uploads/2014/09/ASD-Comparison-092214.pdf.

[2] Leo Kanner, 'Autistic Disturbances of Affective Contact,' *Classic Readings in Autism*, ed. Anne M Donnellan (New York: Teachers College Press, 1985), 41.

[3] This list, and each quote, comes from Kanner, 'Autistic Disturbances of Affective Contact,' 42-48.
[4] Michael Rutter, 'Commentary on Kanner's Autistic Disturbances of Affective Contact' *Classic Readings in Autism*, ed. Anne M Donnellan (New York: Teachers College Press, 1985), 50-52.
[5] Ferris Jabr, 'Redefining Autism: Will New DSM-5 Criteria for ASD Exclude Some People?' *Scientific American* (January 30, 2012), viewed on 7 May, 2014, https://www.scientificamerican.com/article/autism-new-criteria/.
[6] D'Vera Cohn, 'Millions of Americans Changed Their Racial or Ethnic Identity from One Census to the Next,' viewed on 22 March 2015, http://www.pewresearch.org/fact-tank/2014/05/05/millions-of-americans-changed-their-racial-or-ethnic-identity-from-one-census-to-the-next/.
[7] JAMA, 'A Definition of Irreversible Coma,' *Journal of the American Medical Association* 205.6 (Aug. 5, 1968): 85.
[8] See Peter Singer, *Rethinking Life and Death* (New York: St. Martin's Press, 1994), chapter 2.
[9] Amy Harmon, 'A Specialists' Debate on Autism Has Many Worried Observers,' *New York Times*, January 20, 2012.
[10] Benedict Carey, 'New Definition of Autism Will Exclude Many, Study Suggests,' *New York Times*, January 19, 2012.
[11] Ari Ne'eman and Steven Kapp, 'What Are the Stakes? An Analysis of the Impact of the DSM-5 Draft Autism Criteria on Law, Policy and Service Provision,' *Autistic Self Advocacy Network (ASAN) Policy Brief*, June 2012.
[12] Young Shin Kim, et al., 'A Comparison of DSM-IV Pervasive Developmental Disorder and DSM-5 Autism Spectrum Disorder Prevalence in an Epidemiologic Sample,' *Journal of the American Academy of Child & Adolescent Psychiatry* 53.5 (2014): 500-508.
[13] Susan L. Hyman, 'New DSM-5 Includes Changes to Autism Criteria,' *AAP News*, originally published online June 4, 2013, viewed on 22 March, 2015, http://aapnews.aappublications.org/.
[14] Colleen Harker and Wendy Stone, 'Comparison of the Diagnostic Criteria for Autism Spectrum Disorder across DAM-5, DSM-IV-TR, and the Individuals with Disabilities Act (IDEA) Definition of Autism.'
[15] Evelyn Hooker, 'The Adjustment of the Male Overt Homosexual,' *Journal of Projective Techniques* 21 (1957): 18-31.
[16] Hyman, 'New DSM-5 Includes Changes to Autism Criteria.'
[17] I go into this in more detail in Simon Cushing, 'Autism: The Very Idea,' *The Philosophy of Autism*, eds. Anderson and Cushing (Lanham: Rowman and Littlefield, 2013), 17-45.
[18] See Jennifer Richler, 'Is It Possible to Recover from Autism?' *Scientific American* 24.3 (2013): np, viewed on 26 May 2015,

http://www.scientificamerican.com/article/is-it-possible-to-recover-from-autism/.
[19] *Littleton v. Prange*, 9 S.W.3d 223 (1999).
[20] Alison Carlson, 'When is a Woman Not a Woman?' *Women's Sports & Fitness* 13 (1991): 25. See also Anne Fausto-Sterling, *Sexing the Body* (New York: Basic, 2000): chapter 1. Patino agreed to fake an injury at the Kobe games so that the reason for her dismissal did not get out and cause embarrassment, and she was encouraged to keep training. However, 4 months later, at the first meet of the Spanish indoor season the head of the Spanish federation told her she would have to fake another injury—this time supposedly career-ending—or risk exposure in the media. She refused, won her race, and, as promised, she was exposed in the media, lost her boyfriend and many friends and all of her records were stripped from the books.
[21] Similar issues arise concerning race, see Charles Mills, '"But What Are You Really?" The Metaphysics of Race,' *Blackness Visible: Essays on Philosophy and Race*, ed. Charles Mills (Ithaca, NY: Cornell University Press, 1998), 41-66.
[22] Hilary Putnam, 'Meaning and Reference,' *Journal of Philosophy* 70.19 (1973): 699-711.
[23] See the papers by Sample, Pentzell, Stubblefield and Maiese in Anderson and Cushing, *The Philosophy of Autism*, for more in depth critiques of Baron-Cohen's various views.
[24] See Jill Boucher, *The Autistic Spectrum: Characteristics, Causes and Practical Issues* (London: Sage, 2009), 211, 213. This theory presents what I think is a caricature of the autistic individual as one who cannot see the forest for the trees. But note also Baron-Cohen's most recent theory posits instead that autistic individuals are *superior* 'systemizers' (sic) where 'systemizing is the drive to analyze *or construct* systems'. Simon Baron-Cohen, *Autism and Asperger Syndrome: The Facts* (Oxford: Oxford University Press, 2008), 63, emphasis added.
[25] I say 'purported' because there seems to be ample evidence of creativity even amongst quite severely autistic individuals. Consider Derek Pavancini, the blind British pianist, who, while he has memorized 'an enormous repertoire' of jazz songs, is also able to improvise on the spot. Baron-Cohen, *Autism and Asperger Syndrome*, 104. There are more and more examples of autistic visual artists as well.
[26] 'Hyper-or hypo-reactivity to sensory input or unusual interest in sensory aspects of environment; (such as apparent indifference to pain/heat/cold, adverse response to specific sounds or textures, excessive smelling or touching of objects, fascination with lights or spinning objects).' The best candidate would be Frith's WCC theory, but even that does not seem equipped to explain the insensitivity to heat/cold. Uta Frith, *Autism: Explaining the Enigma* (Oxford: Blackwell, 1989.)
[27] Boucher, *The Autistic Spectrum: Characteristics, Causes and Practical Issues*, 139.

[28] For an illustration, see Cushing, 'Autism: The Very Idea,' 31-33.
[29] Joseph Piven, et al., 'Broader Autism Phenotype: Evidence From a Family History Study of Multiple-Incidence Autism Families,' *American Journal of Psychiatry* 154 (1997): 185.
[30] Boucher, *The Autistic Spectrum: Characteristics, Causes and Practical Issues*, 118.
[31] Piven, et al., 'Broader Autism Phenotype: Evidence From a Family History Study of Multiple-Incidence Autism Families,' 185. As evidence, the authors offer: 'Wolff et al… interviewed the parents of autistic children and the parents of nonautistic mentally retarded comparison subjects and found that the parents of the autistic children were more often judged to lack emotional responsiveness and empathy, show impaired rapport with the examiner, and have histories of oversensitivity to experience, special interest patterns, and oddities of social communication… Gillberg, in a study of the parents of 23 children with Asperger syndrome, reported social deficits in 11 of the 23 fathers that were similar to, but milder than, those seen in Asperger syndrome.' Piven, et al. 'Broader Autism Phenotype: Evidence From a Family History Study of Multiple-Incidence Autism Families,' 186.
[32] Baron-Cohen, *Autism and Asperger Syndrome*, 93.
[33] Rebecca Muhle, Stephanie V. Trentacoste and Isabelle Rapin, 'The Genetics of Autism,' *Pediatrics* 113.5 (2004): e482.

Bibliography

Anderson, Jami and Simon Cushing, eds. *The Philosophy of Autism*. Lanham, MD: Rowman & Littlefield, 2013.

Baron-Cohen, Simon. *Autism and Asperger Syndrome: The Facts*. Oxford: Oxford University Press, 2008.

Boucher, Jill. *The Autistic Spectrum: Characteristics, Causes and Practical Issues*. London: Sage, 2009.

Carey, Benedict. 'New Definition of Autism Will Exclude Many, Study Suggests.' *New York Times*, January 19, 2012.

Carlson, Alison. 'When Is a Woman not a Woman?' *Women's Sports & Fitness* 13 (1991): 24-29.

Cushing, Simon. 'Autism: The Very Idea.' *The Philosophy of Autism*, edited by Jami L. Anderson and Simon Cushing, 17-45. Lanham: Rowman and Littlefield, 2013.

Donnellan, Anne M., ed. *Classic Readings in Autism*. New York: Teachers College Press, 1985.

Fausto-Sterling, Ann. *Sexing the Body*. New York: Basic, 2000.

Frith, Uta. *Autism: Explaining the Enigma*. Oxford: Blackwell, 1989.

Harker, Colleen and Wendy Stone. 'Comparison of the Diagnostic Criteria for Autism Spectrum Disorder across DAM-5, DSM-IV-TR, and the Individuals with Disabilities Act (IDEA) Definition of Autism.' The Iris Center 2004. Viewed on 4 November 2014.
http://iris.peabody.vanderbilt.edu/wp-content/uploads/2014/09/ASD-Comparison-092214.pdf.

Harmon, Amy. 'A Specialists' Debate on Autism Has Many Worried Observers.' *New York Times*, January 20, 2012.

Hooker, Evelyn. 'The Adjustment of the Male Overt Homosexual,' *Journal of Projective Techniques* 21 (1957): 18-31.

Hyman, Susan L. 'New DSM-5 Includes Changes to Autism Criteria.' *AAP News*, originally published online June 4, 2013. Viewed on 22 March 2015.
http://aapnews.aappublications.org/.

Jabr, Ferris. 'Redefining Autism: Will New DSM-5 Criteria for ASD Exclude Some People?' *Scientific American* (January 30, 2012). Viewed on 7 May 2014.
https://www.scientificamerican.com/article/autism-new-criteria/.

JAMA. 'A Definition of Irreversible Coma.' *Journal of the American Medical Association* 205.6 (Aug. 5, 1968): 337-340.

Kanner, Leo. 'Autistic Disturbances of Affective Contact.' *Classic Readings in Autism*, edited by Anne M. Donnellan, 11-50. New York: Teachers College Press, 1985.

———. 'Follow-up Study of Eleven Autistic Children Originally Reported in 1943.' *Classic Readings in Autism*, edited by Anne M. Donnellan, 223-234. New York: Teachers College Press, 1985.

Kim, Young Shin, Eric Fombonne, Yun-Joo Koh, Soo-Jeong Kim, Keun-Ah Cheon, and Bennett Leventhal. 'A Comparison of DSM-IV Pervasive Developmental Disorder and DSM-5 Autism Spectrum Disorder Prevalence in an Epidemiologic Sample.' *Journal of the American Academy of Child & Adolescent Psychiatry* 53.5 (2014): 500-508.

Littleton v. Prange. 9 S.W.3d 223 (1999).

Mills, Charles. *Blackness Visible: Essays on Philosophy and Race*. Ithica, NY: Cornell University Press, 1998.

———. '"But What Are You *Really*?" The Metaphysics of Race.' *Blackness Visible: Essays on Philosophy and Race*, edited by Charles Mills, 41-66. Ithica, NY: Cornell University Press, 1998.

Muhle, Rebecca, Stephanie V. Trentacoste, and Isabelle Rapin. 'The Genetics of Autism.' *Pediatrics* 113.5 (2004): e472-e486.

Ne'eman, Ari, and Steven Kapp. 'What Are the Stakes? An Analysis of the Impact of the DSM-5 Draft Autism Criteria on Law, Policy and Service Provision.' *Autistic Self Advocacy Network (ASAN) Policy Brief*, June 2012.

Piven, Joseph, Pat Palmer, Dinah Jacobi, Debra Childress, and Stephan Arndt. 'Broader Autism Phenotype: Evidence from a Family History Study of Multiple-Incidence Autism Families.' *American Journal of Psychiatry* 154.2 (1997): 185-190.

Putnam, Hilary. 'Meaning and Reference.' *Journal of Philosophy* 70.19 (1973): 699-711.

Richler, Jennifer. 'Is It Possible to Recover from Autism?' *Scientific American* 24.3 June 6, 2013. Viewed on 26 May 2015. http://www.scientificamerican.com/article/is-it-possible-to-recover-from-autism/.

Rutter, Michael. 'Commentary on Kanner's Autistic Disturbances of Affective Contact.' *Classic Readings in Autism*, edited by Anne M. Donnellan, 50-52. New York: Teachers College Press, 1985.

Singer, Peter. *Rethinking Life and Death.* New York: St. Martin's Press, 1994.

Simon Cushing is Associate Professor of Philosophy at the University of Michigan-Flint. He is the co-editor, along with Jami Anderson of *The Philosophy of Autism*, published in 2013 by Rowman & Littlefield.

Creativity and 'Madness': Myths, Constructions and Realities

Jonathan Appel, Dohee Kim-Appel, Erin Snapp, Claire Whiteman, Mary Cassidy and Rebecca Stanic

Abstract

The definition and depiction of madness can greatly alter the opinion on whether or not creativity and 'madness' are related. 'Madness' is often a social construction of non-conformity and creativity, even in its more modern edifices of medicalization, psychiatrization, and even criminalization; with the Diagnostic and Statistical Manual (DSM) as the current mythology to explain human behaviour. This chapter will discuss the relationship between mental states and creativity, both as the construction and an expression of neurological and psychological diversity and as a tool for healing a wounded psyche. Both cutting edge research and intervention suggestions are offered to illuminate the connections between creativity, and the multiple constructions of 'madness.'

Key Words: Creativity, madness, mental illness, expressive arts, art therapy, schizophrenia, bi-polar disorder, autism.

*****

1. Construction of Terms: 'Madness' and Creativity

The definition and depiction of 'madness' can greatly alter the opinion on whether or not creativity and madness are related. Typically, today 'madness' is often seen as a synonym for mental or psychiatric illness. Currently, if one is diagnosed with a mental illness then one is stigmatized. In the early 19th centuries, maybe this was not the case. In the 19th century, the thought of madness 'could serve as a distinguishing factor, one that could mark a person as separate, unique and even divinely chosen.'[1] George Becker found the relationship between creativity and madness has been a subject of controversy in Western society from about the 19th century to the present. He explains, 'Although speculations regarding the mental state of creative individuals predate this period by centuries, they typically fell short of the verdict of clinical insanity.'[2]

We have all been exposed to the view of the tortured artist. Salvador Dali's and Vincent van Gogh's bizarre behaviours or Sylvia Plath's depression have been well documented. A possible link between mental illness and creative output has been documented throughout history. As far back as the 4th century B.C., the connection between 'divine' inspiration and altered mental state had already been made, prompting Plato to declare in the dialogue to Phaedrus: 'Madness' provided it comes as the gift of heaven, is the channel by which we receive the greatest blessings… Madness comes from God, whereas sober sense is merely human.' In fact, some researchers even declare that creativity and mental illness are almost the exact state of mind. Adrienne Sussman notes:

> The list of afflicted artists is staggering, and spans all areas of art. Many of the most iconic figures in the modern Western canon, including the poet T.S. Eliot, the composer Irving Berlin, and the painter Georgia O'Keefe were formally institutionalized at some point in their careers. Others, including the writer Virginia Woolf and the artist Vincent van Gogh, actually ended their own lives because of mental illness. It seems almost impossible that so many central figures in the arts could be connected in such a specific way serendipitously – merely listing the artists who have suffered from mental illness suggests that mere chance isn't responsible, that a scientific explanation for the link must exist.[3]

Creativity has been demarcated as the process of thinking up new and original ideas, methods, and concepts, and has been defined as being original and effective.[4] Understanding what creativity is a challenge when one is asked to view creativity in purely objective terms. Creativity also often has a non-reductive subjective nature, not unlike consciousness.[5]

Creativity has also been defined as 'the production of something both new and valued.'[6] During the period of the Italian Renaissance individuals who possessed superior ability in creativity were called 'genio' or what we call 'genius.' Genio had the definition of being an 'imitation of established masters of nature'.[7] While there may be some relationship between genius and creativity -they are not necessarily the same thing. Creativity may have a thinking function, such as novel and divergent problem solving; it also possesses a production of creative artifacts. Modern research has focused on the multidimensional nature of both creativity and madness, but both these definitions remain in flux as they are socially constructed. Differences in Western and Eastern cultures' views of creativity has been found to vary on the ideas and purposes of creativity, thereby changing what different cultures view creativity as, this research gives support that creativity is not regarded similarly by different cultures; while there may be a shared concept of creativity, what that creativity is entirely depends on one's social values and their culture.[8] Such findings challenge the concept that creativity can be judged objectively; instead it would seem that creativity is subjective by its very nature, being at least partially constructed by one's birthplace and culture. Knowing that such influences can affect ideas of creativity notes the limitations of a purely universal definition of creativity.

2. Research into 'Madness' with Creativity Prevalence

Scholars have been long interested in comparing rates of mental disorders (as defined by psychiatric nomenclature) among artistically inclined individuals. Researcher Nancy Andreasen compared average business professionals to creative writers and found that 80% of writers have experienced manic depressive disorder or prolonged periods of depression while only 30% of the business professionals have experienced one of these mood disorders.[9] Another study found that 38% of poets, playwrights, sculptors, and painters, who had received distinguished honours in their field, had been treated for depression or manic depressive disorder (bi-polar) in opposition to the general population's treatment of only 6%.[10] Andreasen also notes 'affective disorder may be both a 'hereditary taint' and a hereditary gift.'[11]

Other researchers have concluded that bipolar disorder is around 10 and 40 times more common among artists than among the general public.'[12] American clinical psychologist Kay Redfield Jamison found that creative individuals, especially poets, reported that their mental and physical states during periods of great creative productivity were very similar to those during manic episodes.[13]

Arnold Ludwig researched and diagnosed 1,004 eminent professionals, by reading biographies, which had made significant contributions to society throughout human history. In his results, he found that creative artists had a much higher chance of having a severe mood disorder than did any other professional. He also found that as adults, anywhere from 59-77% of the prominent artistic field could be diagnosed with a mood disorder.[14] Power et al more recently tested whether risk scores for schizophrenia and bipolar disorder would predict creativity. These researchers did find higher risk scores were associated with artistic society membership or creative profession[15]

Image 1: Some believe that Salvador Dali's mental disorders may also have been the key to his creativity. Picture is in public domain htttp://publicdomainclipart.blogspot.com/2009/04/salvador-dali-cats-and-water-caught-in.html

3. Biological Constructions of 'Madness'

One view constructs how madness and creativity may be influenced by biological factors. It is noted that Einstein, Newton, and James Joyce all have close relatives or offspring that may have suffered from schizophrenia. This suggests to some that creativity and madness may have a genetic and/or biological link.[16] Mental illness is often viewed as a biological disease of the brain. This research asserts that creativity is neurologically linked to mental illness. Some mood disorders are even listed with the side effects of heightened and creative thoughts in the Diagnostic and Statistical Manual of Mental Illness.[17] The biological view thus suggests that the possible link between creativity and mental illness may be found in the brain's cerebral cortex. This brain region holds the parietal, temporal, and frontal lobes–locations where knowledge, meaning, and mental concepts are stored. Researchers find that people with mental illness commonly have abnormalities in this lobe. This research indicates that those with schizophrenia, depressive disorders, and substance abuse are most likely to see a dysfunction in these brain regions.[18] Sussman suggests, 'hyperactivity found in the parietal and temporal lobes, may cause one to make strange connections between unrelated ideas, thoughts, and emotions. These thoughts may seem abstract and bizarre to the average person, making an artist's expressions of their mind seem creative and unusual.'[19]

The brain of a 'mentally ill' individual also shows imbalances in neurotransmitters which are seen as adversely impacting the normal functioning of the frontal and temporal lobes. Those with schizophrenia have high levels of dopamine that can cause hallucinations, delusions, and scattered or tangential thought processes. Many with the label of bipolar disorder have cycling levels of norepinephrine in the frontal lobe that result in hyper or low thought levels and unusual, creative ideas.[20] Neurotransmitter variations may alter perception and cognitive thoughts.[21] These imbalances, it is suggested, can allow the mentally ill to draw, paint, hear, and think differently from the average individual.[22] Dr. Kinneth Helman at the University of Florida asserts:

> These hallucinations and delusions thus can be expressed through a person's art, literature, or musical expression. Activities in the brain from atypical neurotransmitter variations allow combining of information in the parietal and temporal lobes in overwhelming ways. Distorted images created by artists, such as those by Pablo Picasso and Salvador Dali, are thus then seen as having a powerful impact on the normal human, due to the fact that many 'normals' are not able to imagine these distortions in their heads.[23]

The biological view has also noted that recent research has also made an intriguing link between creativity and schizophrenia.[24] This line of research indicates that a genetic mutation linked to psychosis and schizophrenia may also influence creativity. Szabolcs Kéri, a geneticist at Semmelweis University in Budapest, Hungary, who carried out a genetic study on schizophrenia notes that biological research could help to explain why mutations that enhance a person's risk of developing mental illnesses such as schizophrenia or bipolar disorder have been preserved, even selected, during the course of human evolution. Kéri studied a gene called neuregulin 1, which has been discovered to be involved in brain development. Prior research has linked this gene mutation to vulnerability towards schizophrenia and psychosis. Kéri looked at the relationship between these gene variations and creative thinking. He found that individuals with two copies of the neuregulin 1 mutation were much more likely to score higher on measures of creativity compared to subjects with one or no copy of the mutation. Those with one copy were also judged to be more creative, on average, than subjects without the mutation.[25] How exactly neuregulin 1 impacts the link between creativity and mental illness isn't entirely clear. It is noted that the subjects with two copies of the mutation were no more likely than others to also possess traits, such as paranoia, odd speech patterns, inappropriate emotions, or other features associated with psychosis. This may suggest that the mutation's connection to mental illness is likely mediated by other variables.

There are also indications that the mutation may impact the prefrontal cortex – which serves as the logic controls for the brain. It is thought that Neurgulin 1 (as well as other biological vulnerabilities) may impact prefrontal lobe activity. It has been reported that the reduction of prefrontal functions may lead to disinhibition and creative peaks in highly functioning people, even if they are in the pre-symptomatic stage of severe neurodegenerative illnesses.[26] This modification may release creative potential in some –but may also result in psychotic delusions in others. Kéri's work indicates intelligence could be one factor that determines whether the neuregulin 1 mutation enhances creativity or contributes to psychosis. Nevertheless in relation to psychosis the greatest degree of creativity is shown in the relatives of persons with psychosis who have minor genetic loadings for psychosis and don't have a formal diagnosis of psychosis.[27]

A. Autism

Autism Spectrum Disorders (ASD) are typically described as a biologically based neurodevelopmental conditions with a wide range of dysfunctional social and cognitive adaptations. The focus in the study of ASD, to a smaller extent, has also been on the observation of a superior narrowing of intellectual skills, with a substantial minority of ASD individuals displaying some exceptional creative abilities (reaching genius proportions in some cases). According to the Diagnostic and Statistical Manual (DSM), individuals with ASD are likely to have communication deficits, such as responding inappropriately in conversations, misreading nonverbal interactions, or having difficulty building friendships appropriate to their age. In addition, people with ASD may be overly dependent on routines, highly sensitive to changes in their environment, or intensely focused on inappropriate items. The DSM 5 suggests that individuals with ASD will fall on a continuum, with some individuals showing mild symptoms and others having much more severe symptoms. For the majority of ASD, creativity as a skill is seen as lacking.[28] Some elements of a creativity deficit in autism have been investigated, including a possible developmental precursor of pretend play.[29] There are a growing number of experimental studies of creativity in autism. Researcher Uta Frith found that when given the freedom to create patterns using images or sounds, children with autism produced less varied patterns relative to normal controls.[30] That is, they were indeed less creative. A similar conclusion was determined by Lewis and Boucher when examining the drawings produced by children with autism.[31] The contents of these drawings were less varied– implying a lack of creativity. The research is consistent with the classical portrait of autism, that of rigid, stereotyped behaviours, a preference for sameness and a resulting lack of imagination.

Lyons and Fitzgerald however, offer a challenge to this impoverished creativity in ASD. They point out the enormous achievements that some people with ASD show in creative and scientific fields. They suggest:

> The results of our evaluation suggest that many features of ASD are advantageous for great creativity. Creativity is an extremely complex and multifaceted construct and no cognitive theory or model of brain function has so far been able to fully account for it. We suggest that the distinctive gifts of perception, attention, memory and information processing combined with personality attributes can give rise to the extraordinary creativity seen in some individuals with ASD.[32]

The biological construct and evidence supports some form of association between creativity and mental disorder, but the direction of any simple causal link remains uncertain. Results of various studies do suggest an increased rate of schizophrenia, bi-polar disorder, depression, and personality disorder as well as alcoholism/drug addiction in creative individuals.[33] The link between mental disorder and creativity is likely not to be a simple one-to-one correlation.

4. Cognitive Constructions of 'Madness'

Cognitive models suggest that factors of intelligence, cognitive flexibility, and communication mediate with biological factors to produced different outcomes. Keri notes:

> My clinical experience is that high-IQ people with psychosis have more intellectual capacity to deal with psychotic experiences, it's not enough to experience those feelings, but you have to communicate them.[34]

It may be the process of communication and expression of divergent or novel thought processes that holds a critical role in increasing coping and healthy adaptation, in the mentally ill. This certainly has implication for understanding the conditions associated with constructions of 'madness' and the link with creativity.

Jeremy Hall, a geneticist at the University of Edinburgh, found a connection between the neuregulin 1 mutation and psychosis, also supports the notion that the gene's impacts are probably influenced by cognitive and personality factors, including intelligence.[35] Psychologist Shelley Carson sees cognitive flexibility as a protective factor. Cognitive flexibility is the ability to shift thoughts or actions as demanded by the situational context. This includes the ability to shift attentional focus from one stimulus to another with conscious control. Carson notes, 'Deficits in this ability have long been considered a hallmark of schizophrenic thought.'[36] Cognitive flexibility is also associated with the personality trait of openness to experience, which is the psychological trait most often linked with not only creativity, but 'madness' as well. But the openness and sensitivity of creative people can expose them to much suffering and pain, which can be debilitating. As Sylvia Plath said, 'When you are insane, you are busy being insane—all the time ... when I was crazy, that's all I was.'[37]

This relationship does not fully suggest the overly romantic notion that psychotic states and creativity are the same thing. Hall states: 'Madness is often madness and doesn't have much genetic association with intelligence.'[38] Another researcher of the creativity/madness link notes, 'Few would argue that full-blown psychosis is conducive to creative accomplishment, but perhaps a little bit helps.'[39] Psychologist David Schuldberg suggests, 'While it remains clear that emotional instability is usually detrimental to creativity, it may also be valuable. Emotionality may provide the intense motivation, the conviction, imagination, and the inspiration necessary for future discoveries and breakthroughs.'[40] Creativity or 'madness' may also allow the artist, poet, writer, composer, and scientist to escape the powerful cultural or social constraints that they would otherwise face in today's society. Schuldberg notes that conformity often hinders the ability to facilitate the amount of creativity or 'madness' needed to develop cultural progression.[41]

As mentioned, research often notes that many suffering with psychotic disorders such as schizophrenia show clinical signs of frontal lobe dysfunction, including blunted affect, difficulty with problem solving, and impoverished thinking. What is mentioned less often in the behavioural sciences literature is that those with the conditions of schizophrenia and bi-polar actually perform better, cognitively, once they are medicated and the extremes of the conditions are under control. The functional and stabilized mentally ill are often able to organize myriad pieces of information (ones that are both cognitive and sensory in nature) to yield unique and often highly insightful solutions to problems. Those with schizophrenia may actually perform better, cognitively, once they are medicated and the mental illness is under control.[42]

Psychosis and the non-normative experiences of those suffering from bi-polar and/or schizophrenia conditions often can be viewed as the inability to filter and organize information normally; these experiences include additional sensory stimulations that result in creating abundant unprocessed and/or unfocused material from which one can gain either cognitive errors or novel insights. Divergent thinking can equally result in cognitive error or in originality. While the creativity of those with schizophrenia and bi-polar conditions may or may not be organized, their additional sensory experience provides a wealth of material for the feeding of potential creative thought that is greater than the norm. If a level of cognitive organization can be restored (via medication and various psychosocial or even spiritual therapies) - novel insights can be translated to the language of valued and understood narratives.

The implication (of the biological and cognitive factors research) is that there are radically different routes to creativity, including normal and so-called abnormal neurocognitive developmental patterns. The rise in reported and continuing cases of people being born with conditions such as autism spectrum disorder or psychotic disorders may indicate a possible evolutionary trait. Thus, these neuro-diverse conditions may be mutations that can be seen as enhancing the ability of a sub-set of high-functioning people with these conditions (often with unusual or specialized interests) to intensively focus on problems and creative solutions without the normal social constraints.

5. Cultural Constructions of Defining and Assessing 'Madness'

> *Everything that can be counted does not necessarily count; everything that counts cannot necessarily be counted.*
> *- Albert Einstein.*[43]

The constructed western worldview is exemplified by science, inductive logic, and a more linear reductionist reality. This worldview seeks to analyse, categorize, objectify. We narrow our version - believing the parts are the whole story. Typically, we have the tendency to approach the challenge of understanding our world categorically through a narrow lens. Categorical thinking while developmentally has helped our thinking (e.g. helps understand and encode information in our memory)—it also distorts our ability to see the differences and similarities between two different facts or concepts. If you pay too much attention to the boundaries, you have trouble seeing the big picture. How psychiatry or psychological science (as an extension of the western worldview) defines and assesses 'madness' is often no different. Developing a diagnostic system (the DSM) biased towards a biological (and pathological) worldview tells a distorted and partially informed story. The introduction of the DSM 5 notes, 'DSM is a *medical* classification of disorders'.[44] Dr. Allen Frances, best known for chairing the task force that produced the fourth revision of *Diagnostic and Statistical Manual* (DSM-IV) asserts that the newest edition of the DSM (5) is often replacing normality and with a reductionistic biomedical model. Frances states,

> Psychiatric diagnosis is facing a renewed crisis of confidence caused by diagnostic inflation... These changes will probably lead to substantial false-positive rates and unnecessary treatment. Drug companies take marketing advantage of the loose DSM definitions by promoting the misleading idea that everyday life problems are actually undiagnosed psychiatric illnesses caused by a chemical imbalance and require a solution in pill form. This results in misallocation of resources, with excessive diagnosis and treatment for essentially healthy persons (who may be harmed by it).[45]

This worldview also strongly suggests that symptoms (diagnosis) result almost exclusively from a 'disease' process that resides mostly within individuals. This reductionism often misses the whole contextual picture or a 'wide lens view' that includes sociocultural and other multiple systemic and reciprocal processes that may produce troubled behaviour as a reaction to situation. This localization of 'illness' often results in segregation in the 'inflicted'.

It is well known that the United States incarcerates a greater percentage of its population than any other nation on Earth, with nearly 2.4 million Americans behind bars (with over 6 million altogether either in jail, prison or community control).[46] Of great concern is the fact that prisons are exceedingly being filled with more inmates who suffer from mental illness.[47] The increased incarceration rate of the mentally ill has been one of the consequences of the 'deinstitutionalization' movement of the mentally ill in the 1980s and 1990s in the United States. Many were told that this was the 'humane' way to treat the mentally ill -in the community rather than locked up in cold and sterile institutions. Many were also assured the money would follow the patients into the community- as millions would be saved by closing state- run mental hospitals. Anyone who has worked through the process into the current era—knows that this did not happen. Deinstitutionalization of the public mental health system in the United States since the 1980s has resulted in correctional institutions becoming the' poor person's mental health facility'. Services have been cut, and there are not enough needed supportive resources in the community. Some have commented that the mentally ill were not deinstitutionalized in the United States—we 'trans-institutionalized' them into our jails, prisons and court systems (and did so without much guilt).[48] Our future generations may look back on this time with shame- unless fears of a psychopathic society come true.[49]

'Madness,' for better and for worse, is not seen the same way worldwide. Mental disorders are often considered to be the product of multiple factors, but mostly get described through medicalized language in the West. Culture may also be thought to determine the pattern and expression of certain specific states of 'madness' or mental disorders. There is acknowledgement that mental disorders, at least in part, can represent culture-specific expressions although they are not part of the standard nomenclature of traditional Western psychiatry and the behavioural sciences. 'Madness' often takes the form of scientific paradigms produced in 'Western' countries and is not necessarily sensitive to traditional views or epistemologies. Researchers Leighton and Hughes comment about cultural mental disorders:

> A list would include 'amok' and 'lâtah' both found in Malay, 'imu' among the Ainu of Japan, 'koro' in China, 'witiko' among the Ojibwa Indians of the Northeast Woodlands, 'piblokto' in the eastern Arctic, and 'arctic hysteria' in Siberia. Each one embodies a constellation of symptoms found primarily in a given culture area, and often there is association between cultural beliefs or practices and the content of the symptoms.[50]

Culture may impact the understanding, course, and severity of mental disorders. Even biological and genetic states and conditions express and adapt themselves in a cultural and social context. The questions of cultural patterns and their shaping of hereditary processes are rarely fully contemplated. If one views 'madness' through the lens of 'extended time' and dynamic cultural and physical evolutions, the impact may be more profound than the snapshot picture we often take.

Additionally, whether in research or assessment in the behavioural sciences one should be collecting 'holistic' multi-method data. The examination of this data should also take both the 'objective (empirical-behavioural-external) view–as well as the 'subjective' (internal-qualitative and/or narrative) view or meanings in account. One-dimensional assessment can be helpful, but never should be used as the *only* piece of information. We need both (mixed) approaches to research as neither quantitative nor qualitative may be sufficient by itself. Any knowledge of a phenomenon is enlightened by a 'multiple angles' argument – quantitative and qualitative approaches provide different 'pictures.' One must be cognizant of the inherent limited vision, particularly when defining and describing mental states—as numbers are one thing—but discovering of both the horrid as well as the insightful subjective and narrative experiences may be required to humanize the intervention approaches. As noted by Kara Holmes and Fiona Ann Papps – in their chapter 'The Consumer Movement and the Social Construction of Mental Illness' – professionals pathologies mental illness through social construction, particularly language.

The Behavioural Sciences is strongly associated with positivist leanings and scientific language.[51] The values and methods guiding traditional psychology and related fields have sought to strengthen links with biology, biochemistry and the 'real sciences,' rather than with the symbols and languages associated with literature and the creative arts. Fathali Moghaddam, an Iranian psychologist, does suggest this view is limiting, and notes literature can serve both as a source of psychological data and as a source of insights for psychology and views about mental illness in a social and cultural context.[52]

The artist's soul will intuit something is missing in a purely limited mechanical view of defining humans, which is psychiatry's DSM system. In fact, many will fiercely resist this quantification. We must recognize such tools are also a product of the same human frailty and underdeveloped vision, and take them with a huge grain of salt - learning to use them in the least harmful ways. The intentions are good, but partially blinded by professional apparatus. The study of abnormal mental states is complex and influenced by historical time and culture. No single explanation fits all situations. We should not mistake the map for the territory - and most of all we must listen with our hearts as well as our brains.

6. The 'Professional' Constructions of 'Madness'

> *There is a congruity between our apparatus for acquiring knowledge and the nature of the things known*
> *-C.H. Waddington.*[53]

What the above quote may mean is that, as mentioned, we are often blinded by our own cultural 'maps' that we acquire as well as the limits of our brains and sensory systems. This idea also refers to what society has imprinted on our biology as well as what our *professional cultures* have constructed or even imposed on us. The 'psychiatric bible' of The Diagnostic and Statistical Manual of Mental Disorders (DSM-5) defines abnormal behaviour as:

> A behavioural or psychological syndrome or pattern that reflects an underlying *psychobiological dysfunction* that is associated with distress or disability and is not merely an expectable response to common stressors or losses.[54]

The environment is only mentioned as part of a deviation from what is considered normal in a sociocultural context, which is usually expressed as distress or disability. The 'problem' is always seen as being located within the individual, rather than the dysfunction of the larger reciprocal content between the individual and larger systems of organization. As noted by Kara Holmes and Fiona Ann Papps – in their chapter 'The Consumer Movement and the Social Construction of Mental Illness' – Drawing on the contextualization discourse subverts the institution of mental health care that locates the object of mental illness inside a person. As noted in their research consumers mostly draw on this discourse and are calling for an acknowledgment of wider discourses to explain the social construction of mental illness.

There has been a supposed attempt in the new DSM-5 to move beyond the system of merely putting people into categorical 'boxes'. Clinicians are supposed to capture the symptoms and severity of mental illnesses, by using dimensional assessments. These would allow clinicians to systematically evaluate patients on the full range of symptoms they may be experiencing. Dimensional assessments, so the thinking goes, allow clinicians to rate both the presence and the severity of symptoms, such as 'very severe,' 'severe,' 'moderate' or 'mild.' The concern is that they have just stretched the 'box' – because just a small amount will now qualify as a 'diagnosable disorder.' The DSM 5 also very consciously added the phrase 'psychobiological dysfunction' in describing, what the DSM system was defining. This still suggests being trapped in a linear, medical, and categorical conceptual model of human behaviour. But would that not be what one would expect from a manual that was for the most part designed by American M.D.s? This is consistent with Holmes and Papps's view that the dominant discourse has assumed that mental illness can be measured, assessed and recorded, with standardized formats and techniques, all in which power relationships are inherently defined in these constructions of standardization.

If one takes a systems view, one would also need to view the individual – particularly children or adolescents – as only the 'symptom bearer' of the series of embedded systems. A system has multiple levels and sub-systems including the family, the community, peers, and society in general – all which may initiate, hold, and contribute to the dysfunction. Children become the symptom barriers of the ills of the culture. So what do we see? ADHD and Autism, which perhaps represent two extreme expressions of (mal) adaptation seen through the forms of 'symptoms' for the brain-mind to keep up with the increasing frantic pace of our information culture (and lost ability to focus and contemplate) – and/or (2) a turning off and a turning inward to screen the distress of what is only described as an oversensitive 'biology,'– but likely that has multi-level and reciprocal causal factors. This is consistent with the view that 'madness' is a sane reaction to a mad culture. The societal goal often becomes targeted towards convergence rather than divergence. Adaptation is more likely to occur with conditions and structures that do not support creativity thinking, or creative vision. With the DSM, one can only recognize there is a problem, but its view is but a snapshot or a fragment of the full context. An example of this limitation is that the DSM views symptoms arising from processes occurring within individuals while family therapy sees symptoms as arising from processes occurring within family or other connected systems.[55]

7. Construction of Intervention: Creativity

Working with individuals with mental health issues is always a complicated thing. Very few programmes give *inclusive* training to do this. There are many programmes of systematic intervention aimed at modifying clients' behavioural, emotional, and/or cognitive state. Therapy is often used to control abnormal behaviour.[56] Psychological intervention has been criticized as merely being a means the state (however surreptitiously) uses to help its citizenry adapt to the cultural norm.

The bias in contemporary psychiatric-biological construction is towards medication. Recent concerns have been raised that perhaps psychiatric medications are being over-prescribed.[57] This over-medication can result in the numbing of the emotional system or can even thwart creative ability. The bias in counselling and psychotherapy programmes is often towards verbal therapy – which also often falls short. The dialogue of the therapy also is usually defined to language that in constructed or standardized around the medicalized terminology of controlling symptoms, diagnosis, and 'disordered thinking'. Once again this construction reflecting that the nature of seeing things is unknowingly limited by how we look at things. It is no accident that most of the 'best practices' in assessment, counselling, and psychotherapy are often touted as cognitive-behavioural. This construction represents the easiest paradigm to turn into reductionistic research products–and is done by individuals who are cognitive behavioural creatures themselves. Other interventions of systems of counselling and therapy (such as emotionally focused theorists) do not necessarily partake in much external/objective oriented data based research. There is other research that states success is not so much a result of the unique factor (therapy type) as from those common factors of human warm, genuineness, and engagement.[58]

Traumatic experiences (in all its forms) and social exclusion or oppression is often recognized as a core experience of many psychological problems and a root influence to many differently expressed forms of 'madness' or psychiatric diagnoses.[59] Traumatic memories or associations appear to take root not in the verbal, analytical parts of the brain but in the nonverbal emotional regions of the limbic system, from which cognition is often disconnected. Verbal therapy is often limited in its ability to initially access required emotional and cognitive content present in clients with traumatic histories. Many individuals are at an either pre-verbal (or pre-personal) level of experience (such as children) or may not have the skills to identify and express thoughts and feelings in an integrated manner (particularly with embodied trauma).[60] This might impact the important stage of therapeutic engagement as well. Premature verbalization or interpretation of meaning may either be inaccurate or emotionally overwhelm the person in therapy. Both errors of technique may result in disengagement from the therapy process.

Effective therapeutic work with trauma or highly emotional charged issues often requires training in non-verbal and creative methods as well (e.g. art therapy, or play therapy, music therapy, etc.) as well as verbal counselling methods. Some clients' initial therapeutic work may need to be 'bottom-up' through pre-personal images and emotional states, which others may need to build the narrative through a symbolic and expressive lens where development of meaning and/purpose are often critical issues. Traditional counselling approaches usually reside in language and intellectual routes, often ignoring alternative pathways. A larger assessment map and an expressive therapeutic approach provide multiple access points to address what are usually multi-level and multi-layered problems. Expressive interventions, including art and music, may provide an essential role in the developmental of more effective and integrative therapeutic trauma-informed counselling and psychotherapy.

Alice Flaherty, an American neurologist, notes, 'When clinicians treat patients with disorders that affect their creativity, they need to protect patients' creativity, both from the side effects of treatment and from the very conditions that partly gave rise to the creativity.'[61] Thus, medication in the absence of other non-verbal psychosocial intervention cannot fully provide comprehensive treatment. Creative individuals such as writers, poets, artists and singers have often used their art as part of the 'healing' process of mental illness. Expressive therapies such as art, dance and music are often recognized as effective means to treat emotional disorders.[62] These forms of therapies can provide ways to reframe organize and express divergent as well as painful experiences.

8. Conclusion

While there is no universal or static definition of 'madness' or even creativity, many authors and researchers have tried to define, construct, and explain the relationship and identify the link between emotional and mental states and creativity.[63] The connections between madness and creativity are more likely found in highly complex relationships with multiple reciprocal and mediating variables and various constructions.

Thus, certain personality traits, cognitive flexibility, and/or brain functioning of creative individuals may overlap with socially constructed clinical syndromes of mental illness or 'madness.' This overlap does appear to intersect—but not with a one-to-one correspondence. This area of overlap may serve to illuminate constructs of both creativity and madness. The connection between 'madness' and creativity may be found in the shared biological, cognitive, or personality features, related to the presence of cognitive and social disinhibition.[64] Hence, 'madness' may mean something more than merely 'bad' genetics and malfunctioning neurotransmitters, or cognitive variation (although it may still be helpful to describe these associations). We suspect that the current picture may be incomplete. The study of human behaviour, including madness and creativity, involves numerous biological, psychological, and social substrates– and perhaps can best be illuminated by a truly multidisciplinary analysis and multidimensional intervention. Each version or construction of 'madness' develops and maintains its own language and definitional system, which require linkage and 'multilingual' or multidisciplinary proficiency. Future inquiry needs to tease out these connections and clarify these multi-dimensional constructions and associations.

Notes

[1] George Becker, 'The Association of Creativity and Psychopathology: Its Cultural-Historical Origins,' *Creativity Research Journal* 13, no. 1 (2001): 48.
[2] Ibid., 45.
[3] Adrienne Sussman, 'Mental Illness and Creativity: A Neurological View of the "Tortured Artist",' *Stanford Journal of Neuroscience* 1, no. 1 (2007): 21.
[4] Mark A. Runco and Garrett J. Jaeger, 'The Standard Definition of Creativity,' *Creativity Research Journal* 24, no. 1 (2012): 92-96; Jennifer Diedrich, Mathias Benedek, Emanuel Jauk, and Aljoscha C. Neubauer, 'Are Creative Ideas Novel and Useful?' *Psychology of Aesthetics, Creativity, and the Arts* 9, no. 1 (2015): 35
[5] Michel Pham, 'Emotion and Rationality: A Critical Review and Interpretation of Empirical evidence.' *Review of General Psychology* 11, no. 2 (2007): 155.
[6] Maureen Neihart, 'Creativity, the Arts, and Madness,' *Roeper Review* 21, no. 1 (1998): 47.
[7] Becker, 'The Association of Creativity and Psychopathology,' 46.
[8] Weihua Niu and Robert J. Sternberg. 'The Philosophical Roots of Western and Eastern Conceptions of Creativity,' *Journal of Theoretical and Philosophical Psychology* 26, no. 1-2 (2006): 18.
[9] Nancy C. Andreasen, 'Creativity and Mental Illness,' *American Journal of Psychiatry* 144, no. 10 (1987): 1288-1292.
[10] Kay Redfield Jamison, *Touched with Fire* (New York: Simon and Schuster, 1996).
[11] Nancy C. Andreasen, 'Creativity and Mental Illness,' *American Journal of Psychiatry* 144, no. 10 (1987): 1292.
[12] O. Somasundaram, 'The Seeds of Creativity and the Soil of Poet Kannadasan.' *Indian Journal of Psychiatry* 53, no. 1 (2011): 82.
[13] Kay Redfield Jamison, 'Mood Disorders and Patterns of Creativity in British Writers and Artists,' *Psychiatry* 52, no. 2 (1989): 125-134.
[14] Arnold M Ludwig, *The Price of Greatness: Resolving the Creativity and Madness Controversy* (New York: Guilford Press, 1995).

[15] Robert Power, Stacy Steinberg, Gyda Bjornsdottir, Cornelius A. Rietveld, Abdel Abdellaoui, Michel M. Nivard, Magnus Johannesson et al. 'Polygenic Risk Scores for Schizophrenia and Bipolar Disorder Predict Creativity.' *Nature Neuroscience* (2015), 1-4.
[16] Edward Hare, 'Creativity and Mental Illness,' *BMJ* 295, no. 6613 (1987): 1587-1589.
[17] Sussman, 'Mental Illness and Creativity,' 24-27.
[18] Edmund S. Higgins and Mark Stork George, *Neuroscience of Clinical Psychiatry: the Pathophysiology of Behavior and Mental Illness* (Philadelphia: Lippincott, Williams & Wilkins, 2013).
[19] Sussman, 'Mental Illness and Creativity,' 22.
[20] Ibid., 24-27.
[21] Ibid., 24-27.
[22] Ibid., 24-27.
[23] Quoted in Sussman,, 'Mental Illness and Creativity,' 24.
[24] Alice W. Flaherty, 'Brain Illness and Creativity: Mechanisms and Treatment Risks,' *Canadian Journal of Psychiatry. Revue Canadienne de Psychiatrie* 56, no. 3 (2011): 132-143.
[25] Ibid., 1070-1073.
[26] William W. Seeley, et al., 'Unravelling Boléro: Progressive Aphasia, Transmodal Creativity and the Right Posterior Neocortex,' *Brain* 131, no. 1 (2008): 39-49.
[27] Szabolcs Kéri, 'Genes For Psychosis And Creativity: A Promoter Polymorphism of the Neuregulin 1 Gene Is Related to Creativity In People with High Intellectual Achievement.' Psychological Science 20, no. 9 (2009): 1070-1073.
[28] Fiona J. Scott and Simon Baron-Cohen, 'Imagining Real and Unreal Things: Evidence of a Dissociation in Autism,' *Journal of Cognitive Neuroscience* 8, no. 4 (1996): 371-382.
[29] Simon Baron-Cohen, 'Autism and Symbolic Play,' *British Journal of Developmental Psychology* 5, no. 2 (1987): 139-148.
[30] Uta Frith, 'Cognitive Mechanisms in Autism: Experiments with Color and Tone Sequence Production,' *Journal of Autism and Childhood Schizophrenia* 2, no. 2 (1972): 160-173.
[31] Vicky Lewis and Jill Bouchet, 'Skill, Content and Generative Strategies in Autistic Children's Drawings,' *British Journal of Developmental Psychology* 9, no. 3 (1991): 393-416.
[32] Viktoria Lyons and Michael Fitzgerald. *Critical Evaluation of the Concept of Autistic Creativity*, INTECH Open Access Publisher, (2013): 33. Viewed on 15 April 2015, http://www.intechopen.com/books/recent-advances-in-autism-spectrum-disorders-volume-i/critical-evaluation-of-the-concept-of-autistic-creativity.

[33] Arnold M. Ludwig, 'Reflections on Creativity and Madness.' *American Journal of Psychotherapy* 43 (1989): 4-14.
[34] Quoted in E. Callaway, 'Artistic Tendencies Linked to Schizophrenia Gene,' *New Scientist*, 15:58, and (2009): 12.
[35] Jeremy Hall et al., 'A Neuregulin 1 Variant Associated with Abnormal Cortical Function and Psychotic Symptoms,' *Nature Neuroscience* 9, no. 12 (2006): 1477-1478.
[36] Shelley Carson, 'Creativity and Psychopathology: Shared Neurocognitive.' *Neuroscience of Creativity* (2013): 175.
[37] Quoted in Alice W. Flaherty, 'Brain Illness And Creativity: Mechanisms and Treatment Risks.' *Canadian Journal of Psychiatry. Revue Canadienne De Psychiatrie* 56, no. 3 (2011): 132.
[38] Callaway, "Artistic Tendencies Linked to Schizophrenia Gene, 13.
[39] Emma Young, 'What's the Link Between Creativity And Mental Illness?' *New Scientist* 206 (2010): 31.
[40] David Schuldberg, 'Creativity and Psychopathology: Categories, Dimensions, and Dynamics,' *Creativity Research Journal* 13, no. 1 (2001): 107.
[41] Schulberg, , 'Creativity and Psychopathology,' 108.
[42] Örjan, De Manzano et al., 'Thinking Outside a Less Intact Box: Thalamic Dopamine D2 Receptor Densities are Negatively Related to Psychometric Creativity in Healthy Individuals,' PLoS One 5, no. 5 (2010): np. Viewed on 15 April 2015, http://www.ncbi.nlm.nih.gov/pmc/articles/PMC2871784/.
[43] Quoted in Charles Garfield, *Peak Performers* (New York City: Harper Collins, 1987).
[44] American Psychiatric Association, and American Psychiatric Association. *'Diagnostic and Statistical Manual of Mental Disorders Fifth Edition (DSM-5).'* Washington, DC: American Psychiatric Association (1994), 11.
[45] Allen Frances, 'The New Crisis of Confidence in Psychiatric Diagnosis.' *Annals of Internal Medicine* 159, no. 3 (2013): 221-222.
[46] Elliott Currie, *Crime and Punishment in America* (London: Macmillan, 2013).
[47] Irina R. Soderstrom, 'Mental Illness in Offender Populations: Prevalence, Duty and Implications,' *Journal of Offender Rehabilitation* 45, no. 1-2 (2007): 1-17.
[48] Ashley Primeau, Thomas G. Bowers, Marissa A. Harrison, and XuXu. 'Deinstitutionalization of the Mentally Ill: Evidence for Transinstitutionalization from Psychiatric Hospitals to Penal Institutions,' *Comprehensive Psychology* 2, no. 1 (2013): 1-10.
[49] Gary Olson, *Empathy Imperiled: Capitalism, Culture, and the Brain*, Vol. 10 (Berlin: Springer Science & Business Media, 2012).
[50] Alexander H., Leighton and Jane M. Hughes, 'Cultures as a Causative of Mental Disorder,' *Milbank Quarterly* 83, no. 4 (2005): 12.
[51] Hare, 'Creativity and Mental illness,' 1587-1589.

[52] Fathali M. Moghaddam, 'From 'Psychology in Literature to Psychology is Literature': An Exploration of Boundaries and Relationships.' *Theory & Psychology* 14, no. 4 (2004): 505-525.
[53] Conrad Hal Waddington, *The Evolution of an Evolutionist* (Cornell: Cornell University Press, 1975).
[54] American Psychiatric Association, *Diagnostic and Statistical Manual of Mental Sisorders, (DSM-5®)*. (Washington D.C.: American Psychiatric Pub, 2013).
[55] Jonathan Appel, and Dohee Kim-Appel. 'The Multipath Approach to Personality: Towards a Unified Model of Self,' *Psychology* 1, no. 04 (2010): 273.
[56] Donald Black, *Toward a General Theory of Social Control: Fundamentals* (New York: Academic Press, 2014).
[57] B. Smith, 'Inappropriate Prescribing,' *Monitor on Psychology* 43, no. 6 (2012): 36.
[58] Bruce E. Wampold, 'Humanism as a Common Factor in Psychotherapy,' *Psychotherapy* 49, no. 4 (2012): 445.
[59] María-José Alvarez et al., 'Prevalence and Clinical Impact of Childhood Trauma in Patients with Severe Mental Disorders,' *The Journal of Nervous and Mental Disease* 199, no. 3 (2011): 156-161.
[60] Eliana Gil, *Helping Abused and Traumatized Children: Integrating Directive and Nondirective Approaches* (NY: Guilford Press, 2006).
[61] Alice W. Flaherty, 'Brain Illness and Creativity: Mechanisms and Treatment Risks,' *Canadian Journal of Psychiatry, Revue Canadienne de Psychiatrie* 56, no. 3 (2011): 133.
[62] C. A. Malchiodi, 'Creative Arts Therapy Approaches to Attachment Issues,' *Creative Arts and Play Therapy for Attachment Problems* (2014): 3-18.
[63] Erika Lauronen, et al., 'Links between Creativity and Mental Disorder,' *Psychiatry* 67, no. 1 (2004): 81-98.
[64] Emilie Glazer, 'Rephrasing the Madness and Creativity Debate: What Is the Nature of the Creativity Construct?' *Personality and Individual Differences* 46, no. 8 (2009): 755-764.

Bibliography

American Psychiatric Association. *Diagnostic and Statistical Manual of Mental Disorders, (DSM-5®)*. Washington, DC: American Psychiatric Association, 2013.

Andreasen, Nancy C. 'Creativity and Mental Illness.' *American Journal of Psychiatry* 144, no. 10 (1987): 1288-1292.

Alvarez, María-José, Pere Roura, Anna Osés, Quintí Foguet, Judit Sola, and Francesc-Xavier Arrufat. 'Prevalence and Clinical Impact of Childhood Trauma in Patients with Severe Mental Disorders.' *The Journal of Nervous and Mental Disease* 199, no. 3 (2011): 156-161.

Appel, Jonathan and Dohee Kim-Appel. 'The Multipath Approach to Personality: Towards a Unified Model of Self.' *Psychology*,1, no. 04 (2010): 273-281.

Baron-Cohen, Simon. 'Autism and Symbolic Play.' *British Journal of Developmental Psychology* 5, no. 2 (1987): 139-148.

Becker, George. 'The Association of Creativity and Psychopathology: Its Cultural-Historical Origins.' *Creativity Research Journal* 13, no. 1 (2001): 45-53.

Black, Donald, *Toward a General Theory of Social Control: Fundamentals*. New York: Academic Press, 2014.

Callaway, E. 'Artistic Tendencies Linked to Schizophrenia Gene,' *New Scientist*, 15:58 (2009): 12-13.

Carson, Shelley. 'Creativity and Psychopathology: Shared Neurocognitive.' *Neuroscience of Creativity* (2013): 175-203.

Garfield, Charles. *Peak Performers*. New York City: Harper Collins, 1987.

Currie, Elliott. *Crime and Punishment in America.* London: Macmillan, 2013.

De Manzano, Örjan, Simon Cervenka, Anke Karabanov, Lars Farde, and Fredrik Ullen. 'Thinking Outside a Less Intact Box: Thalamic Dopamine D2 Receptor Densities are Negatively Related to Psychometric Creativity in Healthy Individuals.' *PLoS One* 5, no. 5 (2010): np. Viewed on 15 April 2015. http://www.ncbi.nlm.nih.gov/pmc/articles/PMC2871784/.

Flaherty, Alice W. 'Brain Illness and Creativity: Mechanisms and Treatment Risks.' *Canadian Journal of Psychiatry. Revue Canadienne De Psychiatrie* 56, no. 3 (2011): 132-143.

Frith, Uta. 'Cognitive Mechanisms in Autism: Experiments with Color and Tone Sequence Production.' *Journal of Autism and Childhood Schizophrenia* 2, no. 2 (1972): 160-173.

Frances, Allen. 'Saving Normal: An Insider's Revolt Against Out-Of-Control Psychiatric Diagnosis, DSM-5, Big Pharma and The Medicalization Of Ordinary Life.' *Psychotherapy in Australia* 19, no. 3 (2013): 14.

Frances, Allen. 'The New Crisis of Confidence in Psychiatric Diagnosis.' *Annals of Internal Medicine* 159, no. 3 (2013): 221-222.

Gil, Eliana. *Helping Abused and Traumatized Children: Integrating Directive and Nondirective Approaches*. NY: Guilford Press, 2006.

Glazer, Emilie. 'Rephrasing The Madness And Creativity Debate: What Is The Nature of the Creativity Construct?' *Personality and Individual Differences* 46, no. 8 (2009): 755-764.

Hall, Jeremy, Heather C. Whalley, Dominic E. Job, Ben J. Baig, Andrew M. McIntosh, Kathryn L. Evans, Pippa A. Thomson. 'A Neuregulin 1 Variant Associated with Abnormal Cortical Function and Psychotic Symptoms.' *Nature Neuroscience* 9, no. 12 (2006): 1477-1478.

Hare, Edward. 'Creativity and Mental Illness.' *BMJ* 295, no. 6613 (1987): 1587-1589.

Higgins, Edmund S., and Mark Stork George. *Neuroscience of Clinical Psychiatry: The Pathophysiology of Behavior and Mental Illness*. Philadelphia: Lippincott, Williams & Wilkins, 2013.

Jamison, Kay Redfield. *Touched with Fire.* New York: Simon and Schuster, 1996.

Jamison, Kay Redfield. 'Mood Disorders and Patterns of Creativity in British Writers and Artists.' *Psychiatry* 52, no. 2 (1989): 125-134.

Jarrold, Christopher, Jill Boucher, and Peter Smith. 'Symbolic Play in Autism: A Review.' *Journal Of Autism And Developmental Disorders* 23, no. 2 (1993): 281-307.

Kéri, Szabolcs. 'Genes For Psychosis And Creativity: A Promoter Polymorphism of the Neuregulin 1 Gene Is Related to Creativity In People with High Intellectual Achievement.' *Psychological Science* 20, no. 9 (2009): 1070-1073.

Landreth, Garry L. *Play Therapy: The Art of the Relationship.* London: Routledge, 2012.

Lauronen, Erika, Juha Veijola, Irene Isohanni, Peter B. Jones, Pentti Nieminen, and Matti Isohanni. 'Links Between Creativity and Mental Disorder.' *Psychiatry* 67, no. 1 (2004): 81-98.

Leighton, Alexander H., and Jane M. Hughes. 'Cultures as a Causative of Mental Disorder,' *Milbank Quarterly* 83, no. 4 (2005): 12-37.

Lewis, Vicky, and Jill Bouchet. 'Skill, Content and Generative Strategies in Autistic Children's Drawings.' *British Journal of Developmental Psychology* 9, no. 3 (1991): 393-416.

Ludwig, Arnold M. *The Price of Greatness: Resolving the Creativity and Madness Controversy*. New York: Guilford Press, 1995.

Ludwig, Arnold M. 'Method and Madness in the Arts and Sciences.' *Creativity Research Journal* 11, no. 2 (1998): 93-101.

Ludwig, Arnold M. 'Reflections on Creativity and Madness.' *American Journal of Psychotherapy* 43 (1989): 4-14.

Lyons, Viktoria, and Michael Fitzgerald. *Critical Evaluation of the Concept of Autistic Creativity*, INTECH Open Access Publisher, (2013): 33. Viewed on 15 April 2015.
http://www.intechopen.com/books/recent-advances-in-autism-spectrum-disorders-volume-i/critical-evaluation-of-the-concept-of-autistic-creativity.

Malchiodi, C. A. 'Creative Arts Therapy Approaches to Attachment Issues.' *Creative Arts and Play Therapy for Attachment Problems* (2014): 3-18.

Moghaddam, Fathali M. 'From Psychology in Literature to Psychology is Literature: An Exploration of Boundaries and Relationships.' *Theory & Psychology* 14, no. 4 (2004): 505-525.

Neihart, Maureen. 'Creativity, the Arts, and Madness.' *Roeper Review* 21, no. 1 (1998): 47-50.

Niu, Weihua, and Robert J. Sternberg. 'The Philosophical Roots of Western and Eastern Conceptions of Creativity.' *Journal of Theoretical and Philosophical Psychology* 26, no. 1-2 (2006): 18.

Olson, Gary. *Empathy Imperiled: Capitalism, Culture, and the Brain*, Vol. 10. Berlin: Springer Science & Business Media, 2012.

Pham, Michel Tuan. 'Emotion and Rationality: A Critical Review and Interpretation of Empirical Evidence.' *Review of General Psychology* 11, no. 2 (2007): 155.

Power, Robert, Stacy Steinberg, Gyda Bjornsdottir, Cornelius A. Rietveld, Abdel Abdellaoui, Michel M. Nivard, Magnus Johannesson et al. 'Polygenic Risk Scores for Schizophrenia and Bipolar Disorder Predict Creativity.' *Nature Neuroscience* (2015), 1-4

Primeau, Ashley, Thomas G. Bowers, Marissa A. Harrison, and XuXu. 'Deinstitutionalization of the Mentally Ill: Evidence for Transinstitutionalization from Psychiatric Hospitals to Penal Institutions.' *Comprehensive Psychology* 2, no. 1 (2013): 1-10.

Runco, Mark A. 'Reasoning and Personal Creativity.' *Creativity and Reason in Cognitive Development* (2006): 99-116.

Schuldberg, David. 'Creativity and Psychopathology: Categories, Dimensions, and Dynamics.' *Creativity Research Journal* 13, no. 1 (2001): 105-110.

Scott, Fiona J., and Simon Baron-Cohen. 'Imagining Real and Unreal Things: Evidence of Dissociation in Autism.' *Journal of Cognitive Neuroscience* 8, no. 4 (1996): 371-382.

Somasundaram, O. 'The Seeds of Creativity and the Soil of Poet Kannadasan.' *Indian Journal of Psychiatry* 53, no. 1 (2011): 82.

Smith, B. 'Inappropriate Prescribing.' *Monitor on Psychology* 43, no. 6 (2012): 36.

Soderstrom, Irina R. 'Mental Illness in Offender Populations: Prevalence, Duty and Implications.' *Journal of Offender Rehabilitation* 45, no. 1-2 (2007): 1-17.

Seeley, William W., Brandy R. Matthews, Richard K. Crawford, Maria Luisa Gorno-Tempini, Dean Foti, Ian R. Mackenzie, and Bruce L. Miller. 'Unravelling Boléro: Progressive Aphasia, Transmodal Creativity and the Right Posterior Neocortex.' *Brain* 131, no. 1 (2008): 39-49.

Sussman, Adrienne. 'Mental Illness and Creativity: A Neurological View of the "Tortured Artist".' *Stanford Journal of Neuroscience* (2007): 24-27.

Waddington, Conrad Hal. *The Evolution of an Evolutionist*. Cornell: Cornell University Press, 1975.

Wampold, Bruce E. 'Humanism as a Common Factor in Psychotherapy.' *Psychotherapy* 49, no. 4 (2012): 445.

Young, Emma. 'What's the Link Between Creativity and Mental Illness?' *New Scientist* 206 (2010): 31-31.

Jonathan Appel, Ph.D., has worked in the field of Behavioral Health for three decades. He has worked with individuals, groups, families, and organizations as a Counsellor, Psychotherapist, Clinical Supervisor, Director of Behavioral Health Services, Consultant, Researcher, Department Chair, IRB Director, and Educator. He is currently a Full Professor in the Department of Behavioral and Social Sciences, within the School of Criminal Justice and Social Sciences at Tiffin University in Tiffin, Ohio, U.S.A.

DoHee Kim-Appel, Ph.D., is an associate Professor in the Department of Counseling and Art Therapy at Ursuline College in Pepper Pike, Ohio. Kim-Appel has presented papers and training sessions regionally, nationally, and internationally in such topics as workplace violence, family violence, mindfulness, substance abuse and mental illness, and creativity and mental health. Kim-Appel has more than a decade of experience in the field of Behavior Health working with a diverse population of clients across the spectrum of emotional and substance related issues,
including youth, individuals, couples, and families.

Erin Snapp holds a BA in Psychology from Tiffin University and an MS in Clinical Psychology from Eastern Michigan University. She will be starting a PhD in Kinesiology with a specialization in Exercise and Sport Psychology at Wayne State University in August of 2016. Her research focus involves understanding the relationship between cognition and physical activity in populations of brain injury and athletes.

Claire Whiteman, LPC, CDCA, and art therapist, currently works with inner city adults and children at The Centers for Families and Children. She is pursuing additional training in trauma therapy and strives to incorporate art in her daily activities while parenting two teenagers.

Mary Cassidy, M.A. is an art therapist and licensed professional counsellor. She currently works in a residential therapeutic farm community that serves adults with chronic mental illness. Her research interests center on the connection between the mind and body and the significance of creativity for wellness.

Rebecca Stanic, M.A., L.P.C. completed a graduate program at Ursuline College of Pepper Pike, Ohio, in Art Therapy and Counselling in December of 2014. She is now a Licensed Professional Counselor working with children and adolescents who face emotional and behavioral issues. While volunteering as an advocate for mental health consumers, she continues to seek out knowledge to educate oneself and others on the challenge of living with an emotional or behavioural disorder.

The Lived Experience of Mental Health Issues as a Constructive Asset for Redefining and Measuring Citizenship: A Social Enterprise

Jean-François Pelletier

Abstract

A good way of making sense of the lived experience of mental illness, is to transform this experience into a constructive asset for redefining and measuring citizenship. This chapter discusses the perspectives of a diverse group of persons in recovery from mental illnesses who were engaged as members of a Co-research Team to perform a series of focus groups with other research participants. The project was about developing a new measure of citizenship and social inclusion. The development of this measure was conducted through a Community-based Participatory Research (CBPR) design. CBPR is an approach to research that involves persons of primary interest in all aspects of the process. Co-learning, a strength-based approach, and acknowledgement of privilege and power are hallmarks of CBPR. This chapter is based on focus groups that were held to discuss the benefits and challenges of being involved in CBPR, both personally and for the scientific community. Qualitative analysis points to ways that are helpful in maximizing the engagement and inclusion of persons in recovery through CBPR. Persons with the lived experience of recovery in mental health were fully included in all aspects of this project that led to the creation of a new consumer-led social enterprise.

Key Words: Community-based participatory research, citizenship, social inclusion, finding meaning, user-led social enterprise.

*****

1. Introduction

A good way of making sense of the lived experience of mental illness and its socio-political aftermaths is to transform this experience into a lever of change in reinterpreting and measuring citizenship. This hermeneutical essay discusses the perspectives of a diverse group of persons in recovery (consumers) who were engaged as co-researchers in the development of a new measure of citizenship. They discussed in focus groups the benefits and challenges of their involvement in the Co-research Team (CRT), both personally, and for the research community. CRT members were trained and engaged in conducting a series of focus groups and concept mapping sessions with other research participants in a Community-Based Participatory Research (CBPR) project for the creation of a measure of citizenship from the perspective of persons in recovery. They thus developed an expertise that can be offered through a new consumer-led social enterprise, which is based at the Montreal Mental Health University Institute (MMHUI), in the province of Quebec, Canada.

CBPR is a capacity-based approach to research in mental health that involves persons of primary interest in all aspects of the process. In addition, co-learning, and acknowledgement of privilege and power are hallmarks of CBPR. CRT members discussed the meaning of their contribution to CBPR. Of symbolic importance is that CRT members gradually became agents of change in their own communities, conveying a new and more inclusive interpretation of citizenship that goes well beyond a deficit-based definition of mental illness.

Since antiquity, psychosocial suffering and distress has been given many different names and has been studied from many different conceptual angles. From melancholy to madness, and to psychiatric disorders, for instance, such conditions were associated with stigma and social exclusion, and were defined as an incapacity to exert reason and therefore to claim citizenship.[1] Nowadays, we know that recovery, even from a serious mental illness like schizophrenia is possible. In the literature on recovery, finding meaning and a purpose in life is a key for hope of a better future and of a fulfilling life in the community for everyone, including persons with serious mental illness. Meaning, as a sense of belonging, has been shown to enable people to take control, to re-write a personal and collective history and to restore dignity with self-agency. This hermeneutic essay points to ways that are helpful in maximizing the engagement and inclusion of persons with the lived experience of mental health issues, and in interpreting and understanding the lived experience of civic recovery. To that end, a specific tool to measure citizenship has been tested and used to support the active engagement of CRT members in creating a new social enterprise, namely the International Program for Participatory Action Research (IPPAR). The IPPAR is a non-profit community organisation whose members are people with the lived experience of mental illness (consumers and carers). The aim of the IPPAR is twofold: to translate the experiential knowledge of consumers and carers into scientific evidence and to transform the research and scientific milieu as an inclusive workplace for them. As members as the IPPAR as a social enterprise, persons in recovery engage their responsibility when they vote in Annual General Assemblies or on the Board of Direction. This chapter chronicles the creation of the IPPAR through the development and use of a first measure of citizenship, which was completed by 802 MMHUI patients who were met by some of their peers of the IPPAR who acted as research assistants, thus promoting and exemplifying a new vision of civic recovery.

2. Civic Recovery

Nowadays, after decades and even centuries of pessimism forecasting a life-long deteriorating process – the *Kraepelian* theory of schizophrenia – recovery is the goal of contemporary mental health policies, for instance in several English speaking countries.[2] In the literature on recovery, finding meaning and a purpose in life is a key for hope of a better and fulfilling life.[3] But stigma is a major obstacle to recovery, even within research and health services.[4] The World Health Organization considers that stigma attached to mental illness is the greatest obstacle to the improvement of the lives of people with mental illness and their families, this being particularly true in the case of schizophrenia.[5] Stigma is a 'deeply discrediting attribute'[6] that keeps the persons to whom it is attached to from being full and equal citizens. Stigma manifests itself through attitudes, judgments and discriminating behaviours propagated through invalidating discourses regarding the person suffering from mental illness.

There are many arenas of recovery for persons living with mental health issues, including the political one with people participating, at various and complementary levels, as citizens and as the main agents of their own wellbeing. 'Political developmental tasks' involve developing advocacy skills, at the individual level, and advocating for system change toward greater involvement of service-users as decision-makers.[7] Consumers have been working to reclaim their 'rightful place in society', but one realm in which it has been difficult to find opportunities and resources to engage fully, is in the development of a research agenda at a policy and system level.

Recovery involves the development of new meaning and purpose in one's life as one grows beyond the catastrophic effects of mental illness.[8] Such recovery principles have influenced how research can be conducted.[9] In fact, one of the more important innovations involved in recovery-oriented systemic transformation has been to involve people in recovery in the transformation process itself. In other words, one of the significant roles people in recovery can play is in contributing to the improvement of the very mental health services intended to support them in their journey towards civic recovery.[10] As a result of this innovation, systems have been experimenting with involving consumers in all aspects of system reform including design, implementation, and evaluation of services. These principles are also the basis of Community-Based Participatory Research (CBPR), where stakeholders work in partnership throughout the research.[11] This chapter emanates from such a CBPR project that is getting more and more 'patient-led',[12] with people in recovery being research assistants and co-investigators, and even entrepreneurs in the IPPAR.

In general, research priorities and objectives of people in recovery tend to focus more on social determinants of well-being than on individual attributes of impairment.[13] Reducing stigma and self-stigma are among the most important research priorities that people in recovery would like to see addressed.[14] One way to reduce the impact of self-stigma is to re-interpret this experience by trying to decipher a meaning in its narrative. Finding meaning is a theme very often reported in the narratives of consumers when they talk or write about themselves and about their struggles to overcome suffering and despair. Mental healthcare systems are now trying to focus on the enhancement of people's sense of wellbeing.[15] Finding meaning is also a way to take control, to re-write a personal and collective history and to restore dignity with self-agency.

Beyond reduction or remission of psychiatric symptoms, recovery-oriented mental health policies and systems not only help the individuals with mental illness to live in their community – to be in the community – but also aim at enabling them to become and remain members of the community.[16] Several evidence-based interventions exist that focus on the psychiatric rehabilitation and social inclusion of people living with mental illness. Social interaction, which is essential to community membership, involves the development and maintenance of reciprocal relationships between members of a community in which each of its components are co-citizens to each other. Citizenship relates to the strength of people's connections to the rights, responsibilities, roles, and resources that society offers to people through public and social institutions, and relationships involving close ties, supportive social networks, and associational life in one's community.[17]

As early as 1994, in the early ages of the recovery movement, Daniel Fisher developed an empowerment model of recovery based on the principles that emerged from the experiences of consumers in recovery. Among those principles is that persons with the lived experience of mental illness are full human beings who deserve respect and full citizenship.[18] More recently, Larry Davidson et al. suggest that, as a sense of empowerment and control over one's life emerges, people in recovery may start to demand the same rights and responsibilities as other citizens.[19] Supporting people with mental illness in exercising the rights and responsibilities of citizenship might be a pre-condition for their recovery, not an eventual reward contingent on the person overcoming his or her disability first. Indeed, almost from inception, recovery proponents have alluded to citizenship, albeit rarely defining the term and without attempts to measure it empirically.

Generally speaking, two portrayals of recovery stand out amidst the diversity of views: restoration of functioning and deepening wellness.[20] When recovery is mainly seen as symptom management, the primary focus of personal choice and responsibility in the process of recovery becomes seeking and complying with treatment. Such a 'clinical' model does include social functions, but from a professional point of view. Instead of focusing primarily on symptom relief and management, a second view casts a wider spotlight on restoration of self-esteem and identity and on attaining meaningful roles in society. While the clinical-recovery model has focused upon the remission of symptoms and restoration of functioning, a rehabilitative view of recovery has been a more subjective and consumer-oriented concept that focuses on the full lives that are lived in the face of, or despite, enduring disability.

Although the recovery literature has now and then alluded to citizenship, clinicians' and scientists' references or pledges to citizenship have been sparse and, generally, vague. Several tools have been developed to assess recovery, but until very recently no measure was available to assess citizenship from the perspective of persons in recovery. In a rapid review of the literature[21] based on a MEDLINE search with the key words 'citizenship', 'measure', and 'mental health', the new measure of citizenship is the only referenced tool specifically designed to assess the degrees to which individuals with psychiatric disorders perceive themselves to have full citizenship. On the other hand, the search with 'recovery', 'measure', and 'mental health' yielded 392 references. Among those is the Recovery Assessment Scale, which was developed as an outcome measure for programme evaluation.[22] Mark Salzer and Eugene Brusilovskiy have published an in-depth review of the quantitative properties of the Recovery Assessment Scale, based on 77 articles that included psychometric data. They found that these studies indicate very good results for internal consistency, test-retest reliability, and internal reliability.[23] Among the tools that were developed to empirically assess recovery, the Recovery Assessment Scale has been the most published,[24] whereas the measure of citizenship is the only published tool developed to assess citizenship. Although citizenship is a distinct concept, it overlaps somewhat with the Mental Health Consumer/Survivor Movement's view of recovery, and we have recently demonstrated a correlational relationship between citizenship and recovery.[25] Citizenship and recovery would appear to be two intertwined and complementary concepts for civic-recovery: a process of rehabilitation not merely from an illness, but more broadly a restoration of a sense of active citizenship that was impacted by the socio-political aftermaths of a stigmatizing social representation of mental illness. This chapter reconsiders the symbolic significance of this lived experience of civic recovery according to a group of individuals who share their experience of cohabitation as teammates.[26]

3. Principles of Hermeneutic Phenomenology and the Symbolic Order

Hermeneutic theory is part of the social constructivist paradigm in which meaning is inter-subjectively constructed,[27] in contrast to the empirical universe of assumed created scientific realism.[28] It focuses on the significance that an aspect of reality takes on for the people under study. Hermeneutics focuses on defining shared linguistic meaning for a representation or symbol, where the process of understanding moves from parts of a whole to a global understanding of the whole and back to individual parts in an iterative manner.[29] Hermeneutic phenomenology can also be used to inform the conduct of interpretive research. This essay suggests that consumers with the lived experience of social exclusion due to mental illness are the best placed stakeholders to discover and recognize pathways to civic recovery and social-symbolic inclusion.

Paul Ricoeur's theory of interpretation provides an intervention through which researchers using hermeneutics can achieve congruence between philosophy, methodology and method in interviewing and textual analysis for research purposes. Interpretation moves forward from simple understanding,

> to deeper understanding, where the interpreter understands the parts of the text in relation to the whole and the whole of the text in relation to its parts (the hermeneutic circle).[30]

Hermeneutic phenomenology can be defined as the process of interpreting and describing human experience. This methodology helps to understand the central nature of this experience and hermeneutic phenomenology is gaining popularity in human sciences research, for instance, in qualitative mental health research.[31] In effect, hermeneutic phenomenology can be useful in considering the totality of human experience and to understand its meaning. Such a holistic approach has two main benefits.

> First, it legitimates the claims made by [psychiatric patients] that their experiences are intrinsically meaningful. Second, it can provide a framework for those who work with [them] and who are interested in understanding these experiences,[32]

experiences which can make sense within the symbolic order.

A symbol may not have the quality of conceptual specificity. In fact, the power of symbol lies in its vagueness. What it lacks in conceptual clarity is filled up by the power of its suggestiveness.[33] To try to find the real meaning that may be hidden in a narrative, for example, is to make an exegesis of it. Exegesis is a way to ontologically interpret a message as it relates to a background that is filled with meaning and being. It is within this dynamic between the forefront and the background that lays the symbolic, true meaning of the message. Seeking to understand a narrative, 'to understand it from its intention, on the basis of what it really means'[34] is a way of conceptualizing psychotic thinking as symbolist. This rationale we seek to unfold is not formal, but transcendental, deliberately avoiding 'the charmed circle of the problem of subject and object, and addressing the question of being'.

> The common element, which is found everywhere, from exegesis to psychoanalysis, is the architecture of meaning, which can be termed "double meaning" or "multiple meaning", whose role in every instance [...] is to show while concealinging.[35]

Ricoeur proposes to call *symbolic* these multiple-sense messages. He calls a symbol any structure of meaning in which a direct sense, primary and literally, also has another indirect meaning, secondary, figurative, which can only be apprehended through the first. Texts, documents, and monuments are expressions of life from which to extract an exegesis that focuses on meaning and being. Irrationality and meaninglessness is what defined mental illness in the first place,[36] and hermeneutics helps to see that, quite to the contrary, it is saturated with meaning as a quest and is thus very far from being *non-sense*.

Interpreting and reading a text is always within a community, a living tradition or school of thought, which develops assumptions and requirements. And when it comes to texts, what is at stake is the speech as a whole, expressed through writings, sculptures, paintings, etc. Traditional hermeneutics refers to the study of the interpretation of written texts, especially texts in the areas of literature, religion and law. Contemporary hermeneutics encompasses not only issues involving the written text, but everything in the interpretative process. This includes verbal and nonverbal forms of communication such as occurs with practical research procedures like focus groups, through which participants interact and can collectively position themselves independently from social and discursive mechanisms of exclusion. A hermeneutic analysis of the transcript of such a focus group can reveal a symbolic order that restructures the place of the lived and collective experience of SMI, this time to the advantage of consumers in their civic recovery journey.

Unlike the technical signs that say what they mean, the symbolic signs are opaque because the primary obvious and literal meaning has a secondary meaning that is only accessible by the first one. Here, we need to talk to the person to understand his experience. The phenomenology of symbols reveals an inner consistency, something like a symbolic system, and to interpret is to demonstrate this consistency. By revealing such consistency, the narrative no longer has this meaningless attribute that was initially diagnosed as a symptom of a deeper psychiatric disorder. It is precisely meaningful – full of meaning – because it relates to the ontology of being.

4. The Meaning of Engagement

The Citizens Social Inclusion project that goes on at the Yale Program for Recovery & Community Health[37] combined CBPR and concept mapping methodologies[38] to explore the perspectives and processes involved in claiming or reclaiming citizenship for persons in recovery from a life disruption due to mental health issues. In order to substantially involve these new co-researchers in a way that was rigorous, supportive and reflexive, a Co-Research Team (CRT) was formalized, comprised of these members along with academics and research assistants.

CRT members were trained in all aspects of the research process, but assisted more actively with conducting and analysing focus groups and in conducting concept mapping sessions. Concept mapping integrates input from multiple stakeholders, uses sophisticated multivariate data analysis, and creates a series of 'maps' or visual representations of data that can be used to guide action planning, programme development, and measurement development. This method has been used extensively in the public health field,[39] including with people in recovery.[40] In order to reflect on this CBPR initiative and to better understand the needs and expectations of the CRT members, they were asked what they thought about their active participation throughout the project, in particular in conducting focus groups and concept mapping sessions with study participants. As discussed below with excerpts from the focus group verbatim transcript, five major themes emerged from the analysis of the focus group among CRT members: 1) recognition of competencies, 2) wanting and creating change, 3) building relationships, 4) learning about self through others; and 5) lending credibility.

4.1. Recognition of Competencies

The experience as CRT members began by first learning about the research goals and deciding whether they still wanted to participate as co-researchers. They were thus involved '*from the jump*' and their responsibilities grew over time, gradually, with the appropriate, yet often informal training and support from faculty members of the research team. '*When we go through our own battles, they are there supporting us*', says one CRT member. This highlights the importance of a supportive and inclusive work environment and culture for consumer researchers to be able to assume this new role of co-investigators in the CRT. This welcoming approach trickled down as CRT members were able to feel relaxed and to make study participants feel welcomed and respected, as they were.

A CRT member said that he would most probably never have applied to a research position: '*If I saw that in the [news]paper I would think automatically that I don't qualify*'. To several, who had been away from the work market for extended periods, or who had, at times, occupied job positions which were not highly valued or in which they felt exploited, being a respected teammate meant a lot.

> I just felt like, I just can't believe that doctors would want us on their team and be equal. I felt overwhelmed, felt joy to be sitting next to them equally knowing that they have all that education, went to school all that time. I did go to college but I don't have what they have and still [here I am at Yale] on the same page. … I felt amazed.

Then, CRT members were naturally communicating this kind of amazement to other study participants, for them to also have a positive influence in their community lives.

4.2. Wanting and Creating Change

CRT members gradually became agents of change in their respective communities, and within the research community to start with. The word change comes back several times in the focus group transcript. For instance, they were able to notice that it was a genuine preoccupation for academics and research assistants: '*it feels like it's more of the gut of the change*'. Being a CRT member was a different and new status for them, just in the fact that they could tell that something was changing. Even outside this small research-CBPR community, this change in their lives made them '*more confident*' generally.

> I think by us being people with lived experiences it kind of like validated to study participants; *yes, you're going to be involved in this next step and next step and this is going to come to something.* Like; *your information isn't just worthless, we are not going to just put it in a book somewhere.*

4.3. Building Relationships

Being valued and recognized as CRT members, with their vulnerabilities and strengths, somehow proved that they '*can get things done*' and that they are '*competent and effective.*' Not in spite of their mental condition, but because they found their own way to civic recovery and are now in a position to share that unique knowledge with others to help them go through, and beyond, their own difficulties. '*It's like expanding on what I've already done. You know, taking that next step, the next level and seeing how that part works.*' Having dealt with and suffered from severe judgemental attitudes in the past, CRT members were very aware that not feeling judged is essential for study participants to effectively participate and open up. A CRT member says that; '*there was also an effect on the people we didn't know, because they saw that we were warm and friendly and approachable, which I think made it easier for them too.* […] *We laugh, we relate.*' '*We are all in this together*', says another about the relations with the academic researchers on the project.

4.4. Learning about Self through Others

With faculty members, CRT members felt validated. '*They took what we said and used it and we were being heard even though they have all that education. It wasn't me just sitting next to them; it was when I spoke they listened and then validated what I said.*' In their connection to study participants, CRT members gave back this confidence. They exemplified this hope that some persons with SMI and with very difficult life trajectories can be in recovery and perform complex research tasks. This is directly related to the possibility of contributing to one's community, just as the CRT members were able to contribute to research as a more and more inclusive workplace.

4.5. Lending Credibility

'*We were able to relate* […]. *What they're going through, we've been through. So, it was like, I could identify with what they were going through.*' The lived experience of CRT members helps them in quickly rephrasing the information they gather through a 90 minute focus group, for example. It is thus possible for them to delve deeper and to extract more subtle personal information about daily life challenges. This also helps study participants to feel comfortable in confiding. Even though it would probably be possible to have an acceptable '*body language*' and '*attitude*' while dressed with '*a suit and a tie*', such artefacts usually represent a higher social-economic status that can be intimidating to many who do not have the chance to be as wealthy. In such circumstances; '*I'm going to tell you what I think you want to know but I'm not going to tell you everything about me*'. Persons with the lived experience are well placed to get a better reaction. This capacity lends scientific, as well as social credibility to this overall CBPR endeavour, and this expertise has been transposed in Montreal, Canada, with the creation of new consumer-led social enterprise, namely the International Program for Participatory Action Research (IPPAR).

5. A Citizenship-Oriented and Consumer-Led Social Enterprise

For a study on the development of a new computational and mobile application, we have asked to form three groups of 9 participants each to complete the *Consumers' Checklist of Participatory Action Research* [14] in order to identify what objectives a research project should have to promote consumers' citizenship and social inclusion. To better understand the hopes and expectations of consumers who might be invited to get involved as partners in a CBPR project that would aim at addressing inclusion, for each 30 items of the Checklist they were asked to score on a 5-point Likert scale how important they thought it would be to undertake a research project on that topic. Then, ten of the 27 focus groups participants where engaged in a complementary focus group to discuss the very participatory nature of the project and to discuss the results of the Checklist (Table 1).

The focus group was conducted by a consumer. He prompted discussion with this question: *What would you gain in being engaged as research partners in a participatory research project aiming to address some on the topics suggested by study participants with the Checklist?* Four main themes emerged from the focus group.

5.1. Breaking Free from Poverty

Breaking free from poverty is the ultimate goal for many participants, once the symptoms are under control and the recovery process is under way. If people are economically better off, their mental health will improve. Paying consumers to become involved as CBPR partners is a way to help them financially, and the amount of money they are granted for their work, although relatively modest, is meaningful. A participant said that this extra money can be used to pay for small pleasures of life, like going out to have coffee with a friend, which is not always easy to do when the social assistance allocation is fully budgeted for in advance.

Table 1: Results of the Consumers' Checklist of Participatory Action Research (*n*=27)

Topics: *For me, research should aim at…*	**%**
Breaking free from poverty	88
Facilitating the recognition of competencies	86
Improving access to information	85
Taking responsibilities	84
Facilitating the recognition of the need for accommodations	83
Overcoming multiple bereavements	83
Fighting stigma in the workplace	82
Facilitating the recognition of credentials and work experiences	82
Finding access to housing	82
Finding access to transportation	81
Supporting decision making and one's voice and influence	81
Supporting social integration (work, volunteering etc.)	80
Fighting against stigma amongst family members and loved ones	79
Fighting against stigma within health services	79
Breaking free from isolation	78
Disclosing	78
Supporting employees	78
Recognizing civic contributions other than work	77
Improving the interactions with the Justice system	76
Insuring decent retirement revenues	76
Supporting employers	75
Supporting access to insurance	74
Negotiating and coping with own stigma	74
Providing guardianship	74
Fighting against stigma present in society in general	73
Fighting against stigma within emergency services	72
Facilitating the recognition of limitations and challenges	72
Fostering more inclusive values	70
Supporting parental role	68
Enabling the right to vote	66

5.2. Recognition of Competencies

Recruiting and training consumers to conduct interviews or focus groups with peers is a meaningful way to recognize their specific competencies and contributions, and to influence the symbolic representation of their experience. Being recognized as important contributors within a research team demonstrates that they have specific and useful skills. This confers social legitimacy to the process, as well as scientific credibility. In fact, consumers can obtain more information from study participants because participants in interviews or focus groups and peer research assistants can relate to each other.

5.3. Improving Access to Information

Participants like to have access to first-hand information. Being actively involved in research is a good way to have access to first-hand information and new technologies, even more so with newly discovered findings. In the IPPAR, participants are exposed to new findings about citizenship and they can test new ways of exercising it for their own civic recovery process.

5.4. Taking Responsibilities

Playing an active role in CBPR is an opportunity to get trained and supported in assuming some responsibilities, and to be accepted and recognized as a teammate within an inclusive scientific unit located at the very heart of a university institute, namely the Montreal Mental Health University Institute.

With these findings in mind and in reflecting on the experience, a group of consumers based in Montreal, province of Quebec, Canada, developed and proposed a new Social Support Program (SSP) to the Quebec Ministry of Employment and Social Solidarity (MESS). In the province of Quebec, SSPs are designed for people who face various forms of disabilities, including mental health problems. These disabilities are severe enough to have had major impacts on their life trajectories, particularly in terms of their significantly lower socio-economic status. Participants in these SSPs receive a monthly supplement to their government social welfare allocation. There are SSPs in different economic sectors, offering mostly basic manual or clerical work experiences. The new SSP is the only one to offer scientific trainings for persons with life disruptions due to severe mental health problems who need special employment support and who have an interest in academia and research. To be eligible for this SSP, participants have to be living on social welfare with severe mental health problems that kept them away for extended periods from the workforce. They are persons with a high school diploma as a minimum requirement and they have to be able to work up to 20 hours per week. Upon entry, they have to select up to five objectives they want to pursue in order to develop their socio-professional skills, and are expected to have reached at least one of these targets after 12 months of participation, renewable for up to three years of participation.

The activities offered to participants are designed to explore their potential. They are supported to develop their self-confidence, social skills and problem solving skills through oral or written presentations and through respectfully deliberating with teammates. They are asked to maintain a regular work schedule with assiduity, punctuality and commitment and also to develop an individualized social and professional project to accomplish after their participation. Some participants will choose to go back to college or university afterward. However, regardless of what they chose, while in this citizenship-oriented SSP, they participate in research activities by conducting preliminary literature reviews, transcribing and codifying interviews, and assisting with the analysis and knowledge translation processes. For example, they may be asked what they think of a new questionnaire to be used in research or evaluation projects in development.

In February and March 2015, the IPPAR was contracted by the MMHUI to approach MMHUI patients, for them to complete the short 24-item version of the measure of citizenship [27] (Table 2).

6. Conclusion

The results to the measure of citizenship indicate that there is still a lot of progress to be achieved in terms of citizenship, particularly with regards to community involvement. But process-wise, the active participation of the IPPAR members has shown that persons in recovery can definitely be involved in research as an inclusive community. Their lived experience of mental health issues is often associated with a difficult and dramatic life trajectory of marginalization, but it can also be a unique and constructive asset when translated into transformative action through CBPR. This hermeneutic essay discussed the contribution of people in recovery to the Co-research Team and to the development and use of a new measure of citizenship, and to a sense of belonging that is more inclusive of otherness. While conducting focus groups or concept mapping sessions with their peers, the lived experience of IPPAR members proved to be a priceless resource. It also allowed real-time interpretation in summarizing and reformulating statements made by study participants. For example, it was suggested that when patients come to the MMHUI, they could be better informed about how the MMHUI, as a public institution, is "involved in the community" too, and also informed of the different opportunities for recovery through community involvement. IPPAR members thus used their lived experience to ensure that their interpretation was correct in order to capture the symbolic and subjective essence of participants' input. Reflecting on the CBPR potentialities, this experience paved the way for the foundation of the IPPAR as new consumer-led social enterprise. This approach generated a meaning to the experience of mental illness, and made it a *deeply validating attribute*, to paraphrase Goffman.[41] Translation of the lived experience through hermeneutics is central in understanding the symbolic dialectic of exclusion and inclusion, and *the translation from parts of a whole to a global understanding of the whole and back to individual parts in an iterative manner*, to quote Ricoeur.[42]

Table 2: Results to the measure of citizenship

Dimensions and items of the citizenship scale (5 dimensions, 24 items, *n*=802)	%
Basic needs (5 items)	69
Your basic needs are met	72
You do things to take care of your home	74
You are safe in your community	74
There are laws that will protect you	73
You have or would have access to employment	50
Involvement in community (4 items)	58
You are included in your community	66
You have responsibilities to others in the community	56
You can influence your community or local government	50
You have knowledge about your community	59
Self-determination (6 items)	72
You or your family have choices in education	63
You stand up for what you believe in	70
You have the right to be in a relationship with a partner of your choice	74
You have privacy	76
You have the right to disagree with others	75
You can make choices about how you spend your money	77
Access to services (4 items)	73
You have access to adequate healthcare	77
You have or could have access to adequate and affordable housing	75
You would have access to public assistance, if needed	71
You have choices in your mental healthcare	71
Respect by others (4 items)	69
You are treated with dignity and respect	77
Others feel accepted by you	76
Others listen to you	70
Your personal decisions and choices are respected	71
Total	71

Notes

[1] Michel Foucault, *Madness and Civilization: A History of Insanity in the Age of Reason* (New York: Pantheon books, 1965).
[2] Mike Slade, Julie Williams, Victoria Bird, Mary Leamy and Clair Le Boutillier, 'Recovery Grows Up,' *Journal of Mental Health* 21.2 (2012): 99.

[3] Patricia E. Deegan, 'Recovery: The Lived Experience of Rehabilitation,' *Psychosocial Rehabilitation Journal* 11.4 (1988): 18.
[4] Graham Thornicroft, *Shunned: Discrimination Against People With Mental Illness* (New York: Oxford University Press, 2006), 252.
[5] Nadia Kadri and Norman Sartorius, 'The Global Fight against the Stigma of Schizophrenia,' *PLoS Medicine* 2.7 (2005): np.
[6] Erving Goffman, *Stigma: Notes on the Management of Spoiled Identity* (New York: Simon and Schuster, 1963), 31.
[7] Roberto Mezzina, Marit Borg, Izabel Marin, Dave Sells, Alain Topor and Larry Davidson, 'From Participation To Citizenship: How to Regain a Role, a Status, and a Life in the Process of Recovery,' *American Journal of Psychiatric Rehabilitation* 9.1 (2006): 42.
[8] William A. Anthony, 'Recovery from Mental Illness: The Guiding Vision of the Mental Health Service System in the 1990s,' *Psychosocial Rehabilitation Journal* 16.4 (1993): 15.
[9] Larry Davidson, Courtenay Harding and LeRoy Spaniol, *Recovery from Severe Mental Illnesses: Research Evidence and Implications for Practice*, vol. 1 (Boston: Boston University Centre for Psychiatric Rehabilitation, 2005).
[10] Jean-François Pelletier, Patrick Le Cardinal, Jean-Luc Roelandt and Michael Rowe, 'Le Rétablissement Civique,' *Les conceptions du rétablissement en santé mentale: recherches identitaires, interdépendances et changements sociaux* 20.2 (2013): 9-21.
[11] Meredith Minkler and Nina Wallerstein, *Community-Based Participatory Research for Health: From Process to Outcomes* (San Francisco: Jossey-Bass, 2003).
[12] Larry Davidson, Judith Shaw, Selina Welborn, Brian Mahon, Margaret Sirota, Paul Gilbo, Michael McDermid, James Fazio, Carol Gilbert, Sheryl Breetz and Jean-François Pelletier, 'I Don't Know How to Find My Way in the World: Contributions of User-Led Research to Transforming Mental Health Practice,' *Psychiatry* 73.2 (2010): 101-113.
[13] Diana Rose, Pete Fleischman and Til Wykes, 'What are Mental Health Service User's Priorities for Research in the UK?' *Journal of Mental Health* 17.5 (2008): 524.
[14] Jean-François Pelletier, Alain D. Lesage, André Delorme, Ann C. Macaulay, Jonathan Salsberg, Catherine Vallée and Larry Davidson, 'User-Led Research: A Global and Person-Centered Initiative,' *International Journal of Mental Health Promotion* 13.1 (2011): 12.
[15] Patrick W. Corrigan, Jonathon E. Larson and Nicholas Rüsch, 'Self-Stigma and the 'Why Try' Effect: Impact on Life Goals and Evidence-Based Practices,' *World Psychiatry* 8.2 (2009): 79.

---

[16] Norma Ware, Kim Hopper, Tony Tugenberg, Barbara Dickey and Daniel Fisher, 'Connectedness and Citizenship: Redefining Social Integration', *Psychiatric Services* 58.4 (2007): 469-474.
[17] Michael Rowe, *Crossing the Border: Encounters between Homeless People and Outreach Workers* (Berkeley: University of California Press, 1999); Michael Rowe and Jean-François Pelletier, 'Mental Illness, Criminality, and Citizenship Revisited', *Journal of the American Academy of Psychiatry Law* 40.1 (2012): 8-11.
[18] Daniel Fisher, 'Health Care Reform Based on an Empowerment Model of Recovery by People with Psychiatric Disabilities', *Hospital & Community Psychiatry* 45.9 (1994): 913-915.
[19] Larry Davidson, Maria O'Connell, Janis Tondora, Martha Lawless and Arthur Evans, 'Recovery in Serious Mental Illness: A New Wine or Just a New Bottle?' *Professional Psychology: Research and Practice* 36.5 (2005): 480-487; Larry Davidson and David Roe, 'Recovery From Versus Recovery in Serious Mental Illness', *Journal of Mental Health* 16.4 (2007): 459-470.
[20] Jacob Hess, Jeffrey Lacasse, Jordan Harmon, Daniel Williams and Nathan Vierling-Glaassen, '"Is There a Getting Better From This, Or Not?" Examining the Meaning and Possibility of Recovery from Mental Health Disorder', *Child and Youth Services* 35.2 (2014): 116-136.
[21] Rebacca Ganann, Donna Ciliska and Helen Thomas, 'Expediting Systematic Reviews: Methods and Implications of Rapid Reviews', *Implementation Science* 19.5 (2010): 56.
[22] Patrick Corrigan, Mark Salzer, Ruth Ralph, Yvette Sangster and Lorraine Keck, 'Examining the Factor Structure of the Recovery Assessment Scale', *Schizophrenia Bulletin* 30.4 (2004): 1035-1041.
[23] Mark Salzer and Eugene Brusilovskiy, 'Advancing Recovery Science: Reliability and Validity Properties of the Recovery Assessment Scale', *Psychiatric Services* 65.4 (2014): 442-453.
[24] Vicki Shanks, Julie Williams, Mary Leamy, Victoria Bird, Claire Le Boutillier and Mike Slade, 'Measures of Personal Recovery: A Systematic Review', *Psychiatric Services* 64.10 (2013): 974-80.
[25] Jean-François Pelletier, Marc Corbière, Tania Lecomte, Catherine Briand, Patrick Corrigan, Larry Davidson and Michael Rowe, 'Citizenship and Recovery: Two Intertwined Concepts for Civic-Recovery', *BMC Psychiatry* 15 (2015): 37.
[26] Larry Davidsdon, *Living Outside Mental Illness: Qualitative Studies Of Recovery In Schizophrenia* (New York: New York University Press, 2005).
[27] Vivienne Burr, *Social Constructionism*, 2nd ed. (New York: Routledge, 2003).
[28] Stanley Rosen, *Hermeneutics as Politics* (New York: Oxford University Press, 1987): 148.
[29] Paul Ricoeur, *Le Conflit des interprétations. Essais d'herméneutique* (Paris: Éditions du Seuil, 1969).

[30] Rene Geanellos, 'Exploring Ricoeur's Hermeneutic Theory of Interpretation as a Method of Analysing Research Texts,' *Nursing Inquiry* 7.2 (2000): 112.
[31] Alexia Barnable, Alice Gaudine, Lorna Bennett and Robert Meadus, 'Having a Sibling with Schizophrenia: A Phenomenological Study,' *Research and Theory for Nursing Practice* 20.3 (2006): 247-264.
[32] Philip Thomas, Patrick Bracken and Ivan Leudar, 'Hearing Voices: A Phenomenological-Hermeneutic Approach,' *Cognitive Neuropsychiatry* 9.1-2 (2004): 13.
[33] Allan Cacho, 'Symbolism in Religion: Ricoeurian Hermeneutics and Filipino Philosophy of Religion,' *Kritike* 1.2 (2007): 124.
[34] Ricoeur, *Le Conflit des Interprétations*, 7.
[35] Ibid., 10.
[36] Somology Varga, 'Non-Reflective Self-Awareness Towards a "Situated" Account,' *Journal of Consciousness Studies* 19.3-4 (2012): 164-193.
[37] Michael Rowe, Ashley Clayton, Patricia Benedict, Chyrel Bellamy, Kimberly Antunes, Rebecca Miller, Jean-François Pelletier, Erica Stern and Maria J. O'Connell, 'Going to the Source: Creating a Citizenship Outcome Measure by Community-Based Participatory Research Methods,' *Psychiatric Services* 63.5 (2012): 445-450.
[38] William Trochim and Mary Kane, 'Concept Mapping: An Introduction to Structured Conceptualization in Health Care,' *International Journal for Quality in Health Care* 17.3 (2005): 187-191.
[39] Lenor B. Behar and William M. Hydaker, 'Defining Community Readiness for the Implementation of a System of Care,' *Administration and Policy in Mental Health* 36.6 (2009): 384.
[40] Gerdien H. de Weert-van Oene, Victor J. A. Buwalda, Johan M. Havenaar, Wilma Swildens, Albert van Keijzerswaard and Augustinus J. P. Schrijvers, 'Demand-Oriented Care: The Development and Validation of a Measuring Instrument,' *Social Psychiatry and Psychiatric Epidemiology* 41.3 (2006): 216.
[41] Erving Goffman, *Asylums: Essays on the Social Situation of Mental Patients and Other Inmates* (New York: Anchor Books, 1961).
[42] Paul Ricoeur, *Le Conflit des interprétations. Essais d'herméneutique.*

Bibliography

Anthony, William. 'Recovery From Mental Illness: The Guiding Vision of the Mental Health Service System in the 1990s.' *Psychosocial Rehabilitation Journal* 16.4 (1993): 11-23.

Barnable, Alexia, Alice Gaudine, Lorna Bennett and Robert Meadus. 'Having a Sibling with Schizophrenia: A Phenomenological Study.' *Research and Theory for Nursing Practice* 20.3 (2006): 247-264.

Behar, Lenor and William Yydaker. 'Defining Community Readiness for the Implementation of a System of Care.' *Administration and Policy in Mental Health*, 36.6 (2009): 381-392.

Burr, Vivienne. *Social Constructionism.* 2nd ed. New York: Routledge, 2003.

Cacho, Allan. 'Symbolism in Religion: Ricoeurian Hermeneutics and Filipino Philosophy of Religion.' *Kritike* 1.2 (2007): 122-131.

Corrigan, Patrick, Jonathon Larson, and Nicholas Rüsch, 'Self-Stigma and the "Why Try" Effect: Impact on Life Goals and Evidence-Based Practices.' *World Psychiatry* 8.2 (2009): 75-81.

Corrigan, Patrick, Mark Salzer, Ruth Ralph, Yvette Sangster and Lorraine Keck. 'Examining the Factor Structure of the Recovery Assessment Scale'. *Schizophrenia Bulletin* 30.4 (2004): 1035-1041.

Davidson, Larry. *Living Outside Mental Illness: Qualitative Studies of Recovery in Schizophrenia.* New York: New York University Press, 2005.

Davidson Larry, Courtenay Harding and LeRoy Spaniol. *Recovery from Severe Mental Illnesses: Research Evidence and Implications for Practice*, Vol. 1. Boston: Boston University Center for Psychiatric Rehabilitation, 2005.

Davidson, Larry, Judith Shaw, Selina Welborn, Brian Mahon, Margaret Sirota, Paul Gilbo, Michael McDermid, James Fazio, Carol Gilbert, Sheryl Breetz and Jean-François Pelletier. 'I Don't Know How to Find my Way in the World: Contributions of User-Led Research to Transforming Mental Health Practice.' *Psychiatry* 73.2 (2010): 101-113.

Davidson, Larry, Maria O'Connell, Janis Tondora, Martha Lawless and Arthur Evans. 'Recovery in Serious Mental Illness: A New Wine or Just a New Bottle?' *Professional Psychology: Research and Practice* 36.5 (2005): 480-487.

Davidson, Larry, and David Roe. 'Recovery from Versus Recovery in Serious Mental Illness'. *Journal of Mental Health* 16.4 (2007): 459-470.

Deegan, Patricia E. 'Recovery: The Lived Experience of Rehabilitation.' *Psychosocial Rehabilitation Journal* 11.4 (1988): 11-19.

de Weert-van Oene, Gerdien, Victor Buwalda, Johan Havenaar, Wilma Swildens, Albert van Keizerswaard and Augustinus Schrijvers. 'Demand-Oriented Care: The Development and Validation of a Measuring Instrument.' *Social Psychiatry and Psychiatric Epidemiology* 41.3 (2006): 215-220.

Fisher, Daniel. 'Health Care Reform Based on an Empowerment Model of Recovery by People with Psychiatric Disabilities'. *Hospital & Community Psychiatry* 45.9 (1994): 913-915.

Foucault, Michel. *Madness and Civilization: A History of Insanity in the Age of Reason*. New York: Pantheon books, 1965.

Ganann, Rebacca, Donna Ciliska and Helen Thomas. 'Expediting Systematic Reviews: Methods and Implications of Rapid Reviews'. *Implementation Science* 19.5 (2010): 56-65.

Goffman, Erving. *Stigma: Notes on the Management of Spoiled Identity*. New York: Simon and Schuster, 1963.

Geanellos, Rene. 'Exploring Ricoeur's Hermeneutic Theory of Interpretation as a Method of Analysing Research Texts.' *Nursing Inquiry* 7.2 (2000): 112-119.

Hess, Jacob, Jeffrey Lacasse, Jordan Harmon, Daniel Williams and Vierling-Nathan Glaassen. '"Is there a Getting Better from this, or Not?" Examining the Meaning and Possibility of Recovery from Mental Health Disorder'. *Child and Youth Services* 35.2 (2014): 116-136.

Kadri, Nadia and Norman Sartorius. 'The Global Fight against the Stigma of Schizophrenia.' *PLoS Medicine* 2.7 (2005): np.

Mezzina, Roberto, Marit Borg, Izabel Marin, Dave Sells, Alain Topor and Larry Davidson. 'From Participation to Citizenship: How to Regain a Role, a Status, and a Life in the Process of Recovery.' *American Journal of Psychiatric Rehabilitation* 9.1 (2006): 39-61.

Minkler, Meredith and Nina Wallerstein. *Community-Based Participatory Research for Health: From Process to Outcomes*. San Francisco: Jossey-Bass, 2003.

Pelletier, Jean-François, Patrick Le Cardinal, Jean-Luc Roelandt and Michael Rowe. 'Le Rétablissement Civique.' *Développement humain, handicap et changement social* 20.2 (2013): 9-21.

Pelletier, Jean-François, Alain Lesage, André Delorme, Ann Macaulay, Jonathan Salsberg, Catherine Catherine Vallée and Larry Davidson. 'User-Led Research: A Global and Person-Centered Initiative.' *International Journal of Mental Health Promotion* 13.1 (2011): 4-12.

Ricoeur, Paul. *Le conflit des interprétations. Essais d'herméneutique*. Paris: Éditions du Seuil, 1969.

Rose, Diana, Pete Fleischman and Til Wykes. 'What Are Mental Health Service User's Priorities for Research in the UK?' *Journal of Mental Health* 17.5 (2008): 520-530.

Rosen, Stanley. *Hermeneutics as Politics*. New York: Oxford University Press, 1987.

Rowe, Michael, Ashley Clayton, Patricia Benedict, Chyrel Bellamy, Kimberly Antunes, Rebecca Miller, Jean-François Pelletier, Erica Stern and Maria O'Connell. 'Going to the Source: Creating a Citizenship Outcome Measure by Community-Based Participatory Research Methods.' *Psychiatric Services* 63.5 (2012): 445-450.

Rowe, Michael. *Crossing the Border: Encounters Between Homeless People and Outreach Workers*. Berkeley: University of California Press, 1999.

Rowe, Michael and Jean-François Pelletier. 'Mental Illness, Criminality, and Citizenship Revisited'. *Journal of the American Academy of Psychiatry Law* 40.1 (2012): 8-11.

Salzer, Mark, and Eugene Brusilovskiy. 'Advancing Recovery Science: Reliability and Validity Properties tf The Recovery Assessment Scale'. *Psychiatric Services* 65.4 (2014): 442-453.

Shanks, Vicki, Julie Williams, Mary Leamy, Victoria Bird, Claire Le Boutillier and Mike Slade. 'Measures of Personal Recovery: A Systematic Review'. *Psychiatric Services* 64.10 (2013): 974-80.

Slade, Mike, July Williams, Victoria Bird, Mary Leamy and Clair Le Boutilier. 'Recovery Grows Up.' *Journal of Mental Health* 21.2 (2012): 99-103.

Thomas, Philip, Patrick Bracken and Ivan Leudar. 'Hearing Voices: A Phenomenological-Hermeneutic Approach.' *Cognitive Neuropsychiatry* 9.1-2 (2004): 13-23.

Thornicroft, Graham. *Shuned: Discrimination against People with Mental Illness*. New York: Oxford University Press, 2006.

Trochim, William and Mary Kane. 'Concept Mapping: An Introduction to Structured Conceptualization in Health Care.' *International Journal for Quality in Health Care* 17.3 (2005): 187-191.

Varga, Somogy. 'Non-Reflective Self-Awareness towards a "Situated" Account.' *Journal of Consciousness Studies* 19.3-4 (2012): 164-193.

Ware, Norma, Kim Hopper, Tony Tugenberg, Barbara Dickey and Daniel Fisher. 'Connectedness and Citizenship: Redefining Social Integration'. *Psychiatric Services* 58.4 (2007): 469-474.

Jean-François Pelletier is Assistant Professor in the Department of Psychiatry at the University of Montreal, and Assistant Clinical Professor at the Yale School of Medicine. He holds a doctoral degree (PhD) in political science and maintains an interest in all aspects of citizenship, especially as applied to the field of public mental health.

The Experience of Things: Memory, Photographic Representation and Emotions in Psychiatric Field Research

Carlo Orefice

Abstract
Taking as its starting point a number of photographs of a former psychiatric patient – a relative of mine – who was placed in various mental health institutions in Italy for over forty years of his life (between 1945 and 1991), this chapter explores the relationship among memory, photographic representation and emotions. In doing so, it regards field experience as a fundamental tool for the critical investigation of the ways in which, as researchers, we construct forms of knowledge. Indeed, in order to move beyond a reductionist view of mental illness (a view that still has a surprising amount of currency today), those involved in the training of healthcare professionals must not only understand such illness as a 'complex' web of biological, social, cultural and economic factors, but also define it in relation to the implicit meanings that are part of their emotional world and through which they construct their own professional biographies.

Key Words: Representation and construction of madness, pedagogical-educational models, schizophrenia, medical records, photos, emotions, family history.

*****

To Ilaria,
because we have different sensibilities.

1. Introduction

Planned over the course of several cognitive explorations and geographical journeys,[1] this chapter combines different registers and intellectual passions, taking as its starting point a number of photographs of a former psychiatric patient – a relative of mine – who was placed in various mental health institutions in Italy for over forty years of his life. The photographs presented in this chapter can be considered as a nautical chart used to trace the relationship among memory, photographic representation and emotions: they offer a psycho-geographical landscape that is personal as well as social, and at the same time interrogates the field research method by prompting reflection on the theories and practices of mental health education programmes. My reasons for writing this chapter are, therefore, manifold.

The first consideration to be made concerns the ways in which, as researchers, we construct forms of knowledge. Constantly surrounded by a visual culture through which we explore and give sense to our environment, we seek to construct 'objective' academic languages and try to 'limit' our emotions: however, we inevitably end up producing subjective discourses – or, I would say, even autobiographical ones. This notion – of us being engaged in experiences that are frequently based on an emotional cartography which is often implicit and unknown to us, and through which we construct our own professional biographies – seems to me a particularly important aspect for those involved in the training of healthcare professionals.

If it is true that we take possession of the world through narrations which navigate an inner space that is exclusively our own, it is equally true that no way of seeing is independent from the contexts, places and physical (and social) environments that make it possible. In other words, the act of looking is a 'body technique':[2] that is, an act which is culturally interiorized and socially performed. Thus, what we call *meaning* emerges at the intersection of our own present and past experiences and stems from figurative codes that are historically defined.

In promoting 'figural thinking' in the training of healthcare professionals, then, the encounter between the histories of bodies and illnesses becomes a history of representation, making it increasingly clear that any educational intervention must forsake illusory claims to objectivity and make it possible 'to perceive subjective dimensions, as well as the (often) implicit ways in which situations are represented, the meanings attributed to them, and the strategies with which one reacts to them.'[3]

From the above considerations, there follows a methodological premise. The academic world often somewhat distances itself from stories such as those presented here: these appear as 'private,' at times disturbing, and are thus seen as something to be confined to paratexts. Indeed, as researchers operating in a medical faculty, it often does not seem as necessary for us to fully understand the significance of our emotional world as it is to master a solid technical *expertise*: one of the aims of this work is precisely to demonstrate the inadequacy of such an approach. The biomedical paradigm and what we may define as a bio-psycho-social model are not in conflict. On the contrary, they complete and interact with each other.[4]

However, I also detect a risk in all this. When the academic 'censorship' referred to above is not particularly oppressive in its ways, one may fall back into a sort of self-reflexivity leading to self-complacency, thus taking for granted the formative and trans-formative scope of self-narration. In short, one produces self-centred narrations, neglecting to clarify the methodological problems inherent in such reflections. This chapter is, therefore, a personal narration that serves to point out that mental illness combines biological, social and cultural factors, but it is *also* a critical examination of the method we still partly use to train students in medical faculties, especially those working in the psychiatric field. These two aspects are closely connected and raise general methodological issues involving both the anthropological sciences (which have made fieldwork one of their distinguishing features) and educational disciplines (which, like other disciplines in the humanities, have drawn on the former). Read in the context that I deal with in this chapter – mainly from a pedagogical point of view – the fieldwork experience can be viewed as similar to a 'rite of passage,' which may facilitate a certain *way of seeing* and understanding things, thus 'setting us free' from the meanings, values and beliefs that we had considered as *the only* reality up to that point.

In thinking of the infinite series of discourses and institutions that in the course of time have defined, controlled, excluded and 'saved' the *mad person*, this educational approach seems extremely topical;[5] it must begin to operate within an over-medicalized society that (still) seems sometimes incapable of fully recognizing human complexity and usually simply brushes it aside or denies it.

Let me now turn to the last reason that led me to write this chapter. Discussing mental health in an educational context means embarking on a discourse on human *frailty*.[6] Not only because frailty is one of the ontological roots of our existence, but also because it is closely connected to the (familial and social) environment in which we live, that is, to the Other.

Those involved in psychiatric health training should know that, when it comes to approaching the Other, and the Other's horizons of meaning, researchers themselves are not immune to traces of their insecurity – we ceaselessly ask ourselves questions about *our own* frailties and pain. That is, the premise of care is necessarily subordinated to constant research on, and analysis of, who we are and what we feel emotionally. For a large number of the students and professionals with whom I have worked many years now, this has often meant starting from very painful professional experiences where they have had to deal with psychotic dissociation, depression and extreme sensibilities. Treating all of this is particularly difficult: because our existence is not fixed in stone by biology, but, rather, correlated to a 'lived memory' made up of fragments of recollections that one must be able to grasp; but also because students are often taught that the fragile world they will be dealing with in their profession belongs solely to the Other (who by definition needs to be cured), and not to them.[7]

Thus, it seems to me that there is a connection between, on the one hand, an inability to engage with the discourse of frailty and emotion, which is however at the basis of all care professions, and, on the other, the idea – so pervasive in contemporary slogans and our culture of triumphant technology – that frailty is to be regarded as immature, insubstantial, useless, and meaningless. This is clearly a paradox: we live in a society that has achieved technical perfection but in which memory is individualistic, and which thus leads us to try to escape pain, but also happiness, as well as the risk inherent in any exchange. We obsessively seek out other people, not because we really need them in order to establish dialogical relationships based on constructive confrontation, but because we ask others to define our identity.

Why, then, is it so hard for our culture (especially our medical culture) to conceive of frailty as an asset, as a form of loyalty to life and its transformations? Is psychological repression the only viable way, to be taught right from the start in university lecture halls? Or is *teaching and learning* how to turn our frailties into assets a possible solution?

Such are the issues I would like to discuss.

2. The Experience of Things

I will now outline the boundaries of an ongoing field research project[8] in which the professional and personal sides of my life are inextricably connected. I will do so starting from a tiny photograph.

It portrays Angelo (9 September 1919, Gorizia, Italy-19 February 1991, Naples, Italy), my maternal grandfather's brother, who was diagnosed with schizophrenia and placed in various psychiatric hospitals in Italy between 1945 and 1991.[9]

Image 1: Angelo. Naples, around 1960.
© 2015, Carlo Orefice. Used with permission.

> Patient arrived at the [Military] Hospital escorted by another officer, with the following diagnosis: 'Psychosis.' Upon arrival, he showed signs of agitation, uttered disjointed sentences, made rash gestures and threatened bystanders. Restraint of the patient became necessary.[10]

> Patient was transferred from the Military Hospital and admitted yesterday in this ward. He was accompanied by a nurse and wore a straightjacket. When questioned, he gave no answer. He later

> requested the straightjacket to be removed and to be brought something to eat. During the night his behaviour was quiet and orderly.[11]

> He was admitted yesterday at 11 pm; he was restless and uneasy and seemed to be in a dreamy state. He was accompanied by his brother-in-law.[12]

For almost 3 years, this photograph – attached to the cover of a Medical Note [no. 1] – was the only photographic document that allowed me to put a face to this man and, therefore, overcome the 'iconographic void' I had experienced since learning that I had an uncle (19 February 1991, the day of his death). And that he had been *pazzo*. Looking at the photograph, I kept asking myself, *Who was this man?* Turning it in my hands, I thought, *He certainly resembles my grandfather. But who was he really?*

To try and answer these questions, I started examining the medical records in my possession, realizing pretty soon that my professional identity was (almost) the only one benefiting from the perusal – that is, the part of me which is interested in anthropologies of the body, experiences of illness, and the theories and practices of educational work in the mental health field. On the other hand, my family and personal identity seemed to derive little benefit from the frozen and repetitive language of those documents and from the work I was carrying out based on them, important though the work was on a professional level. In short, I knew a lot about Angelo 'the schizophrenic,' but almost nothing about Angelo as a man.

I finally had the chance to reach a deeper level of analysis – one that would satisfy both the professional and personal drives I was agitated by – when, in December 2013, I found a series of photographs of Angelo dating to *before* his hospitalization at the Leonardo Bianchi.[13] These were photographs of ordinary life that, as such, clashed with the neutral and repetitive language used in the medical records: they depicted the life, loves and friendships of this man I had never met, and led me to expand my perspective so as to include the places Angelo had frequented in his day-to-day existence, to go over the relationships and bonds he established with the people who treated him or even just knew him, to look for *traces* of his personality (whether in a letter to one of his relatives or in other photos, etc.) which might free him from the abnormal person category and allow me to catch a glimpse of my uncle.

Today, I consider the bewilderment generated in me by this event as a starting point to attempt to define new interpretive approaches. Indeed, as I briefly mentioned in the Introduction, it allows me to stress the point that medical training must be 'freed' from the prejudice according to which scholars must always be able to keep their personal emotional culture in check, or at least avoid dwelling on it. However, if there is something that field research constantly emphasises, it is that, on certain occasions, what often seems to us inaccessible insofar as it is buried in the depths of our emotional life actually gets 'squeezed out'[14] precisely as we experience it. That is, field research enables us first and foremost to peep into our own human existence – only later do we come to the experience of the Other – and into the representations and relationships that orient us as well as the very order of things. From a pedagogical perspective, this has a highly formative and transformative power, in the sense that the very moment we try to grasp and define the meanings and values of otherness, we can learn a great deal about ourselves.

This idea – which sees access to the Other as always mediated by one's own ontology, one's belonging to a linguistic and historical community, and one's institutional-political-ideological role – is not new; moreover it makes *reflexivity* a fundamental, constitutive feature of both anthropology and medical pedagogy. In the biomedical field, it makes sense to abandon the univocal interpretive framework that has long regarded the study of thought and emotional experience as non-scientific, thus separating the construction of academic identity from the researcher's ability to reflect on his or her emotional states. The different photographs that I found of Angelo have 'squeezed out' of me a series of reflections, whose pedagogical significance is particularly important in view of this new approach.

The first reflection I want to discuss concerns the fundamental distinction made by Dilthey between 'mere experience' and '*an* experience.'[15] Why were Angelo's photos becoming so important to me, whereas the textual analysis of his medical records seemed to require mere – and, I would say, passive – endurance and acceptance of past events? Was it just because they helped to fill the iconographic void I mentioned before? Or because they imposed an interpretative process that called into question an emotional experience in which my past and my present were inextricably linked to each other?

Since, when considered retrospectively, the act of interpretation requires putting a certain experience (*erlebnis*) in its socio-cultural and psychological context, the photos of Angelo required me to work along two lines of enquiry: on the one hand, I had to investigate the (biomedical) categories through which the normal/pathological dualism was defined at the time when the medical records were written, emphasizing that discussing mental illness means taking into account a multiplicity of factors (individual, biological, historical, etc.); on the other, I had to render explicit the family entanglements and implicit meanings through which, over several decades, my family and I have experienced the issue of mental distress.

I will take as an example one of the earliest photos of Angelo, taken before his hospitalization at the Leonardo Bianchi: it portrays a man sitting on a motorbike, with the Neapolitan seafront in the background. The motorbike is not in motion, but I perceive Angelo as moving due to his body posture (slightly leaning forward) and the absence of reference points behind him.

Image 2: Angelo sitting on his motorbike. Naples, around 1948.
© Carlo Orefice. Used with permission

Looking at this photo never fails to touch me. But more than that, it always provokes in me a strong feeling of *unease*.

And it is precisely thanks to such a feeling that, to my mind, one may fully grasp Dilthey's distinction, a notion later expanded by Victor Turner when he wrote that experiences often begin 'with shocks of pain or pleasure' which

> summon up precedents and likenesses from the conscious or unconscious past [...]. Then the emotions of past experience color the images and outlines revived by present shock. What happens next is an anxious need to find meaning in what has disconcerted us, whether by pain or pleasure, and convert mere experience into *an* experience. All this when we try to put past and present together.[16]

Why, then, that feeling of unease?

It stems from the fact that this photo to me evokes the idea of mental illness as a 'place of absence,' as well as that of a mutilated society. However, it also reminds me of my ties to the city where I was born (Naples) and to the places of my childhood, as well as my own sense of uprootedness when I moved away as a teenager. I will expand on these aspects later; for the time being, I wish to stress that an experience is not an isolated occurrence connected to objective data: rather, it contains relations with the past that affect the way in which we structure and give meaning to that experience.

The experience of things, to refer back to the title of this chapter, is thus made up of constant interruptions and re-integrations, of unpredictable cognitive flows that find unexpected forms of signification in personal and individual emotive locations. It is in this perspective that I intend to reflect on the educational role of emotions and their relationship with research in the psychiatric field, as well as on a point that, in my opinion, has yet to be made sufficiently clear: emotions are dependent on, as well as generated and determined by, thought, which, in many cases, is itself emotion.[17]

3. Managing Anger: The Educational Value of Emotions

The idea that experience is 'something one can only undergo but never have,'[18] raises a methodological issue that I would like to investigate further.

According to a methodology that now seems well established (at least, as far as I know, in medical faculties), the interpretive process commonly used by field researchers – I am thinking not only of nurses, but also professional educators – consists in asking a patient questions (based on past medical history), updating and reviewing them in the course of the investigation. Although this method requires complex theoretical skills and, in most cases, is used by professionals having an especially wide-ranging and sensitive skill set, it relies on a particularly insidious assumption: that such theoretical preconditions ensure a *sufficient* degree of 'certainty.' Such an assumption obscures the fact that points of view are not only partial, but they belong to individuals that are culturally and socially situated. As I have noted elsewhere, I have consistently found in my teaching experience that university course syllabi need to provide for serious analysis of the ways in which discursive objects, concepts and notions, enunciative modalities and discursive strategies are formed and transformed – as well as the fundamental impact of such dynamics in the definition of educational models.[19] In this chapter, however, I would like to emphasize how important it is to re-think experience (first and foremost, the experience of researchers and health and care professionals) as a principle of knowledge, and to do so by recognizing the value of the mechanisms of fear, denial, anxiety and identification which field research often brings to the fore.

As a university researcher and lecturer, I have spent the past few years working with students on their personal narratives, examining the events they have experienced (both on a personal and professional level) in order to subject them to shared reflection. Throughout this process, the students' emotions have always been taken into account. However, when focusing on myself, I have tended to exclude certain variables which seemed to me 'unnecessary' (such as the relationship between Angelo's story and my present-day family biography).

But were they unnecessary because of their intimate, personal nature, or because I deemed them unnecessary in the context of the discussion that was taking place?

I have become aware of this issue in recent years, during my work with students of the Degree Course in Professional Education offered at the University of Florence (many of whom are already active in the field) – more precisely, since I started delving with them into the theories and practices of educational processes in the mental health context. Thus, as a teacher I was asking my students to overcome their cognitive/emotional egocentrism, since it often led them to select and prefer what was consistent with the benchmarks and evaluation criteria they had in mind. However, I was not requiring the same of myself.

Should I have investigated Angelo's story – which is also the story of my family – together with my students, or would that have been too intimate a topic? And if so, then didn't excluding variables that I deemed too personal mean distorting that story, depriving it of the transformative value of pain and thus reducing 'madness' to a merely theoretical discourse? And didn't eliminating the strong emotions I felt as a researcher working in the mental health field mean contributing to increase (rather than trying to reduce) the sense of shame and impotence that the stigma[20] of mental illness often carries with it, especially in families (like mine) that have direct experience with such illness?

To avoid misunderstandings, I would like to clarify immediately that maintaining the requisite 'distance' between the observer and the 'objects' of observation has its advantages of course. However, what I wish to advocate is the promotion, as a methodological choice, of an *ethics of responsibility* that turns us, *fragile* individuals, into active subjects and, therefore, regards frailty as a constitutive part of our experiences. I do not wish here to weigh in on the quarrel between theory and practice, or science and emotion: the hierarchy established by the simple fact of making that distinction would lead us away from the connections I wish to investigate in this chapter. The main point raised by the photos of Angelo is that, even before wondering about the contents of our knowledge, we need to examine the ways in which we learn, before interrogating the content of our knowledge.

We may thus say that, from a pedagogical perspective, the investigation of the sense and, most importantly, the value of one's teaching is a tool: the experience of getting cognitively 'lost' – in my case, an experience prompted by Angelo's photos – can cease to be considered as a distraction or mistake to become a fertile starting point for building interpretive processes through which to (re-)think mental illness.

4. Photography and Memory

From all of the above, it is clear that photography is not simply located at the intersection of two distinct procedures, one chemical (the action of light on silver haloid compounds) and the other physical (the formation of the image through an optical device). Indeed, it also involves two aspects that, in a famous essay, Roland Barthes calls respectively *studium* and *punctum*, and which I would now like to discuss.[21]

Studium refers to photographs which arouse a generic interest: that is, photos which – through the object and clothes they depict, photogenic quality, etc. – provide details about the culture to which they belong. In this case, some of the photos of Angelo provide information, for instance, about the type of students that attended a technical high school in Italy around the mid-1930s, or about the dressing style of a young Italian infantry officer during World War II.

Image 3: Angelo (front row, seated on the right) as a technical high school student. Gorizia, around 1937. © Carlo Orefice. Used with permission.

Upon further inspection, they remind me that our behaviour as individuals is the result of processes of imitation, elaboration, repetition and interpretation. Angelo's clothes, as well as the way he positioned his body and occupied spaces, made him feel part of a narrative that was wider and deeper than the mere immediacy of the particular moment 'frozen' in the photograph; in other words, he was the stratified 'product' of individual characteristics, social relations and historical constructs that would start to gradually fade away due to his tragic experiences during the war, and which would eventually be reconfigured only as a clinical truth.

Image 4: Angelo as a soldier. Unknown location, around 1943.
© Carlo Orefice. Used with permission

However, these two photos have no *punctum* in them, that is, nothing in them 'pricks me.' I cannot find in them anything moving – whereas I do find such an element in other photographs, and it is a powerful one.

Thus, when I look at the photo of Angelo's wedding with his bride Olga, who died soon afterwards in an air raid along with her unborn child, I find myself thinking that they must have loved each other very much, and that Angelo's life – marked as it was by a mental illness fed by a constant feeling of loss – must have been unbearable. I also find myself thinking that the medical discourse of the time failed to see that Angelo's distress was marked by underlying structures of meaning based on the experience of guilt, all-consuming sadness, and crushed expectations.

> Five members of his family, including his wife and [unborn] child, died in an air raid in 1944, but he learned about it only in 1945 and, as a consequence, suffered severe mental trauma.[22]

Image 5: Angelo and Olga on their wedding day. Gorizia, 07.12.1942.
© Carlo Orefice. Used with permission

It is thus because of a *punctum* that I am deeply moved by something which finds in a corresponding emotion (tenderness, anger, grief) the conscious sign of that break I mentioned above when quoting Dilthey, and which Barthes seems to allude to when he notes that 'the Photograph is violent: not because it shows violent things, but because on each occasion *it fills the sight by force*.'[23] As I looked at it repeatedly, this photo started working within me, and with time I realized that, for me, the *punctum* was represented by the wedding rings on the bride and groom's fingers. Those objects reminded me of Angelo's loss, which in the medical notes was dealt with in a coldly technical way; moreover, the fact that in other photographs – all discussed in this chapter – Angelo was not wearing his wedding ring, seemed to me a tangible sign of 'what goes by [and] draws us into nothingness even before physical death reaches us.'[24]

However, the pedagogical function of these photos goes even further.

For me, the dates indicated on the back of most of these photos also represent a sort of *punctum*, allowing me to re-read in a different way a series of documents contained in Angelo's medical records: indeed, those apparently neutral numbers enable me to *enter* History. With this term, I am not referring to the history of the psychiatric categories used at the time, which were based on rigid, fixed interpersonal relationships impervious to hope. Rather, I am referring to my family history: a history made of comparisons and cross-references, and of past relationships that seemed lost, but instead had been preserved in implicit meanings that have reached me, so that I might form my own representation of mental illness.

Whether I liked it or not, a photo of Angelo with my grandfather and grandmother introduced into the fabric of my family a procedural dimension as well as a historical depth that, once detected, was bound to have a profound impact on my research.

Image 6: Angelo with his brother, his sister-in-law, and his sister's husband and daughter. Pompei, 30.08.1946. © Carlo Orefice. Used with permission

Indeed, the date written on the back of this photo – 30 August 1946 – allows me to imagine new meanings for the reasons of his first discharge from hospital; interrogate the meaning of Angelo's mental illness; and investigate the medical and familial strategies used to deal with that illness (the man sitting on the left is his sister's husband, later appointed as his 'guardian').

> He was first treated with electroshock therapy and tonic remedies but improvement was partial and temporary, whereas at a subsequent stage insulin therapy yielded excellent results in terms of both his general and mental conditions. The patient has now gained weight, his behaviour is quiet and orderly, and he is a suitable candidate for psychotherapy. As a consequence, he is hereby discharged and entrusted to the loving care of his family.[25]

> [...] he has been admitted to this hospital because he attempted to jump off a balcony as well as throw over one of his little nephews.[26]

> The illness affecting the aforementioned [...] Angelo, as described in the certificate issued by the psychiatric hospital in Naples and attached hereto – dissociative disorder – is so serious that recovery seems almost impossible. Due to the seriousness of the mental illness affecting my brother-in-law [...] Angelo [...] – who is of legal age –, which renders him incapable of making decisions and providing for himself, I hereby request his interdiction with all the legal consequences resulting therefrom.[27]

In other words, in this photo I see reflected one of my family's earliest attempts at bringing Angelo back to a world where human frailty is not just a pathological form of life, but also the distinguishing feature of our existence. At the same time, however, this photo – in which my relatives hold hands, arms around each other – stirs the doubt in me that I may have been able to build part of my sense of security in my family thanks to this man's prolonged hospitalization.[28]

> I, the undersigned, [...] [...], brother of [...] Angelo, hereby declare [...] that my current social and family circumstances will not allow me to take care of my brother within my household if he is discharged from hospital.[29]

And here I come to a further aspect that the passage from *studium* to *punctum* has made me aware of, and which from a pedagogical point of view may well be the most important one of all, due to its transformative significance. In preserving the memory of significant events in the life of my family, the photographs here presented have certainly had a jarring, perturbing effect on me that I feel is relevant to the very meaning and strategies of my field research. However, this is not only because they make a family history structured on guilt, suffering and personal reconciliation even more alive and painful, but also because they slowly erode the very essence of the premise of research: *I can 'dig into' this family history because it is distant from me, and I am excluded from it.*

Therefore, it is not only a matter of seeking to (re-)appropriate a concept – that of schizophrenia and, more generally, 'madness' – by trying to verify the various factors (individual, biological, historical, etc.) through which the normal and the pathological have been defined over time; nor is it a matter of establishing whether Angelo was given a *voice* in the different Medical Notes that concern him. I too am called into question here, with my physical self, including the sense of nausea and deep fatigue that sometimes grips me as I walk the corridors of the Leonardo Bianchi hospital, or when I interview former patients who remember Angelo. All of a sudden, after recovering these photographic memories, I no longer feel at ease in my own body: my genealogy – usually a reassuring factor because, like birth records, it provides 'steady points' of reference – suddenly becomes a source of agitation. It causes me anxiety.

What is the relationship among this ancestor of mine, my family and myself? What if the 'gene of madness' had to be extracted and removed from my own body as well? The family history contained in the Medical Notes reminds me that, if I want to define Angelo's illness, I must take into account the genetic component as one of the several factors (including environmental factors, psychological and social processes, etc.) that contributed to its development. Of course, I am not looking for direct cause-effect relationships; however, in the light of my family's history, I cannot overlook them.

> His father committed suicide aged 33. His mother died following surgery in 1937, aged 43; she had three children, all of whom are alive. A paternal cousin is currently in a psychiatric hospital. Another paternal relative has attempted suicide. A maternal cousin suffers from paranoid psychosis.[30]

Thus, when I look at a photo that shows my mother as a one-year-old baby sitting on Angelo's knees, I know immediately that it was not that porcelain doll-like child who was fragile but, rather, the man who was holding her, overwhelmed as he was by a grief that would forever alter his hopes and expectations for the future.

***Image** 7:* Angelo and his niece Gabriella. Naples, 18.07.1948.
© Carlo Orefice. Used with permission

I thus go back to the medical notes and tell myself that it would be easier if I could focus solely on medical terms and definitions, visiting hours, medicines to be administered, and laundry to be done.

5. Treating Disorder: Objects, Spaces, Identity and Uprooting

The pedagogical function of Angelo's photos lies in their potential to stimulate the reflection skills of the observer. They gradually reveal the implicit meanings through which I have constructed part of my (personal and professional) world, in addition to promoting those of the people they portray. But they also represent a sort of threshold between ambiguous memories consisting of assumptions, conjectures and desires. Faced with this interpretive chaos, as a researcher I would be tempted to subsume all this within the reassuring framework of 'common sense' and scientific rationality, so as to be able to explain to myself *what* mental illness is and *who* Angelo was. As I try to bring some order to my interpretive processes, I would like what I have learned through many years of study and research to come to my rescue and take me by the hand, showing me the sacredness of religious and military traditions, the nature of social ties, the strength of symbols. As if there was no photo to look at. No *punctum* piercing my consciousness and making me feel disoriented. Nevertheless, the more I look at these photos, the more it becomes clear to me that the core problem is not made up of learning processes, practices and contexts: the problem rather lies in the concepts of learning that I am using in order to interrogate the notion of mental illness (and, as a consequence, understand who Angelo was). Starting from this assumption, I would like to reflect about some of the (theoretical and epistemological) 'premises' adopted by the psychiatric discourse of the time in *thinking* of Angelo as a schizophrenic: as I have said, these reflections were 'squeezed out' thanks to the photos presented in this chapter.

The first aspect I would like to emphasize is the relationship between memory and objects. One of the distinguishing features of Angelo's schizophrenia was its 'logical incoherence.' The Medical Notes on his hospital admissions contain many references to this disorder of the thinking process.

> [...] He does not seem to show any signs of hallucination, but [other] behavioural and verbal signs of delirious states (he wishes to go to church, feels guilty, reads and asks for religious books, etc.) have been observed. [31]
>
> During questioning, the patient exhibits a blank demeanour. When answering, his eyes are half-closed or completely closed, his eyelids are clearly trembling, and he speaks in a monotonous tone – at times so softly that it is impossible to understand anything he says. However, when speaking he talks fast, but most of the time he stops mid-sentence without completing his thought and then resumes on a different topic that is usually pointless or even meaningless. He is incoherent, disjointed. His ideas are nonsensical, not systematized, vague.[32]
>
> In the past few days, he has shown mild signs of confusion and depression; when questioned about this, he said he was sure that new events would soon take place in the world [.....]. He should be kept in this ward. We invite the family to request that he undergo electroshock therapy.[33]

Needless to say, Angelo's hospitalizations took place at a time when psychiatry was still in its infancy: antipsychotic drugs and cognitive behavioural therapy were not considered (or were only timidly considered) as possible treatment options. However, one of the limitations of the medical discourse of the time was its incapacity to relate to the objects (and places) that represented a patient's emotional life. That is, in deciphering the complexity of a multi-factor pathology such as the one discussed here, medical practice tended to confirm the model on which it was based: anything else was denied, downplayed and repressed.[34]

From the photos of Angelo, it is clear that our experience of the world (and this holds true for anyone) is not so much the result of exceptional or extraordinary events as the result of everyday life: that is, it is shaped by ordinary *things*. Indeed, things – a technical high school jacket, an army uniform, a pair of round glasses, a striped tie, a wedding ring, etc. – are what represented and constituted Angelo's world, or rather, his ordinary world. Precisely those things, as well as the contexts which have enabled them to endure, inhabited his emotional life when he was in hospital: recalling them was his way of looking for reassurance, a sense of belonging, a familiar face – all these were aspects that medical knowledge had denied, unable as it was to reconcile them with its own driving desire for classification.

> [...] Today he has repeatedly begged to be sent to stay at his brother's in Naples, so that he may end his days with his family....
>
> His doctor being unwilling to grant his requests, he has accused him of being cynical. He has already had electroshock therapy 7 times, without any significant improvement. No critical skills or awareness of [his] illness.[35]
>
> In answering questions [...] he uses meaningless or unrelated sentences: he sometimes talks about ships in a harbour, says that he is surrounded by chaos, mentions islands or cities, and states that confusion is everywhere; there seems to be no continuity in what he says/continuity seems disconnected, words are disconnected. His ideation is chaotic.[36]

Such medical discourse relied on two different but connected considerations.

The first consideration is directly linked to the notion of 'chronological memory,' on which the paradigm of *disease* has gradually been structured, which defines time mainly as clock-time rather than as 'lived memory': the former refers to linear time, whereas the latter points to a place where the memories that feed an individual's inner life accumulate.[37] The second consideration concerns the relationship that we, as individuals, establish with objects, and is connected to the first. The biomedical approach in fact understands illness on one level only (i.e., that of biology), disregarding its complexity or reducing it to a linear succession of causes and effects: as a consequence, not only will such an approach inevitably tend to overlook the contextual and systemic factors and the socio-determinants that contribute to the formation of pathology,[38] but it will regard the ritual and symbolic uses that patients make of their objects as 'unnecessary' levels of investigation.[39]

If this is a paradox that certainly applies to psychiatric institutes (i.e., the past) as well as other highly medicalized settings (i.e., the present), it has now invaded our lives with unprecedented force. We declare ourselves materialists, but we are unable to have an empathic relationship with objects: due to the extent to which we have relied on serial reproduction we have broken all ties between them and their uniqueness. We continue to accumulate objects, but we do not really possess them; we store images, but we do not look at them; we establish virtual relationships, but they rarely go beyond superficial interaction.

This loss of connection with things, which reduces them to mere objects of consumption, is extremely relevant to the issues I am trying to explore. Indeed, when as teachers and researchers working in medical faculties we reflect on the concepts of illness, health and treatment, we often struggle to accept that objects – i.e., things – play a fundamental role in endowing our *being-in-the-world* with meaning, not so much because of the general use we make of them, but because of the local, specific, and thus intimate use we make of them. We are and feel 'at home in the world' precisely because we are defined by a contextual relationship with the things that surround us.

> [Patient exhibits a] slight improvement and more proper behaviour. However, he is still very insistent; extremely keen to be reunited with his brother; wants to wear his uniform and join his division.
>
> He has no grip on reality.[40]

It is by no means new or shocking to say that medical power shuns objects. Not so much, or not only, in order to ensure sanitization of patient environments, or, as in the case of psychiatric institutions, to prevent self-harming (and here is another *punctum*! What happened to your round glasses, Angelo? The ones you always wore before you were committed to a mental hospital?), but because acknowledging their symbolic value would undermine the extraordinary diagnostic and therapeutic efficacy of such power. Once again, we are faced with a contradiction. The main issue, especially in the case of psychiatric patients, is the absence of a 'reliable witness,'[41] that is, of an element that can be extracted from the body of the individual and examined in a laboratory in order to make a diagnosis. But then, one is led to wonder why, if we are unable to find that 'witness' *inside* our patients, we do not look for it in what surrounds them, starting precisely from the objects they own and the meaningful relationships they have with the places they inhabit.

With regard to Angelo's hospitalizations, becoming aware of this inability to acknowledge that, as individuals, we are attached to objects on different levels (instrumental, ritual, symbolic uses) has opened up new research directions for me.

In Angelo's time, suffering from a mental illness meant accepting a world (that of the mental hospital) whose meaning had *already* been established: mental patients had to dress, behave and speak in the way required by the institution in which they were placed.

> [...] upon admission, the patient had in his possession the following items which were collected [...] by the [hospital's] Treasury Officer[s]: Jacket – trousers – shirt – tie – 1 purse – 1 steel ring with engraved initials A.P.[42]

However, that does not necessarily mean that the patients had no opportunities to regain some control. Such opportunities were officially provided for in the mental hospital system, so that every time a patient 'got out,' the objects that had been kept from him/her and deprived of their meaning (inside the hospital) could be reconnected to his/her personal history (outside of the hospital).

> [...] the patient [...] Angelo di Giuseppe has been discharged from this hospital as an "Act of Obligation".
>
> To that end, he has been entrusted to the care of his brother-in-law [.....], who resides in [.....], and the valuables and belongings listed in the admission report dated 16.08.1949 have been returned to him.[43]

But did someone like Angelo, who was hospitalized for a very long time with only brief discharge periods, have any opportunity or hope for 'redemption'? When he was at the Leonardo Bianchi, how did he (if he did at all) elaborate his grief for the loss of his beloved wife, as well as deal with the sense of belonging provided by his connection to the objects that inhabited his inner world and that had been taken away from him upon admission to the hospital? The fact that Angelo had been deprived of those objects imposed on him the need to elaborate not only the loss of his wife and unborn child, but also the grief of separation from the future expectations that had been crushed by that loss: for it seems to me that this deprivation must have irreparably severed Angelo's (already precarious) connection between his past and the heterogeneous (i.e., familial, social and other) environment which gave meaning to those objects. The *steel ring engraved with the initials A.P.*, kept in the Treasury Office of the Leonardo Bianchi hospital during his first course of treatment, did not belong to Angelo, but to his wife Olga: it was the only thing left of her (and of their unborn child) after the air raid in which she died. I presume that, due to that absence, Angelo's sense of guilt, his anxiety, his grief for crushed expectations, and his exhausting nostalgia must have gradually become unbearable.

> [The patient is] lucid, conscious, and oriented. He appears delirious: he says he needs clothes to go to church, experiences pangs of guilt, says he should have been sent to prison at San Vittore because he is a thief...
>
> Disordered associative nerves...a soldier fired a shot, he was frightened, he had [...] a crisis of conscience, he thinks that one can die at any given moment,... [He reflects upon] his faults...[44]

The second premise on which the psychiatric discourse of the time was gradually structured is directly connected to what I have just said with regard to the 'emotional life' of objects. It involves the experience of uprootedness that Angelo's illness carried with it, showing the inability of the medical community of the time to conceive of space not as the specifically human need to 'make a place one's own,' but, rather, almost exclusively as a regularized and ordered dwelling place.

I now turn to two other photos. The first is from September 1938. I think it is a group photo from a sporting competition organized by Angelo's technical high school. My focus (the *punctum*) is not so much on the circle drawn around Angelo's face (another familiar sign attesting to a desire to be close to this man, but also to an inability to recognize him as an 'active' member of the family), but on the writing I can see on the short-sleeved white t-shirt that the man in the middle of the photographed group is wearing while standing.

Image 8: Angelo at a sporting competition. Turin, September 1938. © Carlo Orefice. Used with permission

That writing, which is barely visible, reads, 'GORIZIA': however, the city in Friuli cannot possibly be the location where the photo was taken, since (as stated on the back of the photo) the negative was printed in Turin. This leads me to look at the second photo.

Taken in August 1945, it depicts the wedding of my maternal grandparents. The bride (with a flower in her hair) and groom are sitting at the centre of the table; Angelo stands in the top right corner of the photo, wearing a nice white shirt that contrasts with the grey of the wooden fence behind him. Although I have no direct knowledge of the place (but this time the city is certainly Gorizia, since this is my grandmother's family house), all the people portrayed in the photo were there to attend an event that has become a part of my personal memory and, in a certain sense, a yardstick I have used to measure my affective relationships.

Image 9: Angelo's brother and sister-in-law on their wedding day. Gorizia, 11.08.1945. © Carlo Orefice. Used with permission

When I look at these photos, I realize that settling in a place is a founding gesture, since it means establishing a boundary between the inhabited and the uninhabited:[45] from the moment I am physically there, that place no longer has a generic character but becomes *my own*. The loss of this ability to put down roots, which is particularly apparent in Angelo's case, corresponds to an absence of place that De Martino defines as 'territorial anxiety,'[46] an expression in which the term 'anxiety' refers not only to geographical uprooting, but also to learning and cognitive processes. In other words, 'making a place one's own' is a question of social and cultural survival: vis-à-vis this human need, the psychiatric protocols used in Angelo's time appear as particularly inadequate, at the level of both theory and practice.

Returning to Angelo's comments reported in Medical Note [no.1] from the Leonardo Bianchi hospital: when Angelo spoke about *'ships in a harbour,'* the *'chaos'* surrounding him, and *'islands or cities,'*[47] he was describing the very act of his inhabiting the places that were dear to him, as well as his war experiences. In doing so, he was, in a certain sense, establishing himself: we do not exist 'in the abstract,' but always in a specific place. This consideration – which seems particularly important for the pedagogical sciences, since it points out that our identity is fundamentally dependent on the dialogical relationships we establish with others and with the places we find ourselves in – is what I wish to emphasize in bringing this chapter to a close. I will do so by re-reading a dedication found on the back of another photo (dated 24 March 1943), in which Angelo wrote, *'Absent, but close to you [all].'*

Image 10: Angelo as a soldier. Pavia, 24.03.1943.
© Carlo Orefice. Used with permission

When I look at this face, now so familiar to me, I am reminded of the words of the writer Georges Perec, inviting us to inhabit the world as 'something clear and closer to us: [...] the world, no longer as a journey having constantly to be remade, not as a race without end, a challenge having constantly to be met, not as the one pretext for a despairing acquisitiveness, nor as the illusion of a conquest but as the rediscovery of a meaning, the perceiving that the earth is a form of writing, a "geography" of which we ha[ve] forgotten that we ourselves are the authors.'[48]

> *Which place were you absent from, Angelo? And to whom were you close?*

6. Conclusions

As I bring this chapter to a close, I recall a book by Orhan Pamuk: *Istanbul.*[49] Not only because Pamuk refers to the frailty of the lives of the inhabitants of his city using a Turkish word – *hüzün* – whose Arabic root denotes a collective rather than individual feeling; but also because he portrays that feeling starting from visual memories of his youth, his family, and the places that were dear to him. I return to the photos of Angelo and, realizing the extent to which the story of *my* life depends on sight and touch, I find implicit confirmation of the idea expressed at the beginning of this chapter: there is no thought without figuration, and this holds true especially for those involved in the training of mental health professionals.

Like Pamuk, I need these photos to find myself once more: not only as an individual, but as one of the members of a family in which mental illness has always been a subject of appropriation, explanation, resignation, giving rise to the occupation of geographical spaces and a constant redefinition of meaning. I repeat to myself that we, human beings, are not mere subjectivities, for we come into this world connected to each other: not only as part of the same species, but also as social beings belonging to a culture. In this perspective, identifying the original status of human existence with culture has wide-ranging pedagogical implications. On the one hand, it allows us to reject as completely incorrect the notion that we are all slaves to our animal inclinations: 'human nature' is something that constantly *evolves*, rather than something that has always been the same.[50] On the other hand, recognizing the premise that we are not born good or bad but produce ourselves in the course of historically determined circumstances, makes it possible to radically question the main postulate of 20th-century psychiatry that an entire range of behaviours and attitudes should be considered as falling only within the domain of the pathological,[51] that is, the *ab-normal.*

Thus, as I review the reasons that have led me to write this chapter, I must reiterate that, in establishing a relationship of care, our research efforts should be focused on what we *have in common* as individuals: our capacity to symbolize bodily inclinations; our ability to define ourselves through the experiences of pleasure, pain, and decision-making; and our inescapable need to inhabit a space. Only if we preserve all this from the categorizing and disjunctive language of *disease* (a language that still has a surprising amount of currency today) will we be able to prevent loss from becoming a clinical incident – for mental illness is often the result of an experience of loss, whether real or perceived; only then will loss be understood instead as a *constitutive* experience of human existence.

And here I come again to the eminently pedagogical perspective I mentioned above with regard to the need to 'set education free,' that is, to understand through self-reflection the dynamics that lie inside (and behind) our teaching practices, thus recognizing the formative role of emotions. Our day-to-day life is interspersed with messages that express or convey emotions: not only fear, anger, or sadness, but also love and a sense of sharing and protection. We talk about, listen to, and mediate emotions (through artistic expression as well); in university settings, however, emotions seem to be dealt with in a semi-clandestine manner: we refer to them, but we always take care to preserve our social image as teachers/healthcare professionals who are *immune* from frailty; we assert their educational value, but we exclude them from our syllabi; we study them, but we are unable to translate what they evoke in us into healthcare practice.

In the light of the fieldwork experience inspired by the photos of Angelo, it seems to me extremely urgent that educators and trainers should possess an awareness of their own experiences – as well as of the ways in which they express them – in order to provide emotional education. Facilitating such an exploration of emotion does not simply mean helping individuals to learn how to deal with the disturbing experiences they may have gone through, or preventing the difficulties and pain which may be caused by lack of awareness. First and foremost, it means placing our emotional experiences in a social space-time that, as such, *belongs to all of us*, thus coming to terms with the frailty within us through 'sensibility and gracefulness, extreme kindness and dignity, being able to grasp through intuition the unspeakable and invisible aspects of life' – for such values 'allow us to empathize more easily, and in a more passionate manner, with the states of mind, emotions and existential ways of being of others.'[52]

This can be a good way to move beyond a reductionist view of mental illness, and to propose a reflection of the ways in which – as researchers, but also as individuals – we construct forms of knowledge.

Notes

[1] This chapter is part of a wider multi-disciplinary research project, started in 2011, which concerns the theories and practices of education processes in the mental health sector, with a special focus on the history of 20th-century Italian psychiatry and the deconstruction of the medical categories of normal/pathological that characterized it. The general aim of the research project is to contribute (in empirically and theoretically informed fashion) to wider contemporary international debates on the subject of the relationship between madness and the historical and cultural contexts in which it is observed. Managed within the *Medical Education Laboratory* of the Department of Experimental and Clinical

Medicine (University of Florence, Italy), it arises from a collaboration between the *Polo Archivistico Sanitario ASL NA1 Centro* (Naples, Italy), the *UNESCO Transdisciplinary Chair 'Human Development and Culture of Peace'* (University of Florence, Italy) and the *Medical Anthropology Research Centre* (University of Tarragona, Spain). The field research referred to in this work was carried out at the former psychiatric hospital Leonardo Bianchi in Naples (owned by *Polo Archivistico Sanitario ASL NA1 Centro*) and other in-patient mental health institutions in Naples, mainly between March-August 2013 and January-May 2014.

[2] Marcel Mauss, *Teoria generale della magia e altri saggi* (Torino: Einaudi, 1965).

[3] Carlo Orefice, *Per una pedagogia 'di confine'. Decifrare differenze, costruire professionalità* (Milano: Unicopli, 2013), 35.

[4] To raise awareness about such issues, see also the contribution of ethnopsychiatry and transcultural psychiatry, especially Piero Coppo, *Etnopsichiatria. Un manuale per capire. Un saggio per riflettere* (Milano: Il Saggiatore, 1996); George Devereux, *From Anxiety to Method in the Behavioral Sciences* (Boston: Mouton & Company, 1967); Arthur Kleinman, *Patients and Healers in the Context of Culture: An Exploration of the Borderland between Anthropology, Medicine, and Psychiatry* (Berkeley: University of California Press, 1980); Georges Lapassade, *La découverte de la dissociation* (Paris: Talmart, 1998); Tobie Nathan, *La Folie des autres. Traité d'ethnopsychiatrie clinique* (Paris: Dunod, 1986).

[5] Michel Foucault, *Histoire de la folie à l'âge classique* (Paris: Gallimard, 1972).

[6] Eugenio Borgna, *La fragilità che è in noi* (Torino: Einaudi, 2014).

[7] See Frances J. Allen, *Primo, non curare chi è normale* (Torino: Bollati Boringhieri, 2013); Allan V. Horwitz and Jerome C. Wakefield, *The Loss of Sadness: How Psychiatry Transformed Normal Sorrow into Depressive Disorder* (New York: Oxford University Press, 2007); Jerome C. Wakefield, 'Patologizzare la normalità: l'incapacità della psichiatria di individuare i falsi positivi nelle diagnosi dei disturbi mentali,' *Psicoterapia e Scienze Umane* XLIV, 3 (2010): 295-314.

[8] Regarding the field research referred to in this work, at the moment it concerns: the collection of archival and anthropological data concerning the psychiatric hospital Leonardo Bianchi in Naples and, particularly, the life of Angelo (inside and outside the asylum); the development of video-interviews with survivors of the psychiatric hospital (now in others in-patient mental health institutions in Naples) and with ex healthcare professionals to understand the distinctive ways in which the asylum was designed, constructed and used to control and retain the inmates during specific historical periods; the creation of a specific 'documentation and research inter-university Center' to work on cross-cultural model of medical education and health linked to the *Polo Archivistico Sanitario ASL NA1 Centro*.

[9] During his lifetime, Angelo was hospitalized three times: between 15-16 December 1945 at the Ospedale psichiatrico militare (military psychiatric hospital) in Milan, and between 16 December 1945 - 17 July 1946 at the Ospedale psichiatrico civile (civil psychiatric hospital) Paolo Pini in Milan. [*Medical Note no. 0*, total no. of pages: 56; retrieved on 07 August 2013 from the Niguarda Ca' Granda hospital in Milan]; between 16 August 1949 - 19 February 1991 at the Ospedale psichiatrico civile (civil psychiatric hospital) Leonardo Bianchi in Naples. [*Medical Note no. 1*, total no. of pages: 206; retrieved on 04 March 2011 from the civil psychiatric hospital Leonardo Bianchi in Naples]; [*Medical Note no. 2*, total no. of pages: 85; retrieved on 14 May 2013 from the civil psychiatric hospital Leonardo Bianchi in Naples]. Luckily, having obtained easy access to what can now be considered a complete file record is due to the fact that, at the psychiatric hospital of Naples, the practice of creating an all-in-one folder containing both administrative and health papers, addressed to the patient, was a common practice. Specific regulations addressed to what would have then become the Leonardo Bianchi's Archive, are to be traced (despite for a long time only in the form of principles of declarations) back to 1889 at the time of the approval of the asylum regulation. See Candida Carrino and Raffaele Di Costanzo, *Archivio dell'Ospedale psichiatrico di Napoli 'Leonardo Bianchi'. Inventario* (Napoli: Ospedale psichiatrico Leonardo Bianchi, 2003), 36.

[10] *Proposal for Admission*, 16 December 1945, Medical Note no. 0, 47.

[11] *Clinical chart*, 17 December 1945, Medical Note no. 0, 23.

[12] *Clinical chart*, 16 August 1949, Medical Note no. 1, 3.

[13] Of these photographs, which I found in my mother's family house, there are 22 in total; some dates cannot be established precisely, but, based on a number of checks and comparisons, I can state with certainty that they cover a period running from April 1920 to August 1949, that is, the period immediately preceding Angelo's hospitalization in Naples.

[14] Wilhelm Dilthey, *Esperienza vissuta e poesia. Lessing, Goethe, Novalis, Hölderlin* (Genova: il melangolo, 1999).

[15] Wilhelm Dilthey, *Selected Writing* (Cambridge: Cambridge University Press, 1976).

[16] Victor Turner, 'Dewey, Dilthey, and Drama: An Essay in the Anthropology of Experience', *The Anthropology of Experience*, eds. Victor Turner and Edward Bruner (Urbana and Chicago: University of Illinois Press, 1986), 35-35.

[17] Maria G. Contini, *Per una pedagogia delle emozioni* (Firenze: La Nuova Italia, 1998).

[18] Giorgio Agamben, *Infanzia e storia. Distruzione dell'esperienza e origine della storia* (Torino: Einaudi, 2001), 29.

[19] Carlo Orefice, *Relazioni pedagogiche. Materiali di ricerca e formazione* (Firenze: Firenze University Press, 2013).

[20] Jean-François Pelletier, in this volume.
[21] In *Camera Lucida* (1980) - one of the most important early academic books of criticism and theorization on photography - the French literary theorist and philosopher Roland Barthes develops the twin concepts of *studium* and *punctum*: *studium* denoting the cultural, linguistic, and political interpretation of a photograph; *punctum* denoting the wounding, personally touching detail which establishes a direct relationship with the object or person within it. See Roland Barthes, *La camera chiara. Nota sulla fotografia* (Torino: Einaudi, 1993).
[22] *Family History and Past Medical History*, 16 December 1945, Medical note no. 0, 17.
[23] Barthes, *La camera chiara,* 92.
[24] Ernesto De Martino, *Morte e pianto rituale. Dal lamento funebre antico al pianto di Maria* (Torino: Bollati Boringhieri, 2000), 22.
[25] *Diagnosis*, 17 July 1946, Medical Note no. 0, 16.
[26] *Family History and Past Medical History*, 16 August 1949, Medical Note no. 1, 2.
[27] *Document*, 11 September 1953, Medical Note no. 1, 100-100bis.
[28] As to admittance and discharge dates, Angelo's hospitalizations at the Leonardo Bianchi hospital in Naples were as follows: 16 August 1949 - 17 February 1956; 20 February1956 - 06 June 1957; 02 April 1959 - 20 September 1978; 20 September 1978 - 19 February 1991.
[29] *Document*, 9 May 1979, Medical Note no. 1, 194.
[30] *Family History and Past Medical History*, 16 August 1949, Medical Note no. 1, 1.
[31] *Mental Examination*, 6 January 1946, Medical Note no. 0, 18.
[32] *Mental Examination*, 31 August 1949, Medical Note no. 1, 4.
[33] *Clinical Chart*, 26 April 1950, Medical Note no. 1, 6.
[34] Fiona Ann Papps, in this volume.
[35] *Progress*, 12 February 1946, Medical Note no. 0, 19.
[36] *Mental Examination*, 31 August 1949, Medical Note no. 1, 4.
[37] Eugenio Borgna, *Il tempo e la vita* (Milano: Feltrinelli, 2015).
[38] Jean-François Pelletier, in this volume.
[39] Tobie Nathan, 'Fonction de l'objet dans les dispositifs thérapeutiques,' *Ethnopsy* 2 (2001): 5-42.
[40] *Progress*, 9 March 1946, Medical Note no. 0, 19.
[41] Piero Coppo, *Le ragioni del dolore. Etnopsichiatria della depressione* (Torino: Bollati Boringhieri, 2005).
[42] *Admission Report*, Leonardo Bianchi Civil Psychiatric Hospital, 16 August 1949.
[43] *Discharge Report*, Leonardo Bianchi Civil Psychiatric Hospital, 17 February 1956.

[44] *Mental Examination*, 17 December 1945, Medical Note no. 0, 18.
[45] Franco La Cecla, *Mente locale. Per un'antropologia dell'abitare* (Milano: Elèuthera, 2004).
[46] Ernesto De Martino, *Il mondo magico* (Torino: Bollati Boringhieri, 1978).
[47] *Mental Examination*, 31 August 1949, Medical Note no. 1, 4.
[48] Georges Perec, *Species of Spaces and Other Pieces*, trans. John Sturrock (Harmondsworth: Penguin, 1997), 79.
[49] Orhan Pamuk, *Istanbul* (Torino: Einaudi, 2006).
[50] Marshall Sahlins, *Un grosso sbaglio. L'idea occidentale di natura umana* (Milano: Elèuthera, 2004).
[51] Simon Cushing, in this volume.
[52] Eugenio Borgna, *La fragilità che è in noi*, 3-4.

Bibliography

Aaslestad, Petter. *The Patient as Text. The Role of the Narrator in Psychiatric Notes, 1890-1990*. Oxford: Radcliffe Publishing, 2009.

Admission Report. Leonardo Bianchi civil psychiatric hospital. Naples: Italy.

Agamben, Giorgio. *Infanzia e Storia. Distruzione dell'Esperienza e Origine della Storia*. Torino: Einaudi, 2001.

Allen, Frances J. *Primo, non curare chi è normale*. Torino: Bollati Boringhieri, 2013.

Barthes, Roland. *La Camera Chiara. Nota sulla Fotografia*. Torino: Einaudi, 1993.

Borgna, Eugenio. *La Fragilità che E' in Noi*. Torino: Einaudi, 2014.

———. *Il Tempo e la Vita*. Milano: Feltrinelli, 2015.

Cambi, Franco. *L'Autobiografia come Metodo Formativo*. Roma: Laterza, 2005.

Carrino, Candida and Raffaele Di Costanzo. *Archivio dell'Ospedale psichiatrico di Napoli 'Leonardo Bianchi'. Inventario*. Napoli: Ospedale psichiatrico Leonardo Bianchi, 2003.

Comelles, Josep M. 'Medicine, Magic and Religion in a Hospital Ward: An Anthropologist as Patient.' *AM – Rivista della Società italiana di antropologia medica* 13.14 (2002): 259-288.

Contini, Maria G. *Per una Pedagogia delle Emozioni.* Firenze: La Nuova Italia, 1998.

Coppo, Piero. *Etnopsichiatria. Un manuale per capire. Un saggio per riflettere.* Milano: Il Saggiatore, 1996.

———. *Le Ragioni del Dolore. Etnopsichiatria della Depressione.* Torino: Bollati Boringhieri, 2005.

Davies, James and Dimitrina Spencer, ed. *Emotions in the Field: The Psychology and Anthropology of Fieldwork Experience.* Chicago: Stanford University Press, 2010.

De Martino, Ernesto. *Il Mondo Magico.* Torino: Bollati Boringhieri, 1978.

———. *Morte e Pianto Rituale. Dal Lamento Funebre Antico al Pianto di Maria.* Torino: Bollati Boringhieri, 2000.

De Mennato, Patrizia. 'Medical Professionalism and Reflexivity. Examples of Training to the Sense of "Duty" in Medicine.' *Educational Reflective Practices* 2 (2012): 15-33.

Devereux, George. *From Anxiety to Method in the Behavioral Sciences.* Boston: Mouton & Company, 1967.

Dilthey, Wilhelm. *Selected Writing.* Cambridge: Cambridge University Press, 1976.

———. *Esperienza Vissuta e Poesia. Lessing, Goethe, Novalis, Hölderlin.* Genova: il melangolo, 1999.

Discharge Report. Leonardo Bianchi Civil Psychiatric Hospital. Naples: Italy.

Foucault, Michel. *Histoire de la folie à l'âge classique.* Paris: Gallimard, 1972.

———. *L'Ordine del Discorso.* Torino: Einaudi, 2004.

Horwitz, V. Allan and Jerome C. Wakefield. *The Loss of Sadness: How Psychiatry Transformed Normal Sorrow into Depressive Disorder.* New York: Oxford University Press, 2007.

Kleinman, Arthur. *Patients and Healers in the Context of Culture: An Exploration of the Borderland Between Anthropology, Medicine, and Psychiatry*. Berkeley: University of California Press, 1980.

La Cecla, Franco. *Mente Locale. Per un'Antropologia dell'Abitare.* Milano: Elèuthera, 2004.

La Cecla, Franco and Luca Vitone. *Non è Cosa. Non Siamo mai Soli.* Milano: Elèuthera, 1998.

Lapassade, George. *La découverte de la dissociation*. Paris: Talmart, 1998.

Mauss, Marcel. *Teoria Generale della Magia e altri Saggi*. Torino: Einaudi, 1965.

Medical Note no. 0, Niguarda Ca' Granda hospital. Milan: Italy.

Medical Note no. 1, Leonardo Bianchi Civil Psychiatric Hospital. Naples: Italy.

Medical Note no. 2, Leonardo Bianchi Civil Psychiatric Hospital. Naples: Italy.

Mortari, Luigina. *Apprendere dall'Esperienza. Il Pensare Riflessivo nella Formazione*. Roma: Carocci, 2003.

Nathan, Tobie. *La Folie des autres. Traité d'ethnopsychiatrie clinique.* Paris: Dunod, 1986.

———. 'Fonction de l'Objet dans les Dispositifs Thérapeutiques.' *Ethnopsy* 2 (2001): 5-42.

Orefice, Carlo. *Relazioni Pedagogiche. Materiali di Ricerca e Formazione.* Firenze: Firenze University Press, 2013.

———. *Per una Pedagogia 'di Confine'. Decifrare Differenze. Costruire Professionalità*. Milano: Unicopli, 2013.

Pamuk, Orhan. *Istanbul*. Torino: Einaudi, 2006.

Perec, Georges. *Species of Spaces and Other Pieces*. Translated by John Sturrock. Harmondsworth: Penguin, 1997.

Rosaldo, Renato. *Cultura e Verità. Rifare l'Analisi Sociale*. Roma: Meltemi, 2001.

Sahlins, Marshall. *Un Grosso Sbaglio. L'Idea Occidentale di Natura Umana.* Milano: Elèuthera, 2010.

Turner, Victor. 'Dewey, Dilthey, and Drama: An Essay in the Anthropology of Experience'. *The Anthropology of Experience*, edited by Victor Turner and Edward Bruner, 33-44. Urbana and Chicago: University of Illinois Press, 1986.

Wakefield, Jerome C. 'Patologizzare la normalità: l'incapacità della psichiatria di individuare i falsi positivi nelle diagnosi dei disturbi mentali.' *Psicoterapia e Scienze Umane* XLIV, 3 (2010): 295-314.

Carlo Orefice (PhD in Anthropology) is Associate Professor in General and Social Pedagogy at the "Department of Education, Humanities and Intercultural Communication" of the University of Siena. His current research and teaching activities are focused on Adult Education and Pedagogy of care, with special emphasis on anthropologies of the body and experiences of illness. For the same department, he is Delegate for the Inclusion and Disability. He was a teacher within the Lifelong Learning Programme at Universitat Pompeu Fabra (Barcelona, Spain), and Visiting Researcher at Universidad Autónoma de Coahuila (Saltillo, Mexico) and at Universidad Rovira i Virgili - Medical Anthropology Research Center (Tarragona, Spain).

www.ingramcontent.com/pod-product-compliance
Lightning Source LLC
Chambersburg PA
CBHW071338230926
51846CB00002B/385
* 9 7 8 9 0 0 4 3 5 0 7 8 6 *